Bryan Costales is a C and Unix consultant based in San Francisco. He is also a production designer for motion pictures.

C from A to Z

C from A to Z

Bryan Costales

A SPECTRUM BOOK

Prentice-Hall, Inc.
Englewood Cliffs, New Jersey 07632

Library of Congress Cataloging in Publication Data

Costales, Bryan.
    C from A to Z.

    ''A Spectrum Book.''
    Includes index.
        1. C (Computer program language)   2. Apple II Plus
    (Computer)—Programming.   3. VAX-11 (Computer)—
    Programming.   I. Title.
    QA76.73.C15C67 1985   001.64′24   85-3585
    ISBN 0-13-110057-2
    ISBN 0-13-110040-8 (pbk.)

This book is available at a special discount when ordered
in bulk quantities. Contact Prentice-Hall, Inc., General
Publishing Division, Special Sales, Englewood Cliffs, N.J. 07632

A SPECTRUM BOOK

ISBN 0-13-110057-2

ISBN 0-13-110040-8 {PBK.}

10 9 8 7 6 5 4 3 2 1

Printed in the United States of America

Editorial/production supervision: Joe O'Donnell Jr.
Cover design © 1985 by Jeannette Jacobs
Chapter opening illustrations: Beatrice Benjamin
Manufacturing buyer: Gary Orso

Prentice-Hall International (UK) Limited, *London*
Prentice-Hall of Australia Pty. Limited, *Sydney*
Prentice-Hall Canada Inc., *Toronto*
Prentice-Hall Hispanoamericana, S.A. *Mexico*
Prentice-Hall of India Private Limited, *New Delhi*
Prentice-Hall of Japan, Inc., *Tokyo*
Prentice-Hall of Southeast Asia Pte. Ltd., *Singapore*
Whitehall Books Limited, *Wellington, New Zealand*
Editora Prentice-Hall do Brasil Ltda., *Rio de Janeiro*

To my mother, LaVergne Millard,
and to the loving memory of my uncle Mason Roberts

CONTENTS

PREFACE

This book is a tutorial introduction to the C programming language. It is based on the C *keywords* and on the functions contained in C's *standard library*. It is not intended to be a text on general programming methods, nor is it intended to cover all the subtleties of the language. Rather, it is aimed at the beginning C programmer.

Because this is an introductory text, its focus has been restricted to better clarify and amplify the essentials for understanding the language. There are intentional omissions, for example, that the experienced C programmer will notice at once. Programs using floating-point arithmetic are minimized, and the comma operator is excluded altogether.

To ensure accuracy and portability, every program example was successfully compiled and run on both an Apple II+ under Aztec C65 and on a VAX11-780 under 4.2 BSD Unix. All the program listings were written in machine-readable form and compiled directly from the manuscript. We intentionally kept these examples short so they could be entered and compiled in concert with the text. The emphasis is on writing and then revising these examples, to illustrate new concepts as they arise. As much as possible, they have been made to deal with day-to-day applications rather than abstract mathematical computations.

This book is organized into 20 short, easily digestible chapters, with three appendices for further reference. Each chapter details an individual aspect of the language, focusing on a few closely related keywords or on a single application of standard library functions.

It has been our intention to take the mystery out of C and make it learnable and usable by anyone. Indeed, by the time you finish this book, you will have enough of an understanding of C "under your belt" to write meaningful, useful, and even complex programs.

ACKNOWLEDGMENTS

First and foremost, I must thank Nelson Morgan for recommending this book to my editor, for so diligently correcting my many typos and spelling errors, and for the footnotes with which he has annotated this volume. Equal praise and thanks must go to George Jansen for the many, many hours he spent revising, rewriting, and helping me to clarify my various drafts. Without these two gentlemen, this book would not have been possible.

I must also thank: Beatrice Benjamin for allowing me to use her wonderful illustrations; Eric Allman for his help in achieving technical correctness; Jim Babb for correcting my grammar; and Harry Helms, at Prentice-Hall, for wanting to publish this book in the first place.

Many others have helped in small but indispensable ways. My thanks to Alen Gevins and EEG Systems Lab, Sam and Roz Weston, John Dirlam, Bob Vosse, Jim Shumaker, and Bob Jones for helping me to keep my coffers full this past year. Thanks also to the folks at Toni's Tradewinds Cafe for the times I needed to sit quietly and think and to my dog, Zypher, for her infinite patience and constant companionship. I also thank the many people who so openly shared their knowledge, observations, criticisms, and complaints on the UUCP network in net.lang.c.

Acknowledgment of Trademarks Mentioned

UNIX is a trademark of Bell Laboratories.

CP/M is a trademark of Digital Research.

VAX, PDP/11, and RSX are trademarks of Digital Equipment Corporation.

PC-DOS is a trademark of IBM.

MS-DOS is a trademark of Microsoft Inc.

AZTEC C AND AZTEC C65 are trademarks of Manx Software Systems.

The Latice C Compiler is a product of Latice, Inc.

SUPERSOFT is a trademark of Supersoft Inc.

APPLE and APPLE II are trademarks of Apple Computers Inc.

4.2 BSD is copyrighted by the Regents of the University of California.

C from A to Z

INTRODUCTION

Programming a computer is the art of telling a machine what to do, in a way the machine can understand. Counting to 100 seems second nature to most humans, but computers have to be told how to do it one simple step at a time. Consider the instructions necessary to tell a hypothetical machine to count to 100:

step 1: load 1 into a counter
step 2: increment that counter
step 3: see if the counter is equal to 100
step 4: if not, continue by going to step 2
step 5: if so, we are done.

Essentially, we are "teaching" the computer how to count by giving it five small tasks to perform. Programming, then, is telling a computer what little steps to do and in what order to do them.

In the primitive days of the 1940s, each step had to be specified by physically setting switches (or even repatching a plugboard), very painful methods of programming indeed. Needless to say, better ways were quickly developed, and the C language is one of those better ways.

One advantage of C is that it uses easily understandable words and symbols to tell the computer what to do—what little steps to perform. To count to 100, for example, you might say:

```
counter = 1;
    while ( counter < 100 )
        ++counter;
```

This tells the computer to set the variable *counter* to a beginning value of 1. Then, in a *loop,* it tells the computer to see if *counter's* value is less than 100 and, if so, to increment *counter* (increase its value by 1).

Another nice aspect of C is that it is an efficient language rather than a large one. One measure of a language lies in the number of *reserved words* (keywords) it has. These are words that have special meaning and cause specific actions to be taken by the computer. For C, those reserved words are:

auto	double	if	static
break	else	int	struct
case	enum	long	switch
char	extern	register	typedef
continue	float	return	union
default	for	short	unsigned
do	goto	sizeof	while

Not an imposingly long list, to be sure, yet vast potential lies in its deceptive simplicity.

C is also a free-form language. In C, the "look" of a program—how things are placed on the page—seldom changes the meaning of a program. To illustrate, the previous example of counting to 100 could have as easily been written:

```
counter=1;while(counter<100)++counter;
```

Such a "look" is not recommended, but it in no way changes the program's interpretation or performance and is perfectly legal.

Almost anything you can conceive of programming can be programmed in C. One proof of the power of C lies in the programs that have been written using it. Most of the Unix operating system was written in C. The C compiler itself is written in C.[1] Even other languages, Franz Lisp, for example, have been written in C.

The actual process of programming in C is cyclic. First you write your program using a text editor. Then you compile, assemble, and link it—a process that transforms the text into a program that can be run. When you run it, you may uncover mistakes, *bugs,* in the program, and you go back to rewriting, compiling, assembling, and linking.[2]

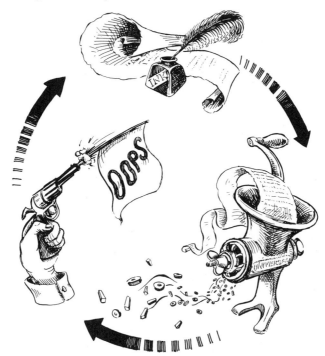

Because programming in C is cyclic, you must not only be comfortable with all these steps, but you must also make this cycle as swift as possible. If you have a choice, choose the system, machine, text editor, and compiler that minimize the nonproductive time you spend in this cycle.

---

[1]This may seem like doing brain surgery on yourself, but it actually works.

[2]The story goes that an early computer failed due to the presence of insects fouling up the hardware, leading to the term *bugs.* Sounds better than *insects in my program.*

1 · THE PROGRAMMING ENVIRONMENT

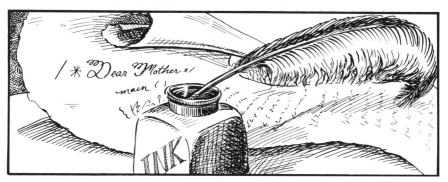

Becoming Comfortable with the Tools You Use.

1.1 AN OVERVIEW OF WRITING AND COMPILING

Turning the Program You Write into a Program that Runs C is a compiled language. That is, before a program can be run or executed, it must first pass through a series of steps that translate a text file into an executable program. Together, these steps comprise what we will call ''writing and compiling a program.'' In brief, they are:

- Write your program's *source text* using a text editor, thereby creating a *source file*.
- Pass that source file through the compiler/assembler, transforming it into an intermediate *object file*.
- Pass that intermediate file through the linker, transforming it into an executable program.

Source Text and the Text Editor

All C language programs begin life as ordinary text files called source files. Aside from a few rules that must be adhered to, creating a source file is no different from writing a letter to Mom. Assuming you have some computer experience, you've probably already used a word processor or text editor. You can use either one to write source files, as long as it produces standard sequential text files. But beware! Word processors that format text directly on the video screen will probably *not* produce the correct kind of text file.

3

Find out what your system offers. Some compilers and/or operating systems include text editors. Life will be much more pleasant if the one you have is what is commonly called a *full-screen text editor*—that is, an editor that allows you to edit a page at a time rather than a line at a time. Before proceeding, spend an hour or so familiarizing yourself with your particular text editor. Write a letter to Mom.

The Compiler and Assembler

The compiler converts your source text file into a file of "human readable" machine instructions. The assembler then converts that file into a machine-readable, relocatable, object file. On some systems, these two steps may appear to be a single step, but this is just an illusion created for your convenience. For the present, you need not understand the nature of these steps, only the mechanics needed to accomplish them.

Find out what your specific system and compiler require to complete these two steps. Take the time now to familiarize yourself with your documentation. Specifically, look for information about compiling and assembling. If documentation is unavailable and you are working on a large multiuser machine, such as a VAX, try typing "man cc" or "help cc". As a last resort, you can always find someone knowledgeable and ask.

Most compilers require the source text file to have a name ending in a ".c" (such as "filename.c"). Naming your files in this manner is good practice, regardless of whether it is required. All the source text file names used in this book will end in a ".c".

Linking and Executing

The final step in getting your program to run is called linking and is invoked with the "link" command. On some systems, linking is called by other names, such as *tkb, load,* or *ln*. Regardless of the name, this is the process of combining a relocatable object file (the result of compiling and assembling) with other files and with libraries of routines to produce a single, executable program.

Now it may seem strange, but many of the things you will put into your programs do not exist within the C language itself. Input and output routines, for example, are supplied in a library called the standard library. The linker looks at your program to see what is needed from the library, then takes those routines from that library and adds them to your program. When linking is finished, you are left with an executable program file, the one that runs on the computer.

1.2 A REAL EXAMPLE

Compiling and Running a Program Using Various Systems   Depending on your system, the steps needed to compile your program can range from simple to complex. We will now illustrate this process for a few different systems. The following program, "welcome.c", is a variation on the traditional first C program. Don't worry about why, or how, it does what it does. It's only a tool you will use to learn the mechanics of compiling.

Using your text editor, create a text file called "welcome.c". This is a program that produces a surprise message on your video screen. Enter the example exactly as shown in Fig. 1–1. Note that the use of the semicolon is like the period at the end of a sentence. Also note that the "look" of a C program is not etched in stone.[1] (The "look" or style of C programs can vary greatly, a topic we will cover in detail in Chapter 6.) Don't try to compile "welcome.c" yet; we'll do that in a moment. Just type it in for now.

FIGURE 1-1 welcome.c

```
/* welcome.c: a first program for the new C programmer */

main()
{
    int number;
    char language;

    number = 2;
    language = 'C';

    printf( "I'm pleased %d %c you.\n", number, language );
    printf( "Try saying that with any other language!\n" );
}
```

We will now look at how "welcome.c" can be compiled on three different systems. If your compiler is not illustrated, don't worry.[2] Note the common ideas and compare them with those in your own compiler.

Unix

If you are using the Unix compiler, all the compilation steps can be accomplished with the single command "cc". The resulting executable program is named "a.out" and is run by simply typing "a.out".

You Type	What Happens
cc welcome.c	welcome.c is compiled, assembled, and linked.
a.out	The program is run.

[1]A program storage technique predating punched cards.

[2]Even if your compiler *is* illustrated, don't worry. It's not good for you!

Decus C, PDP/11

Under the RSX operating system, running Decus C on a PDP/11 computer, the process is more cumbersome. The resulting executable program is named ''welcome.tsk'' and is run by typing ''welcome''.

You Type	*What Happens*
xcc -a welcome.c	welcome.c is compiled and assembled.
tkb welcome/cp=welcome,lb: [1,1]c/lb	welcome.obj is linked to the standard C library.
welcome	The program is run.

Aztec C65, Apple II

This is the process under the Aztec shell, running the Aztec C compiler on an Apple II computer:

You Type	*What Happens*
c65 welcome.c	welcome.c is compiled and assembled.
ln welcome.rel sh65.lib	welcome.rel is linked to the standard C library.
welcome	The program is run.

1.3 ERRORS

Even the Best Make an Occasional Oops   If anything can go wrong, it will.[3] Trite but true. If you haven't already done so by accident, try omitting a semicolon from ''welcome.c'' before compiling it. Or misspell the word **printf,** and see what happens.

Error messages on different compilers vary from the clear:

```
welcome.c: line 5: missing semicolon
```

to the cryptic:

```
welcome.c 5 #52.
```

In your compiler's documentation, locate the codes, messages, or numbers for the following common errors:

    missing semicolon
    missing closing quote
    missing parenthesis
    undeclared identifier

The phrasing of error messages may differ, but they will always include a line number referring to a line in your original source text. A tip: Because of the way the

---

[3] . . . at the time in which the error will have the most destructive effect.

compiler traps errors, the actual error will often be found on the line preceding that line number.

1.4 SHORTHAND

Compiling a Program with One Swift Stroke   Most operating systems allow secondary *command files* to take the place of commands ordinarily typed in at the terminal. These command files are sometimes called *submit files, exec files,* or *shell scripts*. By creating such a command file, it is possible to compile a program using a single command. If your system requires several commands for compiling, you will save frustration in the long run by creating just such a command file now.

By way of example, under Supersoft C, CP/M-80 the following submit file allows "welcome.c" to be compiled with the command "submit c welcome". Create the following text file using your text editor and save it under the name "c.sub":

```
CC $1.C
C2 $1.COD
ASM $1
LOAD $1
```

Now the process of compiling, assembling, and linking a program can be done with the simple command:

```
submit c filename
```

Under the Aztec Shell, Aztec C on an Apple II, the following shell script file allows "welcome.c" to be compiled with the command "cc welcome.c". Here, the executable file is called "a.out", making the process appear to match that of the Unix version. Create the following text file using your text editor and save it under the name "cc":

```
rm a.out
set -a
c65 -o a.rel $1
ln -o a.out a.rel sh65.lib
rm a.rel
```

Now the process of compiling, assembling, and linking a program can be done with the simple command:

```
cc filename.c
```

1.5 COMMENTS

Documentation Invisible to the Compiler   Comments are used so that people reading your source text, including you, will better understand your intention. All the program examples in this book begin with a comment line giving the program's name and a brief description of what the program does. Observe the first line in "welcome.c":

```
/* welcome.c: a first program for the new C programmer */
```

A comment in C begins with the two-character symbol ''/*'' and ends with the two-character symbol ''*/''. Everything between these symbols, including the symbols themselves, is ignored by the compiler. This means that comments in no way affect the size or speed of your final program.

Comments can be as long as you like and are not restricted to a single line. Once the compiler finds a ''/*'', everything is ignored, including any additional *newlines,* until a terminating ''*/'' is found. For example:

```
/*
** this is a legal comment
*/

/*
    and
          this is also a legal comment
                                                */
```

Be careful, though. The one restriction on the use of comments is that they cannot nest. That is, one pair of ''/* */'' may not enclose, be enclosed by, or overlap another such pair. Unintentionally nesting comments is a common error that occurs when ''commenting out'' text as a part of debugging. For example, suppose you had a line of source text that was causing a problem and you wanted to eliminate it temporarily. If that line were:

```
language = 'C'; /* you betcha */
```

you could not remove it with:

```
/* language = 'C'; /* you betcha */ */
```
                                      ⬆ error

      this text ignored

or with:

```
/*
language = 'C'; /* you betcha */ } this text ignored
*/                               ⟵ error
```

Instead, you must do this:

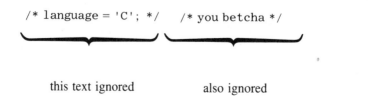

```
/* language = 'C'; */    /* you betcha */
```

      this text ignored   also ignored

Use comments as often as necessary to help clarify your programs. The better you understand what your program is supposed to do, the easier it is to discover why it isn't doing it.[4]

---

[4]Or even why it *is*, when you try to expand the program six months later.

2 · VALUE ASSIGNMENT, TYPE

An Assortment of Types Destined for Many a Need

2.1 VALUE

Put It In and Take It Out   Imagine that the computer's memory is composed of many little boxes, all the same size, lined up one after the other. Into each a value may be placed, and from each a value may be taken. It is these values that are used to represent useful information.

Examine "welcome.c" once again. It is shown in Fig. 2–1.

FIGURE 2-1   welcome.c

```
/* welcome.c: a first program for the new C programmer */

main()
{
    int number;
    char language;

    number = 2;
    language = 'C';

    printf( "I'm pleased %d %c you.\n", number, language );
    printf( "Try saying that with any other language!\n" );
}
```

Notice the statement:

number = 2;

In C, we are saying that something called ***number*** is to be assigned the value 2. That is, ***number*** is the name given to a location in the computer into which the value 2 is placed.

Look at a few of the boxes that make up the computer:[1]

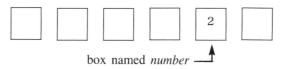

box named *number* ⟶

Notice that the name ***number*** is given to a single box. Here it is the fifth box, but it could as easily have been the 1956th box. The name you give to identify a location in the computer is for your use only. The compiler determines where that location will actually be placed in memory. The "box" referred to by that name could be located just about anywhere in the computer.

All the boxes that make up the computer's memory are the same size, and each can hold a limited range of values. The typical box can contain a value in the range −128 to +127.[2] Such a box is called a *byte*. The value 2 definitely fits in that range. Suppose, however, that you wished to store a value of 1000:

number = 1000;

Clearly, one byte (box) is too small to contain that value. To represent larger values, bytes (boxes) may be combined:

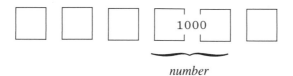

number

The C language provides the means for giving a single name to multiple bytes. This is done by declaring the name to be of a particular *type*. C supports a number of types, each of which reserves an appropriate number of bytes for the particular machine you are on. The three we will look at first are **int, char,** and **float.**

The type **int** can be thought of as short for *integer*. Integers can represent whole numbers, or fixed-point numbers in general. A fixed-point number is one in

---

[1]Remember that they're only *pretend* boxes.

[2]There are 256 different things that can be represented by the electronic configuration of each "box." These can be viewed as numbers (−128 to +127 or 0 to 255), or as 256 distinct symbols of ary variety. For simplicity, just think of them as numbers for now.

which the location of the decimal point does not move. The type **int** frequently reserves a two-byte pair, although on some machines it may reserve four bytes.

The type **char** can be thought of as short for *character*. The letters of the alphabet are characters, as are digits and punctuation marks, and each requires only a single byte.

The type **float** stands for *floating-point number*. Floating-point numbers have a decimal point, the position of which may vary with the value represented.[3] The type **float** generally reserves four bytes, although on some machines it may reserve more.

One way to tell the compiler how many bytes to reserve is:

```
type name;
```

where *type* is either **int, char,** or **float,** and *name* is a name used to *identify* the reserved storage (bytes). As a rule, at least one space (or TAB) must separate the type from the name. Another rule is that the whole declaration must be terminated with a semicolon. Therefore, the declaration:

```
char letter;
```

reserves a single byte identified by the name *letter.* The declaration:

```
int number;
```

reserves a two-byte pair (four bytes on some machines) identified by the name *number.* And the declaration:

```
float temperature;
```

typically reserves four bytes identified by the name *temperature.* However:

```
intnumber;
int number
```

are both incorrect. The first is wrong because there is no space (or TAB) separating the type from the name, and the second is wrong because there is no semicolon at the end.

2.2 IDENTIFIERS

The Rules for Names   The name given to reserved bytes is also called an *identifier,* because it "identifies" those bytes for the compiler. Identifiers, in C, have a particular set of rules governing their formation. Those rules are:

---

[3]For example, 5×10^{-7} and 4×10^{-3} are *floating-point* representations, since the exponent (position of the decimal point) is specified as part of the number represented. If the exponent was always assumed to be a certain value, the representation would be *fixed point.*

1. Identifiers must begin with a letter or an underscore character(_).
2. Identifiers can contain only letters, digits (0 through 9), and the underscore character (_).
3. Uppercase letters are distinct from lowercase letters (on most compilers).
4. Identifiers cannot be the same as any keywords (**char** and **int** are keywords).
5. Identifiers must be different from each other. On some compilers, only the first eight or fewer characters are considered unique.

Before you can use any storage in the computer, you must tell the compiler what *type* of storage you require, and give it an identifier (name). This is called *declaring* an identifier to be of a specified type. Enter program ''identdemo.c'', which is shown in Fig. 2–2, and attempt to compile it. Your compiler may complain about some of the declarations. Be sure you understand what is wrong with the ones it objects to and fix them. This will tell you what limits your particular compiler places on identifier names.

FIGURE 2-2 identdemo.c

```
/* identdemo.c: demonstrate legal variable names */

main()
{
    /*
    ** Differing by case (upper vs. lower)
    */
    int bonzo;
    int Bonzo;
    int BONZO;

    /*
    ** How many lead characters are unique?
    */
    int the;
    int thequick;
    int thequickbrownfoxjumpedoverthelazydog;

    /*
    ** Digits and the underscore allowed.
    */
    int _first;
    int mid_mid;
    int also321;
    int and_123;

    printf( "SUCCESS!\n" );
}
```

2.3 ASSIGNMENT

Putting a Value into Memory Again imagine that the computer's storage memory is composed of empty boxes into which values can be placed and from which values can be taken.[4] You can place the value 1 into a box and it will stay there until you do something to change it. You can add 3 to it. Later, you might subtract 5 from it. Because that value may *vary,* its name, or identifier, is also called a *variable name.* And the storage that name refers to is called a *variable.*

Recall from ''welcome.c'' the two statements:

```
int number;
number = 2;
```

As you have seen, the first statement *declares* the identifier **number** to be of type **int.** The second statement *assigns* (=) the value 2 to the variable named **number.** The assignment operator (=)always assigns the *value* on its right to the variable on its left. That value, terminated by a semicolon, can be a simple thing like the value 2 or the result of a long computation.

The program ''assigndemo.c'' illustrates the proper use of the assignment operator. Note how a variable can be assigned the value of another variable. The program is shown in Fig. 2–3.

FIGURE 2-3 assigndemo.c

```
/* assigndemo.c: demonstrate the assignment operator */

main()
{
    int result, num1, num2, num3;

    num1 = 1;
    num2 = num1;
    num3 = 3;

    result = num1;
    printf( "result = %d\n", result );

    result = num2;
    printf( "result = %d\n", result );

    printf( "result = %d\n", result = num3 );
}
```

This program also demonstrates a bit of shorthand. Multiple declarations can be made with a single *type* keyword. The identifiers involved simply need to be separated by commas:

---

[4]In general, don't assume the ''boxes'' are empty. ''Empty'' them explicitly before using them (you'll see how shortly).

```
int result, num1, num2, num3;
```

This declares all four identifiers to be of type **int.**

2.4 CONSTANTS

I Am What I Am and That's All That I Am   The number 2 is a constant value, be-cause 2 is always 2 no matter what. Two common kinds of constants in C are integer values such as 2 and floating-point values such as 102.5. In C, integer constants are given the storage type **int,** and floating-point constants are given the storage type **float.** The difference between the two is indicated to the compiler by the presence or absence of a decimal point. Thus, 2 compiles to an **int,** and 2.0 compiles to a **float.** For example:

```
int number;
float temperature;

number = 2;
temperature = 102.5;
```

assigns to ***number*** the integer constant value 2 and assigns to ***temperature*** the floating-point constant value 102.5.

As a word of caution, an integer constant should *not* be assigned to a **float** variable, and a floating-point constant should *not* be assigned to an **int** variable. While some compilers make this transformation without complaint, others go bananas.

A third kind of constant is a character constant. Character constants are repre-sented by placing a letter, digit, or punctuation mark between half quotation marks. For example:

```
char letter;
letter = 'C';
```

assigns the letter C (a character constant) to the **char** variable ***letter.***

Character constants can seem confusing because they have numerical values, which differ from the characters they represent.[5] For example, the character con-stant 'C' has a numerical value of 67, and '1' has a numerical value of 49. The assignment:

```
number = '1';
```

assigns the value 49 to ***number*** whereas the assignment:

```
number = 1;
```

assigns the value 1 to ***number.*** The half quotation marks are a signal to the compiler that the numerical value that corresponds to the character should be used. Appendix

---

[5]Character constants are *represented* by strings of ''on'' and ''off'' bits in your computer's mem-ory, just as numbers are. Therefore, any character can also be viewed as a binary number. We refer to this as the ''value'' of the character.

3 contains a list of all the characters and their corresponding values. A brief study of that list will help to clarify which values represent which characters.

Character constants are usually assigned to variables of type **char,** but they may also be assigned to type **int.** This is because characters are actually represented in a computer as numbers whose values range from 0 to +127, and that range can be handled by **int** variables. Thus:

```
int val;
val = '1';
```

is perfectly legal, because the assignment is the equivalent of:

```
val = 49;
```

2.5 INITIALIZING

Declare the Type and Starting Value All at Once When you first declare the storage class of an identifier, all you are doing is reserving bytes. There is no guarantee that those bytes will start out empty, or with a value of 0. If you wish them to begin as 0, you should assign them that value.[6] For example:

```
number = 0;
```

Identifiers may also be assigned a starting value when they are declared. This is called *initializing* a variable. The statement:

```
int number = 0;
```

not only declares **number** to be of type **int,** but also assigns it a beginning value of 0.

The program "initdemo.c" illustrates this concept (see Fig. 2–4). Try omitting the initializing assignments from both *type* declarations. What kind of gar-

FIGURE 2-4 initdemo.c

```
/* initdemo.c: demonstrate initializing variable values */

main()
{
    float temp = 102.5;
    int aspirin = 3;

    printf( "Biff's temperature is %f degrees.\n", temp );
    printf( "He must take %d aspirin hourly.\n", aspirin );
}
```

---

[6]Some compilers may actually do this initialization for you, but it is a bad idea to count on it.

bage gets printed? If you encounter any strange diagnostic messages or compiler errors referring to floating point, you should read the next section.

2.6 FLOAT TROUBLES

Floating-Point Values May Require Special Handling   A few compilers are unable to handle floating-point values without special effort.[7] If your compiler is one of these, you will have gotten a diagnostic warning when you compiled or executed the program "initdemo.c".

Under Aztec C, on an Apple II, you may get the warning:

```
undefined .fltused
```

This means you must include a special floating-point library along with the standard library when you link (Chapter 1) the program:

```
ln initdemo.rel flt65.lib sh65.lib
```
                   └─────────┬─────────┘
                          added

Under Decus C, on a PDP/11, the first line of output might look like:

```
Biff's temperature is {dtoa?} degrees.
```

This means you must include the object file "lb:[1,1]dtoa" along with the standard library when you link (task build) the program:

```
tkb initdemo/cp=initdemo,lb:[1,1]dtoa,lb:[1,1]c/lb
```
                         └──────────┬──────────┘
                               added

Because of this lack of universal easy access to floating point, most of the examples in this book are devised using integer arithmetic only. You don't need floating point to learn the basics of the language, but there will be times when floating point is necessary.[8] Take the time now to learn the ins and outs of using floating point with your compiler.

2.7 THE #define DIRECTIVE

Giving Constants an Alias   The **#define** directive is best thought of as a simpleminded replacement mechanism, something like the global search and replace in a word processor. The directive consists of three parts, each separated by at least one space (or TAB). For example:

```
#define SMALL midgets
```

---

[7]Some can't handle floating point at all! These are only worth mentioning in extremely disdainful tones, perhaps as "C minus" compilers.

[8]If you ever do any scientific or engineering development, you will go nutsy-crazy without floating point.

The first part is the **#define** (pronounced "pound-define") directive itself. Second is the token that will be replaced. And third is the replacement text. This tells the compiler's preprocessor that whenever it sees the token:

```
SMALL
```

in the program text, it should replace it with the text:

```
midgets
```

The **#define** directive must begin a line, and there can be no space separating the # from the **define.**[9] The token to be replaced must be separated from the **#define** by at least one space (or TAB) and is governed by the same rules as those for an identifier. For best readability, that token should be all uppercase. This will prevent you from mistaking constant names for variable names.

One space (or TAB) must separate the replacement text from the token. Everything up to the end of the line is taken as the replacement text:

```
#define TOKEN replacement text is rest of line
```

The replacement text may extend beyond a single line by terminating the line to be extended with a "\". That is, end the line with a backslash followed *immediately* by a carriage return:

```
#define TOKEN this is a big long line of replacement \
text, which had to be continued on another line.
```

Note that token substitution does not occur between quotation marks. That is:

```
#define NAME Biff
printf ( "my name is NAME" ) ;
```

will print "my name is NAME" and not "my name is Biff" as was intended.

Tokens may be **#define'd** using tokens previously **#define'd.** For example:

```
#define BIG 10000. 0
#define SMALL (1. 0/BIG)
```

will substitute for each occurrence of the token SMALL, the text:

```
(1. 0/10000. 0)
```

The program shown in Fig. 2–5, "definedemo.c", illustrates some possible uses for the **#define** directive. Take a moment to experiment and discover the range and limitations of that directive.

As you can see, the **#define** directive is a powerful adjunct to the C language. It can be used to add clarity and simplicity to your programs. If a constant value is **#define'd** at the beginning of a program, for example, it can be changed everywhere in the program by simply changing its definition. You will find **#define** used often throughout the examples in this book.

---

[9]Some compilers are more flexible than others and allow the # to start anywhere. Some also allow space between the # and the **define.** To ensure portability, however, stick to the rules we've stated.

FIGURE 2-5   definedemo.c

```
/* definedemo.c: illustrate use of #define directive */

#define SAYWHAT "num = %d\n"
#define HOWMUCH 5
#define AGAIN SAYWHAT,HOWMUCH
#define LAST printf( AGAIN )

main()
{
    printf( SAYWHAT, HOWMUCH );
    printf( AGAIN );
    LAST;
}
```

3 · FUNCTIONS

Basic Building Blocks of the C Language.

3.1 INTRODUCING FUNCTIONS

What They Are and How to Name Them When you run a program that has been compiled, all the instructions that tell the computer what to do are contained in functions. Look again at the program "welcome.c", which is shown in Fig. 3–1.

FIGURE 3-1 welcome.c

```
/* welcome.c: a first program for the new C programmer */

main()
{
    int number;
    char language;

    number = 2;
    language = 'C';

    printf( "I'm pleased %d %c you.\n", number, language );
    printf( "Try saying that with any other language!\n" );
}
```

Notice that the expression ***main()*** is followed by a left curly brace ({) and that the program ends with a right curly brace (}). This program contains a single function called ***main***.

20

The function named ***main*** is a very special one in C, because every program begins execution at a function with that name, and all other functions in the program are called from it. This special function can be envisioned as the trunk of a tree: Other functions (branches) are called from it and others (smaller branches) are called from those functions, and so on. There is no practical limit to how far this sequence may grow.

The program in Fig. 3–2 is called "minprog.c". It is the minimum legal C program. Go ahead. Take a second to enter, compile, and run it. It compiles without error, and, when run, does absolutely nothing because there is nothing between the curly-brace pair.[1]

FIGURE 3-2 minprog.c

```
/* minprog.c: the minimum C program */

main()
{
}
```

The name given a function, like the name given a variable, identifies it. The rules for creating a legal function name are identical to those for creating a variable name:

1. Identifiers must begin with a letter or an underscore character (__).
2. Identifiers can contain only letters, digits (0 through 9), and the underscore character (__).
3. Uppercase letters are distinct from lowercase letters (on most compilers).
4. Identifiers cannot be the same as any keywords (**char** and **int** are keywords).
5. Identifiers must be different from each other. On some compilers, only the first eight or fewer characters are considered unique.

A function may not be declared (may not begin) within a "{}" pair. Thus:

```
main()
{

sub()
{
}

}
```

is not legal if you intend to declare ***sub()*** as a function because it is enclosed by the curly-brace pair of ***main()*** .The correct way to declare both as functions is:

---

[1]This is a guaranteed bug-free program.

```
main()
{
}

sub()
{
}
```

In this case, **sub()** becomes something akin to a subroutine that can be called from **main()**.

The following program, "callsub.c" illustrates the process of calling another function from **main()**. (See Fig. 3–3.) Note that the program's "flow" is from **main()** to **sub()**, and, when **sub()** has nothing left to do, back to **main()** again.

FIGURE 3-3 callsub.c

```
/* callsub.c: illustrate a function call */

main()                          /* main declared */
{
    printf( "This is main\n" );

    sub();        /* sub called from main  */

    printf( "Back in main\n" );
}


sub()                           /* sub declared  */
{
    printf( "and this is sub\n" );
}
```

3.2 FUNCTION ARGUMENTS

Functions Can Pass Values to Other Functions   Arguments are the means by which values are passed to a function. For example, **printf()** is a function that prints its arguments to the video screen. When you call **printf()** with the statement:

```
printf("hello");
```

you are passing to it the single argument "hello". It then prints that argument to your screen.

A function's arguments are contained within the parentheses following the function's name. A function is said to have an *empty* argument list when the parentheses following the name are empty:

```
main()
```
    ↑— empty, expects no arguments

These parentheses may *not* be omitted, but they may be empty.

When a function is declared, its arguments must be listed in the same order in which it expects to receive them. Thus:

```
sub( arg1, arg2, arg3 )
```
expects three arguments in this order

declares ***sub()*** to be a function that expects three arguments, and expects ***arg1*** to arrive first, ***arg2*** to arrive second, and ***arg3*** to arrive last.

In addition to listing its expected arguments, the *type* of each of those arguments must be declared. That declaration must occur between the right parenthesis ''")'' and before the beginning curly brace ''{'', as:

```
sub( arg1, arg2, arg3 )
....declarations of argument types here
{
```

In the following example:

```
show( firstarg, secondarg )
char secondarg;
int  firstarg;
{
}
```

the function named ***show()*** expects two arguments. The names of the arguments and the order in which they will be received are ***firstarg*** then ***secondarg.*** The first is declared to be of type **int,** and the second is declared to be of type **char.** Notice that the type declarations need not be in the same order as the arguments listed within the parentheses.

To call the function ***show(),*** from ***main()*** for example, state its name followed by two arguments in parentheses:

```
show('A', 65 );
```

The arguments must be listed in the same order that ***show()*** expects to receive them. The type of each should also match, because passing and receiving go hand in hand.

Enter, compile, and run the program in Fig.3–4, which is named ''callfunct.c''. Note that when we call the function ***show()*** we pass it two values, one **char** and one **int,** and that those values are passed using variables.

This program again demonstrates that characters may be interpreted as integers whose values correspond to those of letters, digits, and punctuation marks. The character constant 'A' and the integer constant 65 both have a numerical value of 65.

FIGURE 3-4 callfunct.c

```
/* callfunct.c: calling a function with arguments */

main()
{
    char ch;
    int  num;

    ch = 'A';
    num = 65;
    show( ch, num );

    ch = 65;
    num = 'A';
    show( ch, num );
}

/*
** show(): print the value of a letter and a number.
*/
show( letter, number )
char letter;
int  number;
{
    printf( "The letter is '%c'.\n", letter );
    printf( "and the number is %d.\n\n", number );
}
```

3.3 LOCAL VARIABLES

Passing Variables Doesn't Change Them   When you pass an argument to a function, you are not passing the variable itself. What is passed is a *copy of the value* of that variable. The called function can do anything it wants to that copy without affecting the original variable's value in any way.

Enter, compile and run the following program, "localdemo.c". (See Fig. 3–5.) Observe that variables declared within the functions are *local to each*. The variable *arg* in *modify()* is different from the variable *arg* in *main()*. What happens to one does not affect what happens to the other.

Note that when *main()* calls *modify()* as,

```
modify( arg );
```

all that is passed to *modify()* is the *value* of *arg*, not *arg* itself. The function *modify* then takes that value and assigns it to its own private variable, also named *arg*.

FIGURE 3-5 localdemo.c

```
/* localdemo.c: demonstrate local variable scope */

main()
{
    int arg = 1;

    printf( "In main, arg = %d.\n", arg );

    modify( arg );

    printf( "back in main, arg = %d.\n", arg );
}

/*
** modify(): modifies its personal copy of arg.
*/
modify( arg )
int arg;
{
    printf( "in modify, arg = %d.\n", arg );

    arg = 2;

    printf( "modify made arg = %d.\n", arg );
}
```

3.4 THE return KEYWORD

How to Get Values from One Function Back into the Other   A function can return a value to the function that called it. The mechanism for returning a value is provided by the new keyword **return.** The value returned is of type **int**.

The **return** keyword can be used in two ways. If you want a function to return to the function that called it, regardless of whether it is finished, simply use the **return** keyword followed by a semicolon:

```
return;
```

If you want the function to return a value, simply place that value in parentheses following the **return** keyword:

```
return (value);
```

Some compilers are picky, and will flag as an error:

```
return ();
```

This ought to be the same as:

```
return;
```

that is, returning without providing a return value. However, you should avoid using

```
return ();
```

The parentheses enclosing the returned value are optional (on most compilers), but we will use them for clarity. The space between the **return** and the left parenthesis is cosmetic only, and intended to indicate that:

```
return ( value );
```

is not a function call.

Enter, compile, and run the somewhat longer program, "returndemo.c". It is listed in Fig. 3–6. In the function *main()*, the values returned from *get5()* and *get6()* are each assigned to the variable *number*. The value of *number* is then printed.

FIGURE 3-6 returndemo.c

```
/* returndemo.c: various approaches to return. */

main()
{
    int number;

    number = get5();
    printf( "get5 returned %d.\n", number );

    number = get6();
    printf( "get6 returned %d.\n", number );

    printf( "get7 returned %d.\n", get7() );
}

get5()   /* a function to return a value of 5 */
{
    return ( 5 );
}

get6()   /* a function to return a value of 6 */
{
    int val = 6;
    return ( val );
}

get7()   /* a function to return a value of 7 */
{
    int val;
    return ( val = 7 );
}
```

The use of *get7()* is somewhat different. The *print()* function, like all functions, expects its arguments to be passed by value. All we have done with *get7()* is to pass its returned value directly, without first assigning it to a variable. This illustrates that the value returned by a function can be treated exactly as though the function call itself possesses that value.

The program ''returndemo.c'' also demonstrates alternative ways of using the **return** statement. The function *get5()* returns the *constant value* 5. The function *get6()* returns the *value* of the variable *val.* This variable was assigned the value 6, so the value returned is that of *val* or 6.

The function *get7()* is a bit more roundabout. The value of the assignment

```
val = 7
```

is returned. Almost everything in C yields a usable value.[2] The value of an assignment statement is that of the result of the assignment.

3.5 EXPLAINING printf()

A Real Workhorse for Versatile Output   The *print()* function is a powerful member of the standard library that does a lot more than just print words to your screen. The *f* stands for *formatting,* and *printf()* can be used to print values, sentences, tables, and more.

When you call *printf(),* you must give it two pieces of information. The first piece (the mandatory one) is called the ''control string.'' The second (optional depending on the control string) is a list of values.

```
printf ( "control string" ,val1, val2, ... );
```

The control string *must* be enclosed in *full* quotation marks. With two exceptions, everything so enclosed will be printed. For example:

```
printf ( "hi there" );
```

will print the words ''hi there'' directly to your video screen.

The exceptions are the two special *format control directives,* one of which begins with a backslash character (\), and the other a percent character (%).

The Backslash Directive:\

When placed in the control string, the **backslash** directive is used to imbed control characters into the printed text. Control characters are those that *control* output. They can be produced by holding down the key marked CONTROL (or CTRL) while pressing a letter key. The RETURN and TAB keys also produce control char-

---

[2]Although not always a *useful* value.

acters. The most common control characters are represented in C as "\letter", as shown in this table:

\letter	Control	What It Does
\n	CTRL–J	linefeed or newline
\r	CTRL–M	carriage return
\t	CTRL–I	tab
\b	CTRL–H	backspace
\f	CTRL–L	formfeed
\0	CTRL–@	the value 0

For example, the "\n" in:

```
printf("Try saying that with any other language!"\n");
```

is there to produce a newline. This has the same effect as typing:

```
Try saying that with any other language!
```

on a typewriter, then pressing the RETURN or ENTER key.

The backslash directive can also be used to imbed quotation marks and the backslash character itself into text:

\character	What It Does
\"	imbed a " between full quotes
\'	imbed a ' between half quotes
\\	print a \

For example:

```
printf( "She said, \"Hi mom!\"");
```

will print:

```
She said, "Hi mom!"
```

Enter and compile the short program shown in Fig. 3–7. Try to determine what it will print before you actually run it.

FIGURE 3-7 pfdemo1.c

```
/* pfdemo1.c: illustrate use of the backslash character. */

main()
{
    printf( "name\taka\tage\n----\t---\t---\n" );
    printf( "Nelson\t\"Mo\"\t35\nZypher\t{none}\t2\n" );
}
```

Play with this program. Take a moment to find out what happens when *printf()* is asked to print "\z" if z is not one of those letters listed.

The Percent Directive: %

When placed in the control string, the **percent** directive tells *printf()* to print a value at that place in the text. The type of that value is specified by a letter immediately following the **%.** An unknown letter will either produce an error or some unexpected output.

Directive	Will Print
%d	an integer value
%c	a single character
%f	a floating-point value
%s	a string (Chapter 9)
%o	an octal value (Chapter 19)
%x	a hexidecimal value (Chapter 19)
%%	the character % itself

For each **%** directive appearing in the control string, a corresponding value *must* appear in the value list. To insert, for example, the integer value 5 into your output, you could:

```
printf ( "The number five looks like %d\n", 5);
```

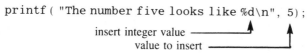

insert integer value ⟶

value to insert ⟶

which prints to your video screen:

```
The number five looks like 5
```

There can be as many **%** directives as you like. Just be sure that there are enough values, that they are in the right order, and that they are the right types.

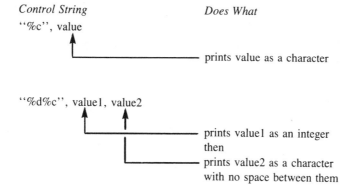

Control String   *Does What*

''%c'', value   prints value as a character

''%d%c'', value1, value2   prints value1 as an integer
then
prints value2 as a character
with no space between them

Compile ''pfdemo2.c'', shown in Fig. 3–8. Try to understand what will be printed before running it. Try changing things around just to see what happens.

In addition to printing a type, the **%** directive can be used to specify a field. This means that when the **%** directive is followed by a number, that number tells

FIGURE 3-8 pfdemo2.c

```
/* pfdemo2.c: illustrate use of the % in printf(). */

main()
{
    char   ch  = 'C';
    int    num = 2;
    float pi   = 3.14159265;

    printf( "%%c prints a character as '%c'.\n", ch );
    printf( "%%d prints an integer value as %d\n", num );
    printf( "%%f prints a float value as %f\n", pi );
    printf( "And %%%% prints the %% character as %%.\n" );
}
```

printf() how many spaces (the field size) to use when printing the value. For example:

```
printf ( ":%5d:", 99 );
```

will print:

```
:   99:
```

If the field is larger than the number of digits, they will be printed to the right side of the field. If the size of the field is negative, the digits will be printed to the left side of the field. If the field is too small, it will be expanded to accommodate the digits. If the field specification begins with a zero, the field will be zero filled from the left. Demonstrate this to yourself by compiling the program "pfdemo3.c" (Fig. 3–9).

FIGURE 3-9 pfdemo3.c

```
/* pfdemo3.c: illustrate field control with printf()   */

main()
{
    int num = 12345;

    printf( "to right     :%20d:\n",  num );
    printf( "to left      :%-20d:\n", num );
    printf( "truncated    :%3d:\n",   num );
    printf( "zero filled :%020d:\n",  num );
}
```

In addition to specifying the size of the field, the **%f** directive allows you to specify the number of *digits of precision*—the number of digits to the right of the decimal point in a floating-point number. To specify digits of precision add a dot (.) to the field specification, then follow the dot with the number of digits of precision you require. For example, ''%7.2f'' will print a floating-point number with two digits following the decimal point, within a field of size 7. Thus:

```
printf ( ":%7.2f:", 1.234):
```

will print:

```
: 1.23:
```

Similarly, ''%.2f'' will print two digits to the right of the decimal point, with no restriction on the size of the field.

If your compiler supports floating point, compile and run the program ''pfdemo4.c'' (Fig. 3–10).

FIGURE 3-10 pfdemo4.c

```
/* pfdemo4.c: illustrate precision control with printf() */

main()
{
    float val = 123.456;

    printf( "just %%f   :%f:\n",      val );
    printf( "%%10f      :%10f:\n",     val );
    printf( "%%10.2f    :%10.2f:\n",   val );
    printf( "%%.2f      :%.2f:\n",     val );
}
```

As you can see, *printf()* provides a general-purpose way to print many things in many ways to your screen. Take some time to experiment. Discover for yourself just how elegant *printf()* can be.[3]

---

[3]Others have pointed to the large *size* of the object code generated by the *printf()* function as a fault of the C language. In its defense, we note: (1) *printf()* is a library function, not strictly a part of the language; (2) it is a large and versatile function, so it is not surprising that it takes a lot of room; (3) for space-critical applications, there are other, smaller functions that can be used.

4. IF AND THE C OPERATORS

Finding Truth and Other Values Through Symbols.

4.1 INTRODUCING OPERATORS

Plus Two New Functions: Getchar () and Rand ()   Operators in C are special symbols which, when properly combined with values, yield a new value as the result. The six different kinds of operators we will cover in this chapter are:

Multiplicative	multiplication, division, modulo
Additive	addition, subtraction
Relational	is greater than, is less than
Equality	is equal to, is not equal to
Logical	and, or
Unary	unary minus, logical negation

In this chapter, you will also be introduced to the **if** keyword. The *if* keyword is one of several that test for the "truth" of a value and peform actions based on the result of that test.

With the introduction of **if** and the six kinds of operators, you will be able to write some slightly more exciting programs. But first, take a look at two new functions we'll be using. The first, ***getchar()***, is a standard library routine for reading a single character from your keyboard. The second, ***rand()***, is a routine that returns a pseudo-random number each time it is called.

Introducing getchar ()

When the ***getchar()*** function is called, it waits for you to press a key on the keyboard, then returns the integer value that corresponds to the value of that key. If you responded to the statement:

```
keypress = getchar();
```

by pressing the letter *A*, for example, the variable **keypress** would be assigned the character value 'A' (Chapter 2). Beware, however. On some systems the character is not returned until you press the RETURN or ENTER key. Your program still gets the same value—the only difference is that you must press an extra key to get it there.

Since **getchar()** returns a value of type **int,** the variable **keypress** should be declared to be of that type. However, since C is very forgiving about types, making **keypress** a **char** will work equally well most of the time. The few cases in which **char** will not work will be covered in Chapter 10.

Note that the program "getchardemo.c" (Fig. 4–1), like all programs that call **getchar(),** begins with the line:

```
# include <stdio.h>
```

This tells the compiler to read the file "stdio.h" as though it is additional text for the program. The file "stdio.h" is a system header file that contains the standard routines and definitions for many input/output functions. The **getchar()** function may not work unless that file is included.

FIGURE 4-1 *getchardemo.c*

```
/* getchardemo.c: character input using getchar()  */

#include <stdio.h>  /* always for getchar() */

main()
{
    int keypress;

    printf( "Press a key: " );

    keypress = getchar();

    printf( "\nYou pressed the '%c' key.\n", keypress );
}
```

Creating rand()

The **rand()** function we've devised for your use differs from the ones supplied with many C libraries. These others use **float** values, but ours is passed an **int** argument and returns an **int** value. How to handle functions that return **float** will be covered in Chapter 12.

Our **rand()** function is called by a statement such as:

```
number = rand( limit );
```

where **number** will be assigned a value between 1 and **limit.** Calling **rand()** with a negative argument will cause it to be "seeded" with a new starting value.

Take the time now to enter the listing provided in Appendix 2. You will understand how it works by the time you finish this book.

4.2 THE MULTIPLICATIVE AND ADDITIVE OPERATORS

The Means of Doing Something Useful with Variables The first two of our six operators are the very same things you learned—it is hoped—in grammar school.

Operator	Description
+ (a+b)	addition (adds a to b)
− (a−b)	subtraction (subtracts b from a)
* (a*b)	multiplication (a times b)
/ (a/b)	division (a divided by b)
% (a%b)	modulo (remainder of a divided by b)

Addition and subtraction act just as you would expect. Multiplication is also very straightforward, but division may be a bit confusing at first. When you divide an integer by an integer, you always get an integer result. Any remainder is simply thrown away (truncated). Should you need to know the remainder, you can use the modulo operator (%). This operator can be applied only to integer type variables. It provides the remainder of a division as an integer result. Thus:

5/2 yields 2 with remainder of 1, hence 5%2 yields 1

1/3 yields 0 with a remainder of 1, hence 1%3 yields 1

The program ''operdemo1.c'' illustrates the use of these operators. It is listed in Fig. 4–2. Note that the value of *keypress* has '0' subtracted from it. This is done to convert character values like '5' into numeric values like 5.[1]

4.3 THE if KEYWORD

The Truth and Nothing but . . . Opposites play an important role in C programming. They are things like yes versus no, living versus nonliving, true versus false, and zero versus not zero. What distinguishes these states is that each has one and only one opposite state—there is ''yes'' and ''no,'' but never ''maybe.''[2]

In C, a value of zero is always considered to be false. Any nonzero value, regardless of how small, is always considered to be true. The **if** keyword, in C, is one process by which the existence of a true state can be determined. In simplified form, the rule for using **if** is:

---

[1]This works because the ASCII representation of the digits have numerical values equal to the ASCII for '0' plus the digit value (see Appendix 3).

[2]You can also program up ''maybe'' by using a sliding (numerical) scale. Still, all-or-nothing variables are very basic to programming.

FIGURE 4-2 operdemo1.c

```
/* operdemo1.c: demonstrate +, -, *, / and % operators */

#include <stdio.h>  /* always for getchar() */

main()
{
    int x, y;

    printf( "enter two numbers, 1 digit each:\n" );

    printf( "x = " );
    x = getchar() - '0';          /* input and convert x */
    getchar();                /* dummy getchar for newline */

    printf( "y = " );
    y = getchar() - '0';  /* input and convert y */
    getchar();                /* dummy getchar for newline */

    printf( "\nx = %d and y = %d, so\n\n", x, y );

    printf( "x + y = %d\n", x + y );
    printf( "x - y = %d\n", x - y );
    printf( "x * y = %d\n", x * y );
    printf( "x / y = %d\n", x / y );
    printf( "x %% y = %d\n", x % y );
}
```

```
            if ( this is true )
                . . . do this;
```

If many statements are to be executed, the form would be:

```
            if ( this is true )
            {
                . . . do this;
                . . . and this;
                . . . and this;
            }
```

The parentheses following **if** must be there, and they must contain a value. The space between **if** and its parentheses is cosmetic and only used here to prevent the **if** statement from bein confused with a function call.

Since the constant value 0 is always considered false, and the constant value 1 is always considered true:

```
            if ( 0 )
                . . . this will never be done;
```

and

```
            if ( 1 )
                . . . this will always be done;
```

4.4 THE RELATIONAL AND EQUALITY OPERATORS

Ways to Measure One Value Against Another   The relational and equality operators are used to determine the "truth" regarding the relationship between two values. These operators are:

Operator	Example	Description
==	(a == b)	is a equal to b?
!=	(a != b)	is a not equal to b?
<	(a < b)	is a less than b?
>	(a > b)	is a greater than b?
<=	(a <= b)	is a less than or equal to b?
>=	(a >= b)	is a greater than or equal to b?

All of these operators perform a comparison of two values and produce a resultant value, which is either 1 (for true) or 0 (for false). Thus:

```
result = ( val1 > val2 );
```

first compares **val1** to **val2** . If **val1** is greater than **val2,** then the value of the comparison is 1 (true). If they are equal or **val1** is less than **val2,** then the value of the comparison is 0 (false). The resulting value of the comparison (1 or 0, for true or false) is then assigned to the variable **result**.

Note that **val1** and **val2** could be just about anything: variables, constants, or values obtained from computations or function calls. A statement such as:

```
if ( sub () == 0 )
```

for example, tests to see if the value returned by the function **sub()** is equal to 0.

The program in Fig. 4–3, "operdemo2.c", uses several of these concepts. The function **tolower()** converts letters from uppercase to lowercase and demonstrates a technique that can be very useful for processing user input of commands. For example:

```
keypress = tolower ( getchar () );
```

can be used to ensure that the program will see only lowercase input, regardless of what the user may type. Also notice how YES and NO are **#define'd** at the start of the program.

A common error in C programming lies in confusing the assignment operator (=) with the equality operator (= =). The former, a single equal sign (=), *assigns* the value on its right to a variable on its left. The latter, a double equal sign (= =), compares the value on its left to the value on its right and yields a value of 1 or 0, representing truth or falsity. Be careful, because:

```
if ( num = 5 )
```

will always be true! Had you wished to test whether **num** was *equal to* 5, a much more likely desire, you should have typed:

```
if ( num == 5 )
```

FIGURE 4-3   operdemo2.c

```c
/* operdemo2.c: demonstrate the equality operators */

#include <stdio.h>
#define YES 'y'
#define NO 'n'

main()
{
    int keypress;

    printf( "Want to know my name? (%c/%c) ", YES, NO );

    keypress = tolower( getchar() );

    if ( keypress == YES )
        printf( "\nMy name is Morris\n" );

    if ( keypress != YES )
        printf( "\n" );
}


/*
** tolower( ch ): If ch uppercase, return it as
**        lowercase. This works because of how
**        ASCII characters are arranged.
*/
tolower( ch )
char ch;
{
    if ( ch < 'A' )
        return ( ch );

    if ( ch > 'Z' )
        return ( ch );

    return ( (ch - 'A') + 'a' );
}
```

4.5 THE else KEYWORD

A Way to Handle False Tests   The C language has a keyword that goes hand in hand with **if**. Called **else,** the rules for its use are shown here. If there is only a single action to take, use:

```
if ( this is true )
    . . . do this;
else
    . . . do this;
```

If there is more than one action to take, use:

```
if ( this is true )
    . . . do this;
else
{
    . . . do this;
    . . . and this;
    . . . and this;
}
```

If the value of the expression in parentheses evaluates to true, the instructions under the **if** are executed, as you learned before. But if that value evaluates to false, **if's** instructions are skipped and the instructions under the **else** are executed.

The program "guessit.c", listed in Fig. 4–4, illustrates one application of **else**. This primitive game, using our *rand()* function, gives you one chance to guess a random number between one and nine. Notice how the function *isdigit()* is used to check whether your guess is a legal one. Also pay special attention to which **else** belongs to which **if**. Note how indenting helps to clarify these relationships.

4.6 THE LOGICAL OPERATORS

Multiple Choices in Tests for Truth The C language provides two operators for choosing between truths. They are the logical-and and the logical-or. The symbols used to represent these operators take a bit of getting used to. The logical-and is represented with a double ampersand (&&), and the logical-or is represented with a double vertical line (| |). For example:

```
if ( this AND that)
```

is written:

```
if ( this && that)
```

and means the instructions following the **if** will be executed only if *both* "this" and "that" are true. Similarly:

```
if ( this OR that)
```

is written:

```
if ( this || that)
```

and means the intructions following the **if** will be executed if *either* "this" or "that" are true, or if **both** are true.

These operators can be used to simplify the flow of your programs. Notice how the function *isdigit()* (Fig. 4–5) from "guessit.c" is reduced to a single line.

A word of caution is in order regarding the | | operator. When a series of test values are evaluated, each separated by an | |, those tests will be made beginning with the leftmost one. The moment a *true* value is found, all further testing is skipped. For example:

FIGURE 4-4   guessit.c

```c
/* guessit.c: demonstrates if/else as a game */

#include <stdio.h>
#define MAX 9
#define TRUE 1
#define FALSE 0

main()
{
    int guess, num;

    rand( -1 );                             /* seed rand() */
    num = rand( MAX ) + '0';            /* make a character */

    printf( "guess a number between 1 and %d: ", MAX );
    guess = getchar();

    if ( isdigit( guess ) == TRUE )
    {
        if ( guess == num )
            printf( "\nYou got it!\n" );
        else
            printf( "\nNope\n" );
    }
    else
        printf( "\nYou must guess with a number.\n" );
}

/*
** isdigit( ch ): return TRUE if ch a digit, else FALSE.
*/
isdigit( ch )
char ch;
{
    if ( ch < '0' )
        return ( FALSE );

    else if ( ch > '9' )
        return ( FALSE );

    else
        return ( TRUE );
}

/** the rand() function goes here **/
```

FIGURE 4-5   isdigit()

```
/*
** isdigit() (revision 1): revised to a single line
*/
isdigit( ch )
char ch;
{
    return ( ch >= '0' && ch <= '9' );
}
```

```
if ( he == who || (c = getchar()); != '\n' )
```

will first test for **he** being equal to **who**. Whenever that test is true, the test for:

```
(c = getchar()) != '\n'
```

will *not* be done. As a consequence, **getchar()** will *not* be called, and the value of **c** will *not* be changed!

4.7 PRECEDENCE AND DIRECTION OF EVALUATION

The Built-in Rules for Resolving Ambiguity   A common problem for programmers is understanding how the compiler will interpret a statement containing several operations. The statement:

```
result = 1 + 2 * 3;
```

for example, can be interpreted two different ways. If the addition is to be done before the multiplication:

```
result = (1 + 2) * 3;
```

the result will be 9. However, if the multiplication is to be done first:

```
result = 1 + (2 * 3);
```

the result will be 7.

When clarifying parentheses are absent, the C compiler has a set of rules that govern which operations will be performed first. These rules, called *operator precedence,* are given in a table in Appendix 3. The higher an operator is in that table, the stronger is its bonding with variables. The multiplicative operator ***** is above the additive operator **+** in the table, meaning that the compiler will multiply before it adds. Using these rules, C will always resolve the ambiguous example above as:

```
result = 1 + (2 * 3);
```

The situation becomes a bit stickier when two operators are of equal height (precedence). Take, for example, the division operator **/** and the modulo operator **%**:

result = 6 / 3 % 2;

Depending on how this is grouped, the result could be 0 or 6. In this situation, C relies on a predefined *direction of grouping*. The third column in the table of Appendix 3 lists that direction of grouping for each level of operators. For the / and % operators, the direction of grouping is left to right. Since they are both of equal height (precedence) in the table, the leftmost one will be done first:

result = (6 / 3) % 2;

We recommend that—if you wish for a calculation to be interpreted only one way—you clearly specify that way using parentheses. This will make your intention clear to both the compiler and to anyone who later reads your source text.[3]

4.8 THE UNARY OPERATORS

Operators that Operate on a Single Variable   As a kind of shorthand, C provides the programmer with some special operators. Two of these are the **not** operator, represented with the symbol ''!'', and the **negation** operator, represented with the symbol ''−''.

A common test in C programming is one to see if an expression or variable is equal to 0. For example, to test the variable *num* to see if it equals 0, you could state:

if (num = = 0)

The *not* (!) operator inverts the truth of a variable or expression. If *num* is not 0 (true) then *!num* will be false. If *num* is 0 (false) then *!num* will be true. This inversion of truth can be used to simplify our test to:

if (! num)

which simply says that if ''*num* = = 0'' (that is, *num* is false), then *!num* is true.

As a word of wisdom, observe that:

if (num = = 0)

is clearer and easier to understand than:

if (! num)

They both achieve the same result, but the former is preferred and is the method we will stick to throughout this book.

Another common inversion in C is that of reversing the sign of a variable. The **negation** operator (−), when applied to a variable or expression, reverses the sign of the value of that variable or expression. If it is positive, it will become negative, and if it is negative it will become positive. For example, the statement:

num = 0 − num;

[3]It also will give your program a better shot at working on another machine or operating system.

can be used to reverse the sign of the variable ***num*** by subtracting its original value from 0. This same effect can be achieved by using the **negation** operator − as:

num = − num;

Both the ***not*** and the ***negation*** operators can be applied to expressions as well as variables. Thus:

! (num = x + y)

yields a truth that is the opposite of the truth of the assignment. And:

- (num = x + y)

yields a value that has a sign opposite that of the assignment. The application of the **negation** operator will become clearer as it is used in program examples throughout the remainder of this book.

5. FOR AND WHILE LOOPS

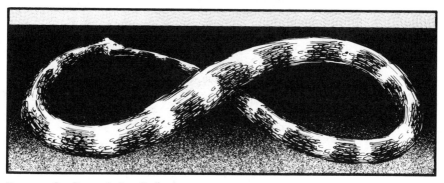

Programs Can Repeat Actions Endlessly.

5.1 INTRODUCING LOOPS

It's Hard to Bore a Computer with the Routine[1] One of the chief strengths of a computer is its ability to perform repeated tasks rapidly, accurately, and without complaint. Up to now, programs you've written have run once and then stopped. You can, however, tell a computer to do the same thing over and over again, millions of times. The C language contains four keywords that allow programs to repeat actions. We will cover three in this chapter. They are:

while	Much like: "While I'm watching you, you had better keep scrubbing that floor."
for	Much like: "For that load of dishes, until there are no dishes left, wash each one and put it away."
do-while	Much like: "Do your homework, while there is homework left to be done."

5.2 THE while LOOP

"While I'm Watching You . . ." Like the **if** keyword, **while** causes a test to be made for truth and certain actions are either taken or skipped based on that test. For a single action, the form is:

```
while ( this is true )
    . . . do this;
```

[1]But it's fun to try.

For multiple actions, the form is:

```
while ( this is true )
{
        . . . do this;
        . . . and this;
        . . . and this;
}
```

But, unlike **if, while** does not necessarily take those actions only once. Instead, it skips back to the truth test and tests it again. This looping (repetition) continues until the test yields a false value, then, like **if,** the program goes on:

```
while ( this continues to be true )
{
        . . . do this;
        . . . and this;
        . . . and this;
        . . . and then skip back
}
    . . . continue here when test becomes false
```

Obviously, if nothing happens to change the test to false, the program will continue looping forever.[2] The program in Fig. 5–1 illustrates one way of terminating a **while** loop.

FIGURE 5-1 blastoff.c

```
/* blastoff.c: illustrating the while loop */

main()
{
    int count;

    printf( "counting down:\n" );
    count = 10;

    while ( count > 0 )        /*  exit loop when count == 0    */
    {
        printf( "%d\n", count );
        count = count - 1;                    /* decrease count */
    }

    printf( "Blastoff!\n" );
}
```

A more practical application for **while** is the creation of a special function for input. Unlike *getchar (),* this function will allow a number more than a single digit long to be entered. See program ''getd.c'', listed in Fig. 5–2.

---

[2]Or until the vacuum tubes in your Apple need changing.

Here the value that **while** is testing is a bit more complex. In the expression:

```
while ((ch = getchar() != '\n' )
```

first ***ch*** is assigned a value returned by ***getchar()***. The result of that assignment, or that of ***ch,*** is then compared to the character constant value of a *newline*. This test provides a means of exiting when the user presses the RETURN or ENTER key.

FIGURE 5-2 getd()

```
/*
** getd(): input digits from the keyboard and return as
**         an integer value.  Non-digits ignored.
*/
getd()
{
    int ch, num, sign;

    num = Ø;
    sign = 1;
    while ( (ch = getchar()) != '\n' )
    {
        if ( ch == '-' )      /* minus sign makes negative */
            sign = -sign;

        ch = ch - 'Ø';        /* convert to integer value */

        if ( ch >= Ø && ch <= 9 )  /* ignore non-digits */
            num = (num * 1Ø) + ch;
    }
    return ( num * sign );
}
```

5.3 THE break KEYWORD

Exit a Loop in Midstream   There are times when you might wish to exit a **while** loop regardless of the result of its test for truth. The **break** keyword does just that, causing the loop to be exited immediately:

```
while (this is true)
{
    . . . do this:
    . . . and this;
    break;
}
. . . continue the program here
```

A very important rule concerning **break** is that it exits only the *current* loop when loops are nested:

```
while ( test )
{
        while ( another test )
        {
      ┌──────── break;
      │ }
      │ └──────►  . . .continue outer while loop here
{
. . . continue program here
```

Usually break is invoked with an **if** statement. Despite its similarity to the **while** loop, **if** is *not* a loop, and a **break** as a result of an **if** test exits the **while** loop.

```
while ( test )
{
        if ( another test )
        {
  ┌──────────── break;
  │     }
  │           . . .continue while here
  │ }
  └►. . . continue program here
```

5.4 THE continue KEYWORD

The Means to Force an Early Repeat   Just as there are times when you might want to *exit* a **while** loop early, there are also times when you might want it to *repeat* early. The **continue** keyword causes an immediate jump to the *test* of a **while** loop.

```
┌►while ( this is true )
│  {
│          . . .do this;
└────────── continue;
           . . .and this;

        . . .rest of program here
  }
```

Again note that **continue** continues only the current loop. Like **break,** the **continue** statement applies only to loops, so a **continue** inside an **if** will skip to the loop containing that **if.**

```
┌►while ( this is true )
│  {
│          if ( test )
└────────── continue;
           . . .

  }
. . .rest of program here
```

Using **while, break,** and **continue,** we will now write the program "wheelo.c", a wheel-of-fortune-style betting game. Look at Fig. 5–3 and notice the statement:

FIGURE 5-3 wheelo.c

```c
/* wheelo.c: betting game demonstrates while/break/continue */

#include <stdio.h>   /* for getchar */
#define MAXNUM 25

main()
{
    int num, guess, bet, coins, woncoins, i;

    printf( "Any key to begin" );
    rand( 0 - getchar() );                        /* seed rand() */

    coins = 100;
    while( 1 )
    {
        printf( "\nYou have %d coins\n", coins );

        printf( "Place your bet (0 to quit): " );
        if ( (bet = getd()) == 0)
            break;

        printf( "Pick a number (0 - %d): ", MAXNUM );
        if( (guess = getd()) > MAXNUM )
            continue;

        num = rand( MAXNUM );
        printf( "Round she goes & it's:  %d\n", num );

        if( guess == num )
        {
            woncoins = bet * (MAXNUM - 1);
            printf( "\nyou win %d coins\n", woncoins );
            coins = coins + woncoins;
        }
        else
        {
            printf( "\nyou lose\n" );
            coins = coins - bet;
        }

        if (coins <= 0)
            break;
    }
    printf( "Game over, you have %d coins\n", coins );
}

/**** place getd() and rand() here ****/
```

```
while ( 1 )
```

The **while** test, like the **if** test, bases its decision on the value it finds between the parentheses. Since 1 is always a true value, the **while** loop will continue to loop forever, or until it encounters a **break.**

5.5 INCREMENT AND DECREMENT

A Little Change Can Be Just the Thing   Since changing value by 1 is so common in programming, especially in loops, C offers two handy operators: **+ +** and **− −**. The first (double plus signs) is used to increment (increase) a value by 1. The second (double minus signs) is used to decrement (decrease) a value by 1. These operators are placed either before or after a variable, depending on *when* you want the value incremented or decremented.

When they are on the left, the value of the variable is incremented or decremented before it is used. Thus:

```
int result, number = 1;
result = ++number; /* both result and number = = 2*/
```

When the operator is on the right, the value of the variable is used as is, and after that, it is incremented or decremented. Thus:

```
int result, number = 1;
result = number ++; /* result = = 1, number = = 2 */
```

The usefulness of these two operators can be seen in this rewrite of "blastoff.c". Look at Fig. 5–4 and notice how much smaller the program has become.

FIGURE 5-4   blastoff.c (revision 1)

```
/* blastoff.c (revision 1): revised to illustrate -- operator */

main()
{
    int count;

    printf( "counting down:\n" );
    count = 10;

    while ( count > 0 )
    {
        /*
        ** note how count is decremented after printing
        */
        printf( "%d\n", count-- );
    }

    printf( "Blastoff!\n" );
}
```

To make sure you fully understand these operators, try to predict the output of the short program listed in Fig. 5–5.³

FIGURE 5-5 incdecdemo.c

```
/* incdecdemo.c: an increment/decrement challenge */

main()
{
    int number;

    number = 1;

    printf( "step 1: %d\n", number++ );
    printf( "step 2: %d\n", --number );
    printf( "step 3: %d\n", ++number );
}
```

5.6 THE for LOOP

"For That Load of Dishes . . ."   The beauty of the **for** loop is that it contains all of its control in one compact line:

```
for ( initialize; test; change )
    . . . do this;
```

and:

```
for (initialize; test; change)
{
    . . . do this;
    . . . and this;
}
```

By way of example, the program "blastoff.c" counted down to 0 from 10. Rewritten with a **for** statement, that countdown would be:

```
for (count = 10; count > 0; --count )
    printf ( "%d\n", count ) ;
```

First *count* is assigned the value 10. This happens only once, when the *for* statement is first entered. Then *count* is compared to 0. While the result of the comparison is true (1)—*count* is greater than 0—the *printf()* statement is executed. Then *count* is decremented, tested again, and the loop continues.

The steps of a **for** loop can be better visualized by comparing them to an equivalent **while** loop:

³You get to read the program first.

```
        initialize        test        change
       _____      _____    _____

for       ( count = 10;   count > 0;    --count )
{
        . . . do this;
}
```

is exactly the same as:

```
count = 10;              ◄——— initialize
while (count > 0 )       ◄——— test
{
    . . . do this;
    --count;             ◄——— change
}
```

A **break** is used to prematurely exit the loop, just as it is used with **while.** A **continue,** however, jumps to the *change* part of the **for** statement rather than the test.

If the middle expression in a **for** statement is missing, it is presumed always true. The first and last expressions are simply ignored if they are missing. Thus:

```
for ( ; ; )
```

just like:

```
while ( 1 )
```

becomes an endless loop.

The three expressions are not required to relate to the same variable. This malleability of **for** can lead to some very strange-looking, but legal, statements:

```
for ( max = 100; last != first; current ++ )
for ( value = 0 ; ; count = 0 )
for (start = end; ; )
```

Examine the rewrite of the *getd()* function listed in Figure 5–6. Note how, in addition to using **for** instead of **while,** the logic has been revised to use **continue.**

5.7 THE do-while STATEMENT

"Do Your Homework While . . . "　One limitation common to both **for** and **while** is that they both *begin* with a test. For these times when you might wish to perform the test last, C provides the **do** keyword. The **do** is always used in combination with **while,** hence the notation **do-while:**

FIGURE 5-6   getd() (revision 1)

```
/*
** getd() (revision 1): revised to illustrate the for loop
*/
getd()
{
    int ch, num, sign;

    sign = 1;

    for ( num = 0; (ch = getchar()) != '\n';  )
    {
        if ( ch == '-' )
            sign = -1;

        else if ( (ch = ch - '0') < 0  ||  ch > 9 )
            continue;

        num = (num * 10) + ch;
    }
    return ( num * sign );
}
```

```
        do
        {
            . . . this;
            . . . and this;
            . . . and this;
        } while ( this is true );
```

The **while** is on the same line as the closing curly brace for cosmetic reasons. This is intended to make it clear that the **while** belongs with the **do** and is not a separate statement. The semicolon following the test at the end of a **do-while** is mandatory. We recommend that curly braces *always* be used to enclose the actions of **do-while** even if there is only a single action:

```
        do
        {
            . . . this;
        } while ( this is true );
```

A **break** behaves just as you would expect. It immediately exits the loop, bypassing the **while**. A **continue** skips immediately to the **while** test. It does not go to the top of the loop at the **do.**

The **do-while** combination is so seldom used that an enlightening example is difficult to find.[4] Examine the following fragment:

---

[4]Even unenlightening examples are hard to find, but they can be produced more easily.

```
do
{
    c = getchar () ;
} while ( c != '\n' ) ;
```

To skip to the end of a line, it is necessary to read at least one character *before* the test.

6 · CLASS AND FORM

Variables Can Be Widely Known and Have Timeless Value.

6.1 auto VERSUS static

Fresh Versus Long-Lasting Variables   In addition to type, variables in C also possess a quality called *class.* One property of class is longevity and refers to the length of time a variable exists and maintains a value. In C, the two possible ways to declare a variable's longevity are with the keywords **auto** and **static.**

The longevity of a variable of class **auto** is brief. Such variables may exist only inside functions. They are created afresh whenever their function is called, then forgotten when it is exited. The program ''autostat.c'' (Fig. 6-1) demonstates this concept. The variable *anum* will possess a new value each time the function *autoplus()* is called, but it will exhibit no memory of anything done to it in previous calls.[1]

The keyword **auto** is reserved but almost never used. The statement:

```
auto int anum;
```

is legal but redundant. Unless otherwise stated, all variables declared inside functions are by default **auto.**

There are other times when you will want a variable with a ''permanent'' longevity, one that maintains a particular value between calls to the function containing it. In C, the class specifier **static** creates such a variable. The statement:

```
static int num;
```

declares *num* to be a **static** (permanent) variable of type **int.** The declaration **static** must precede the type declaration.

---

[1]Unlike your own memory, your computer's will be consistent about what it does or doesn't store. If it isn't, kick it a few times.

53

FIGURE 6-1 autostat.c

```
/* autostat.c:  demonstrates auto vs static. auto first */

main()
{
    int i;                        /* i is auto by default */

    printf( "Auto vs Static\n\n" );

    printf( "auto:\n" );

    for ( i = 1; i < 10; i++ )
    {
        printf( "%d: autoplus() = %d\n", i, autoplus() );
    }
}

autoplus()
{
    int anum;      /* auto by default, value == garbage */

    return ( ++anum );
}
```

Now add to ''autostat.c'' the function *statplus()* containing a **static** variable called *snum*. This revision is shown in Fig. 6–2.

Unlike **auto** variables, **static** variables are guaranteed a beginning value of 0 even if they are not initialized. Thus:

```
main()
{
    static int b;
    int c;
}
```

results in the variable *b* having a beginning value of 0, and *c* having a beginning value of garbage.[2] **Static** variables when initialized as:

```
static int b = 25;
```

will be assigned the initialization value only once, when the program is first executed. But **auto** variables when initialized as:

```
int c = 25;
```

will be assigned the initialization value afresh *each time* their function is called.

[2]This does not mean *c* is initialized to old fish heads. It means the initial value is generally unknown.

FIGURE 6-2 autostat.c (revision 1)

```
/* autostat.c (revision 1):  auto vs static. now static */

main()
{
    int i;

    printf( "Auto vs Static\n\n" );

    printf( "auto:\n" );

    for ( i = 1; i < 10; i++ )
    {
        printf( "%d: autoplus() = %d\n", i, autoplus() );
    }

    printf( "static:\n" );

    for ( i = 1; i < 10; i++ )
    {
        printf( "%d: statplus() = %d\n", i, statplus() );
    }
}

autoplus()
{
    int anum;                /* auto by default, value == garbage */

    return ( ++anum );
}

statplus()
{
    static int snum;              /* declared static, value == 0 */

    return ( ++snum );
}
```

One final rewrite of "autostat.c" will demonstrate this difference. Notice that *autoplus()* and *statplus()* have been combined into the new function *getnew()*, so the variables can be printed together. The variable **anum** begins as 25 each time *getnew()* is called. The variable **snum** remembers what its previous incremented value was and increases with each call to *getnew().* This latest revision of "autostat.c" is shown in Fig. 6–3.

FIGURE 6-3 *autostat.c (revision 2)*

```
/* autostat.c (revision 2):  now both initialized  */

main()
{
    int i;

    for ( i = 1; i < 10; i++ )
    {
        getnew();
    }
}

getnew()
{
    static int snum = 25; /* declared static, starts at 25 */
    int anum = 25;        /* auto by default, starts at 25 */

    printf( "snum =%3d   anum =%3d\n", ++snum, ++anum );
}
```

6.2 LOCAL VERSUS GLOBAL

Variables Can Be Made Known to Many Functions   Another property of class is accessibility, and it refers to which functions know of, and can access, which variables. Variables declared inside a function are only known to and used by that function. You have seen in the declarations:

```
main()
{
    int thisvar;
    ...
}
```

and:

```
sub()
{
    int othervar;
    ...
}
```

that both *thisvar* and *othervar* are each local to the function in which each was declared. The function *main()* knows of *thisvar,* but knows nothing of *othervar,* and vice versa. This is true whether the variables are **auto** or **static.**

By placing a variable outside a function, you are making it known to all the functions that follow. Such variables are called *external,* because they exist externally to functions, and *global* because they are available for use by many functions. Externally placed (global) variables, like **static** variables, last the life of the program.

In the following fragment:

```
int Outside;
main()
{
    int inside;
}
int Otheroutside;
sub()
{
    int otherinside;
}
sub2()
{
}
```

the variable *Outside* is known and accessible to all three functions. The variables *inside* and *otherinside* are each known only to the functions they are in. But the variable *Otheroutside* is known *only* to *sub()* and *sub2()*. Remember that **global** variables are known only to all the functions that *follow* that variable's declaration.

The program "stars.c", listed in Fig. 6–4, illustrates one application for **global** variables. The function *instuff()* is asked to affect two different variables depending on which key is pressed. One easy solution is to make those variables **global,** that is, **static** and external to all functions.

To make our programs more readable, we have chosen to capitalize the first letter of **global** variable names. This sets them apart, and makes it easier to see what is going on inside the program.

Global variables should be avoided when designing functions you may later wish to use in other programs. Notice how often we have used the function *getd()*, for example. This would have been difficult if that function had relied on **global** variables defined in the program in which it originally appeared.[3]

6.3 WHERE THINGS MUST BE

Although Free-Form, C Has Some Positional Constraints   The C compiler is a one-pass compiler, that is, it's a single program that looks at your source text one time and generates the correct assembler code. The disadvantage of this is that it can only look *forward* to find things it needs to know. Because of this design property of the compiler, there are restrictions on where statements may be placed. An external variable, for example, is known only to the functions that follow its declaration, because the compiler compiles from the top down. Until a variable is declared, it does not exist. Similarly, the C compiler requires all declarations inside functions to precede all code. For example:

---

[3]Extensive use of global variables also makes expansions and alterations more difficult, as it is harder to trace "side effects" of actions on those variables. Try to use passed values (function arguments) wherever possible.

FIGURE 6-4 stars.c

```
/* stars.c: draws lines of stars or other characters */

#include <stdio.h>  /* for getchar() */

int Howmany = 9,     /* how many characters to print */
    Letter  = '*';   /* the character which gets printed */

main()
{
    printf( "stars\n" );
    while ( Howmany != 0 )
    {
        instuff();
        outstuff();
    }
}

instuff()
{
    int ch;

    if ( (ch = getchar()) >= '0' && ch <= '9' )
        Howmany = ch - '0';
    else
        Letter = ch;

    printf( "\n" );
}

outstuff()
{
    int i;

    for ( i = 0; i < Howmany; i++ )
    {
        printf( "%c", Letter );
    }
    printf( "\n" );
}
```

```
main()
{
    int num;
    char letter;
    ++num;
    ...
}
```

is correct because all the declarations precede the actions. However:

```
main()
{
     int num;
     ++num;
     char letter;
     . . .
}
```

is incorrect and will cause an error because a declaration follows an action.

In practice, some compilers are less "picky" about these restrictions. Take time to compile the short test program, "wheretest.c", then, by gradually changing it one error at a time, you can discover how much you can get away with on your particular compiler. The program is listed in Fig. 6–5. If you expect to be writing programs that can be transported to other machines and other compilers, you should adhere to positional restrictions we will outline thoughout this book.

FIGURE 6-5 wheretest.c

```
/* wheretest.c: correct to compile without errors */

int Bigboy;

main()
{
    int smallboy;
    Bigboy = smallboy;
    int i;

    for ( i = 0; i < 10; i++ )
        printf( "lastboy = %d\n", Lastboy = ++Bigboy );
}

int Lastboy;
```

6.4 PROGRAM FORM AND WHITE SPACE

The "Look" of Your Program Is Up to You   "White space" is the stuff you don't see. It is the air in which the words and symbols of your program float. It is spaces, tabs, and newlines. But just as with the stuff you *do* see, white space has certain rules that must be obeyed if your program is to compile.

In C, there are certain keywords that are reserved for special use by the compiler. Keywords must be separated from other keywords and from identifiers by at least one piece of white space. In the declaration:

```
static int num;
```

the keywords **static** and **int** must be separated by at least one white space—space, tab, or newline. The keyword **int** and the identifer *num* must also be separated by at least one white space.

Except for preprocessor directives, such as:

```
#define THIS that
```

which are restricted to a single line, C itself views the newline as just another piece of white space. The declaration:

```
char letter, punct, air;
```

may be rewritten, with no change in meaning, as:

```
char letter,
     punct,
     air;
```

The only instance in which C views the newline as special is within quotation marks. A newline can never occur between full or half quotation marks. For example:

```
"This sentence is false"
```

is a legal string, but inserting a newline:

```
"This sentence
is false"
```

will cause the compiler to complain loudly about a missing quote.[4]

Other than this handful of restrictions, the C compiler treats all white space as though it does not exist. It is merely there to make your program clear and readable. In the eyes of the compiler there is no difference between:

```
foo = ( x * y ) / bar ( z ) ;
```

and:

```
foo=(x*y)/bar(z);
```

and:

```
            foo
= (x        *y
) /bar      (z) ;
```

But to human eyes, the difference is between a program that is easy to interpret and debug and a program that's a puzzle.

Consider for a moment the plight of the clever programmer who decided to create two versions of his program—a clean, well-documented version for his own use (Fig. 6-6), and a compact, but ugly version for distribution (Fig. 6-7). Unfortunately, he made a single typo in each version. Even though he knew they both did exactly the same thing (made a pyramid of dots), he found the ugly version much harder to fix. Try to undo his mistakes.

We repeat the assertion that C, while one of the easiest languages to write, can be the most difficult language to read (*if* you abuse your stylistic freedom). The

---

[4]As if that was the big problem with the sentence.

FIGURE 6-6 easy.c

```
/* easy.c: a well written program is easier to debug */

#define MAX 11      /* maximum number of dots */

main()
{
    int dots,    /*     number of dots per line, always odd */
        num,     /*      for loop counter to print the dots */
        spaces;  /* left padding spaces to create triangle */

    /*
    ** increment dots by 2 to keep odd
    */
    for ( dots = 1; dots <= MAX; dots = dots + 2 )
    {
        /*
        ** first print the left padding spaces
        */
        for ( spaces = 0; spaces < (MAX-dots)/2; spaces++ )
            printf( " " );

        /*
        ** then the dots
        */
        for ( num = 0;  num < dots; num++ )
            printf( "." );

        /*
        ** and finish each line with a newline
        */
        printf( "\n" );
    }
}
```

FIGURE 6-7 ugly.c

```
/* ugly.c: an ugly program is very difficult to debug */

main(){int x,y,z;for(x=1;x<=11;x=x+2){for(z=0;z<(11-x)/2;z++
){printf(" ");}for(y=0;y<z;y++){printf(".");}printf("\n");}}
```

responsibility for writing readable code lies squarely on your shoulders.[5] As a benefit to yourself and as a courtesy to others, you should strive to develop a clear, concise programming form.

[5]The buck stops here.

7 · ARRAYS

Organizing Many Items of One Type Together.

7.1 DECLARING ARRAYS

Many Variables Collectively Given a Single Name   An array is a collection of variables, all of the same type, organized sequentially and given a single name. Arrays are always continuous, with each variable placed one after the other, end on end. Each element of an array, a single variable, is accessed by its offset (distance) from the start of the array. The first such variable has an offset of 0, since it is at the beginning of the array, the second an offset of 1 and so forth. The declaration:

```
int nums[6];
```

declares *nums* to be the name of an array of six integers, each of type **int.** This can be graphically represented as:

type:	int	int	int	int	int	int
nums[6]:	val0	val1	val2	val3	val4	val5
offset:	[0]	[1]	[2]	[3]	[4]	[5]

To declare a six-element array named *fred,* each element of type **char,** you would state:

```
char fred[6];
```

where *fred* is a legal variable name. The **char** states that the array will hold items of type **char,** and the "[6]" reserves memory for six of those items. By changing the **car** to **float:**

```
float fred[6];
```

you can reserve space for six items of type **float.**

The rules for declaring an array are identical to those for declaring any other variable, with one addition. The size, or number of elements in an array, must be declared with a *constant expression*. For example:

```
char stack[6];
```

is legal because 6 is a constant, and:

```
#define MAX 6
. . .
char line[ MAX - 1 ];
```

is legal because MAX is **#define'd** as 6, a constant, so 6 minus 1 is a constant expression.

You may not, however, declare an array's size using a variable. That is, a statement like:

```
int size = 6;
. . .
char stack[size];
```

is illegal. The space created for an array *must* be created by the compiler, not by the running program. This unfortunately means there is no way to *dynamically* declare arrays, but techniques will be given in Chapter 15 for circumventing that restriction.

7.2 ARRAY ELEMENTS AS VARIABLES

Accessing Values from an Array Using an Offset   Each element of an array can be used just like any other variable by specifying its offset from the start of the array. That offset is also known as an *index* into the array. By way of example:

```
stack[4] = 15;
```

assigns the constant value 15 to the element offset 4 into the array named *stack*— that is, the *fifth* element of the array. The statement:

```
var = stack[3];
```

assigns the value of element offset 3 into the array named *stack* to the variable named *var.* And the statement:

```
int index = 3;
. . .
var = stack[index];
```

assigns the value of the element whose offset is the value of the variable *index* to the variable *var.*

One common source of errors for beginners is forgetting that arrays start at element 0. When seeing the declaration:

```
int arrayname[100];
```

it is very tempting to access array element number 100. Try to remember that such a declaration allocates 100 elements, all right, but they are numbered 0 through 99, not 1 through 100. C will *not* help you if you forget. The compiler contains no provision to detect an attempt to access an element outside the bounds of an array.[1]

Enter, compile, and run "reverse.c". This short program, listed in Fig. 7–1, first fills an array with characters you type in, then prints them out in the reverse order. If you've ever wondered what a palindrome is, try typing "lewd I did live, evil did I dwel."

FIGURE 7-1 reverse.c

```
/* reverse.c: reverse and print a line of text */

#include <stdio.h>

#define MAX 80
#define DONE '\n'

main()
{
    char line[MAX];
    int  i;

    while ( 1 )
    {
        printf( "Enter line to reverse:\n" );

        for( i = 0; i < MAX; i++ )
        {
            if( (line[i] = getchar()) == DONE )
                break;
        }

        if( i == 0 && line[i] == DONE )
            break;

        for( --i; i >= 0; i-- )
        {
            printf( "%c", line [i] );
        }
        printf( "\n\n" );
    }
}
```

Arrays are also useful for buffering (temporarily holding) information for later processing. The next program, called "calc.c", is a simplified calculator. It is listed in Fig. 7–2. Here an array will be used as a stack (buffer). To add two numbers, first

---

[1]Occasionally, the system will give you an uninformative error message at run time if you try to do this, but don't count on it.

FIGURE 7-2 calc.c

```
/* calc.c:  a simple "reverse polish notation" calculator */

#include <stdio.h>

#define MAXSTACK 20
#define ENTER '\n'

main()
{
    int stack[MAXSTACK], ch, top, temp;

    temp = 0;
    top = 0;
    stack[top] = 0;

    while ( (ch = getchar()) != 'q' )   /* q to quit */
    {
        if ( ch >= '0' && ch <= '9' )
            temp = (temp * 10) + ch - '0';

        else if ( ch == ENTER && temp != 0 )
        {
            if ( top == (MAXSTACK -1) )
            {
                printf( "\nStack overflow. -- aborted.\n" );
                break;
            }
            stack[top++] = temp;
            temp = 0;
        }
        else if ( ch == '+' && top > 0 && temp > 0)
        {
            stack[top] = temp;
            temp = 0;
            stack[top - 1] = stack[top - 1] + stack[top];
            --top;
        }
        else if ( ch == 'p' )
            printf( "\n%d\n", stack[ top ] );
        else
            printf( "?huh?\n" );
    }
    printf( "\n" );
}
```

enter them, then press the PLUS key. The top two numbers on the stack will be added, the top number discarded, and the second from the top replaced with the result. Pressing the p key will print the top number, or that result.

This program has the potential to be made into a useful tool. You might try augmenting it to handle subtraction, multiplication, division, and averaging. Or make it more robust by including tests for anticipated error conditions like division by zero and undefined letters.[2]

7.3 INITIALIZING ARRAYS

Specify a Starting Value for Each Element   Just like a simple variable, an array may have its contents stated at the time it is declared. Thus:

```
int nums[3] = { 1, 2, 3 };
```

declares a three-element array and assigns to those elements the starting values 1, 2, and 3. This is equivalent to saying:

```
int nums[3];
  . . . .
nums[0] = 1;
nums[1] = 2;
nums[2] = 3;
```

The general rule for initializing an array, in its simplest form, is:

```
int name[n] = { val0, val1, . . ., valn-1};
```

where the values are separated from each other by commas and are contained within a curly-brace pair. The array is filled with those values from left to right, beginning at offset 0.

Because of the way the compiler works, values used to initialize arrays must be "already known." Constant values can of course be used, as they are always known.

Unlike ordinary variables, arrays may be initialized *only* if they are either **global** or declared **static.** When declared *inside* a function, an array must be specifically declared **static,** as:

```
main()
{
    static int nums[3] = { 1, 2, 3, );
    . . . . .
```

When declared outside a function (are **global**), the **static** declaration is omitted:

```
int Nums[3] = { 1, 2, 3, };
main()
{
    . . . .
```

If the size of the array (the number of elements it has) is omitted, the compiler will supply the size based on the number of initializers specified. Thus:

```
static int nums[] = { 1, 2, 3 };
```

---

[2]Don't be discouraged that you have to work so hard to make your expensive computer act like a $9.99 calculator. A journey of a thousand miles beings with a single tostada.

is equivalent to:

```
static int num[3] = { 1, 2, 3 };
```

If a **static** array is declared and not initialized, all of its elements are set to a value of 0. Thus:

```
static int nums[3];
```

is equivalent to:

```
static int nums[3] = { 0, 0, 0 };
```

But beware. Arrays of class **auto** are created with values that are garbage. An **auto** array, just as an **auto** variable, is created on the runtime stack, so it will always begin with unpredictable values.

Finally, when the size is declared, but there are fewer initializers than that size, the unspecified rightmost elements are set to 0. Thus:

```
static int nums[3] = { 1, 2 };
```

is equivalent to:

```
static int nums[3] = { 1, 2, 0 };
```

The program in Fig. 7–3, "anagram.c", demonstrates most of these rules. In it you are prompted to enter a word. The letters in that word are then rearranged into alphabetical order and the result printed. Notice that the array *word* is of type **char** because we are storing characters into its elements. It is initialized to contain the word *anagram*, one character per element.

Note how *word* is printed in "anagram.c"—one character at a time, using a **while** loop. If this looks like taking the hard road to what might more easily be written:

```
printf("anagram\n");
```

you are correct.[3] In C, strings (like "anagram\n") are no more than arrays of type **char.**

Since arrays of type **char** (and strings, as you will discover) are so common in C programming, the standard library provides a shorthand function for printing a single character. Called *putchar()*, it is called as:

```
putchar( character );
```

Not only is this easier to type than:

```
printf( "%c", character );
```

it also tends to output characters more rapidly than *printf()*. Take a moment to replace the calls to *printf()* in "anagram.c" with calls to *putchar()*. Note that character constants, such as '\n', must be passed to *putchar()* using half quotation marks:

```
putchar( '\n' );
```

---

[3]Maybe it was harder, but it was *good* for you.

Be careful, though: Many compilers require that your program begin with the line:

```
#include <stdio.h>
```

for *putchar()* to work.

FIGURE 7-3 anagram.c

```
/* anagram.c: alphabetize a word and print it */

#include <stdio.h>

#define MAXWORD 40
#define DONE '\n'

static char word[MAXWORD] = {
    'a', 'n', 'a', 'g', 'r', 'a', 'm', '\n', 0
};

main()
{
    int i, j, index, ch;

    for( i = 0; word[i] != 0; i++ )     /* print "anagram" */
    {
        printf( "%c", word[i] );
    }

    printf( "Enter a word to be alphabetized: " );

    index = 0;
    while ( (ch = getchar()) != DONE )
    {
        if (index == MAXWORD)
            break;
        else
            word[ index++ ] = ch;
    }

    for ( i = 'A'; i < 'z'; i++ )            /* slow sort (ascii) */
    {
        for ( j = 0; j < index; j++ )
        {
            if ( word[j] == i )
                printf( "%c", word[j] );
        }
    }

    printf( "\n" );
}
```

7.4 ARRAYS AND FUNCTIONS

Affect the Array Itself, Not a Copy   Functions can receive arrays as their arguments, but first you must declare those arguments as types appropriate to receive arrays. Such a declaration, for a function called *invert()*, could look like:

```
invert ( ary )
int ary [] ;
{
    . . . .
```

This declares *ary* as the type **array of ints.** In other words, it declares that *invert()* will be *receiving* an array of **ints** as its argument. Note that the number of elements between the square braces is omitted. The **#define** directive can help you remember how many elements you are dealing with. In the fragment.

```
#define MAX 80

. . . main body of program here

invert ( ary )
int ary[]
{
    . . . use MAX here
```

the global search and replace nature of the **#define** directive allows you to write the *invert()* function knowing you are dealing with MAX elements.[4]

When you pass an array to a function [for example, call *invert()* from *main()*], all you have to specify is that array's name. So to call *invert()*, for example, you could write:

```
#define MAX 3

main ()
{
    static nums [MAX] = { 1, 2, 3 );

    invert ( nums ) ;
```

Unlike variables, however, when you pass an array to a function, you are *not* passing a copy of that array. What you are passing is the array's address (explained in the next chapter), which allows you to access that array's elements rather than a copy of those elements. To illustrate this distinction, enter, compile, and run "invert.c". It is shown in Fig. 7–4. In it, the array *nums* is first printed to show its original contents. Then that array is passed to *invert()*, which reverses the order of its elements. Back in *main()*, the array *nums* is printed again to show that *invert()* affected the values of the original elements.

---

[4]However, if your function is more general (that is, called by different routines that might have different length arrays to affect) you will want to send a "size" argument as well. Don't try to dimension the array with this (a fine of two cookies if you forget why).

FIGURE 7-4   invert.c

```c
/* invert.c: show how functions affect arrays directly */

#define MAX 3

main()
{
    int i;
    static int nums[MAX] = { 1, 2, 3 };

    printf( "Before: " );
    for ( i = 0; i < MAX; i++ )
    {
        printf( "%d ", nums[i] );
    }
    putchar( '\n' );

    invert( nums );

    printf( "After:   " );
    for ( i = 0; i < MAX; i++ )
    {
        printf( "%d ", nums[i] );
    }
    putchar( '\n' );
}

invert( ary )
int ary[];
{
    int i, temp;

    for( i = 0; i < (MAX / 2); i++ )
    {
        temp                = ary[i];
        ary[i]              = ary[ (MAX-1) - i ];
        ary[ (MAX-1) - i ] = temp;
    }
}
```

8 · POINTERS

Finding a Value by Way of an Address.

8.1 INTRODUCING POINTERS

A Variable Whose Value Is an Address   One of the more difficult concepts in C is that of *pointers*.[1] A pointer is just a special kind of variable. It is special because it can *contain* as its value the *address* (location in the computer's memory) of another variable. This allows you access to other variables indirectly, based on their locations rather than their names.

Pointers are one of C's most powerful tools and there are two good reasons for learning about them. First, the standard library contains many functions that expect pointers as arguments. If you are to use these functions at all, you need to understand what pointers are and how to pass them. Second, pointers enable you to get your hands on the guts of the machine and produce faster, cleaner code. When sorting data, for example, a sort on pointers can be much faster than a sort on the actual data.

8.2 ADDRESSES

Where Things Are Located in the Computer's Memory   As you have seen, a variable's type must be specified before the compiler can know how many bytes of storage space to reserve for it. When the compiler reserves that space for a variable, it notes where in the machine the beginning (first byte) of that space is located. That location for a variable is called its *address*. Rather than go into the peculiarities of

[1]Setters and retrievers will be covered in a future text.

specific machine addressing, we will illustrate with a simplified model of how variables are stored:

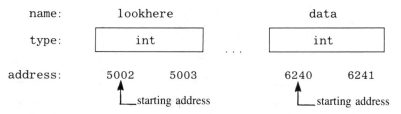

Here, *lookhere* and *data* are the names of two **int** variables, each occupying two bytes of storage. Notice that each also has a starting address associated with it. Those addresses are the memory locations at which each variable begins and are unique to each variable.

Now assume that the variable *lookhere* contains the value 6240:

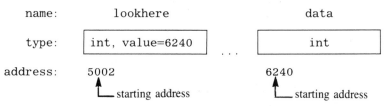

Since that value is exactly the same as the *address* of the variable *data,* it is said to "point to" that variable and can be used to access it.

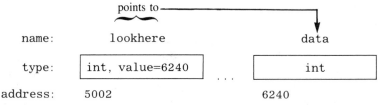

A pointer, then, is merely a variable that contains the address of another variable. You cannot, however, place an address into just any variable. The only type variable that may contain an address as its value is the type **pointer to.** This new type has its own rules for declaration, assignment, and arithmetic.

8.3 DECLARING THE TYPE pointer to

Add a "*" and Presto! a Pointer   To declare a variable to be of type **pointer to** simply begin its name with a "*", as:

```
int *lookhere;
```

This declares the variable *lookhere* to be a **pointer.** The **int** states that *lookhere* will contain the address of a variable of type **int.** In other words, this declares *lookhere* to be a **pointer to int.** Similarly:

```
char *lookhere;
```

declares *lookhere* to be a **pointer to char,** even though the address it will contain is an integer. This may seem somewhat confusing, but all pointers contain integers as their values, no matter what type they point to. The **char** beginning the latter declaration refers to what the pointer will point to, not to the pointer itself. Thus:

```
float *lookhere;
```

declares *lookhere* to be a **pointer to** a variable of type **float,** but the pointer itself is an integer.

A rule in C is that only **pointer** type variables can contain addresses. If you declare a simple **int** variable (one that has no * in front of its name), as:

```
int lookhere;
```

and later try to assign an address to it, you will be given an error message. You must always begin a variable name with a * if that variable will have an address assigned to it:

```
int *lookhere;
```

In other words, you must declare it to be the type **pointer to,** also called a pointer.

8.4 THE & OPERATOR

How to Get an Address into a Pointer   Before a pointer can be used, it must be assigned a value. That is, it must be assigned the address of some other variable. Recall from Chapter 1 that when you declare a variable's name and storage type, you don't know where in the computer that storage will be created. Since that is the case, it might seem impossible to give a variable a value when that value is an address you don't know. Fortunately, C provides a handy operator for achieving just that end.

The **&** operator (pronounced "ampersand") yields the address of a variable when placed in front of that variable's name. Thus:

```
&data
```

yields the address of the variable *data.*

When the **&** operator is used to fetch the address of a variable, that address may then be assigned to a **pointer** type variable. In the example:

```
int *lookhere;     /* pointer to int */
int data;

lookhere = &data;
```

the variable *lookhere* is first declared as the type **pointer to int.** Then the variable named *data* is declared to be of type **int.** Finally, the pointer *lookhere* is assigned a value, and that value is the address of *data.*

The important thing to note in the last line of the example is that the pointer *lookhere* does **not** have a * in front of it. When you assign an address to a pointer, as in:

```
lookhere = &data;
```

the pointer's name is all that is needed—the * is omitted.

Since a pointer's value is an address, the pointer's name (sans *) always yields the address value it contains. If the value of *lookhere* is the address of *data*, as in:

```
lookhere = &data;
```

then the statement:

```
printf ( "%d\n", lookhere );
```

will print the value of *lookhere*, that is, the address of *data*.

Take a moment to compile and run the program in Fig. 8–1, ''addressdemo.c''. Comparing its output to the program steps will serve to illustrate these relationships.

FIGURE 8-1 addressdemo.c

```
/* addressdemo.c: demonstrate the "&" operator */

main()
{
    int *lookhere;   /* pointer to int */
    int data;

    printf ( "\tlookhere is a pointer to int\n" );
    printf ( "\tdata is an int variable\n" );
    printf ( "\n" );
    printf ( "lookhere = &data\n" );

    lookhere = &data;

    printf ( "\n" );
    printf ( "\tthe address of data is:   %d\n", &data );
    printf ( "\tthe value of lookhere is: %d\n", lookhere );
}
```

8.5 POINTER INDIRECTION

Using the Value of a Variable Through Its Address   Now that you can assign the address of a variable to a pointer, the question naturally arises: What can be done with that address? To begin with, you can manipulate the value of a variable indirectly through its address. We use the word *indirectly* to contrast with *direct* accessing of a variable—that is, accessing it by name as you have been doing all along.

To accomplish this indirect accessing, you once again use the * operator. That operator, when placed in front of a pointer name (other than in that pointer's initial declaration) yields the value of *what it points to*, rather than its address.

Expanding the earlier example by adding two lines and initializing **data** will illustrate this concept:

```
int *lookhere;
int data = 5;          ◄────── initialized
int new;               ◄────── added

lookhere = &data;
new = *lookhere;       ◄────── added
```

In other words, if **data** has a value of 5, and **lookhere** points to **data,** then:

```
*lookhere
```

yields the value of **data.** In the last line, the variable **new** is assigned the value of what **lookhere** points to. Since **lookhere** points to **data, new** is assigned the value of **data,** or 5. Thus:

```
lookhere = &data;
new = *lookhere;
```

gives **new** the same value as would:

```
new = data;
```

Putting all this into the form of a short program provides an exercise to illustrate this equivalence. The program is called "equivdemo.c" and is shown in Fig. 8–2.

A possible source of confusion is the multiple use of the * operator. In Chapter 4, you learned that * was the multiplication operator. Here, you have been shown that it both declares a variable to be of type **pointer to,** and returns the value of what a pointer points to. Study the following list of examples. The use of * in each is easily gleaned from context.

```
c * b        multiply c times b
char *c      c declared to be pointer to char
b = *c       b is assigned the value of what c points to
b * *c       b is multiplied times what c points to
*c = b       what c points to is assigned the value of b
```

To summarize, examine the program in Fig. 8–3,"pointerdemo.c". Then enter, compile, and run it. Play with this program. Try different values and approaches. The concept of pointers is basic to the further understanding of C, so take time now to be sure you understand what they are and how they work.

8.6 PASSING POINTERS TO FUNCTIONS

Affect Variables Directly, Rather Than Copies of Values   In Chapter 3, you learned about passing arguments to functions. When you call a function, for example:

```
times2 ( data );
```

you are passing the *value* of **data,** not the variable itself. This ensures that the function **times2()** can *in no way* affect that variable directly.

FIGURE 8-2 equivdemo.c

```
/* equivdemo.c: demonstrate pointer indirection */

main()
{
    int *lookhere;
    int data = 5;
    int new;

    lookhere = &data;
    printf( "lookhere = &data\n" );
    printf( "\n" );

    printf( "data =      %d\n", data );
    printf( "*lookhere = %d\n", *lookhere );
    printf( "\n" );

    new = *lookhere;
    printf( "new = *lookhere\n" );
    printf( "\n" );

    printf( "new =      %d\n", new );
    printf( "\n" );

    *lookhere = *lookhere + 1;
    printf( "*lookhere = *lookhere + 1\n" );
    printf( "\n" );

    printf( "data =      %d\n", data );
    printf( "the value of data was changed using lookhere!\n" );
}
```

FIGURE 8-3 pointerdemo.c

```
/* pointerdemo.c: illustrate the "&" and "*" operators */

main()
{
    char letter = 'A';
    char *ptr;        /* declare ptr as a pointer to char */

    ptr = &letter;   /* assign to ptr letter's address    */

    printf( "The value of letter is %c\n", letter );
    printf( "The value of *ptr is   %c\n", *ptr   );

    *ptr = *ptr + 1;
    printf( "The value of letter is increased by one\n" );
    printf( "using the expression *ptr = *ptr +1, thus\n" );
    printf( "The value of letter is now %c\n", letter );
}
```

On the other hand, when you pass the address of a variable to a function:

```
times2 ( &data ) ;
```

the function can affect the variable itself. For example:

```
lookhere = &data;
*lookhere = *lookhere + 1;
```

permanently changes the value of *data* by adding 1 to the value stored in its location (address).

Passing an address to a function requires that the receiving function declare the argument it is to receive as a pointer. For example, when passing the address of an **int** variable:

```
int data;
```

to the function *times2();*

```
times 2 ( &data ) ;
```

you must declare within the *times2()* itself that the argument it is receiving is a **pointer to** a matching type:

```
times2 ( arg )
int *arg;      /* pointer to receive address of int */
{
     . . . . body of function here
```

The variable *arg* must be of type **pointer to** because it is receiving a value that is an address and only **pointer to** type variables may hold such a value. It must also be declared **pointer to int** because the address it will receive is the address of an **int** variable.

Expanding *times2()* to multiply its argument by 2:

```
times2 ( arg )
int *arg;
{
     *arg = *arg * 2;
}
```

it now doubles what *arg* points to. Since it was passed a value that was the address of *data,* it doubles the value of *data.* Thus:

```
times2 ( &data ) ;
```

is equivalent to:

```
data = data * 2;
```

Since *times2()* only knows it is receiving an address, it could as easily have been called by passing it a pointer. After all, the value of a pointer is an address. Thus:

```
int *lookhere;
int data = 5;
. . . .
lookhere = &data;
times 2 ( lookhere ) ;
```

also passes the address of **data** to **times2()**. Whenever you pass an address to a function, you may also pass a **pointer to** a variable. In both cases, the value that is passed is an address. When a **pointer to** a variable is passed to a function, that function is able to affect the variable itself, just as if it were passed an address. Thus, calling **times2()** with:

```
times2( lookhere );
```

is equivalent to calling it with:

```
times2( &data );
```

In both cases, the address of **data** is passed. The latter case is obvious, because the **&** operator yields the address of **data**. The former passes the value of **lookhere,** and since that value is the address of **data,** it achieves the same result.

To illustrate that passing the address of a variable to a function can affect the variable itself, look at the program "return2.c" (Fig. 8–4). It represents one possible solution to a common programming problem—returning two (or more) values from a function. It does this by returning one value with **return,** and affecting the value of the other through its address.

FIGURE 8-4 return2.c

```
/* return2.c: using a pointer to return two values */

#define DIVISOR 2

main()
{
    int num, result, fract;

    printf( "Enter a number and\n" );
    printf( " I will divide it by %d\n->", DIVISOR );
    while ( (num = getd()) != 0 )
    {
        result = divmod( num, &fract );
        printf( "%d and %d/%d\n->", result, fract, DIVISOR );
    }
}

/*
** divmod: returns val divided by DIVISOR, and places val
**         modulo DIVISOR directly into variable whose
**         address is contained in the pointer ftpr.
*/
divmod( val, fptr )
int val, *fptr;
{
    *fptr = val % DIVISOR;
    return ( val / DIVISOR );
}

/*** place the function getd() here ***/
```

8.7 ADDRESSES AND ARRAYS

Referencing an Array by Its Address   In the previous chapter, you learned that the expression:

```
vals[0]
```

yields the contents of the zeroth element of the array **vals.** Logically, then, the expression:

```
&vals[0]
```

will yield the *address* of the zeroth element of that array. In fact:

```
&vals[anything]
```

will yield the address of the "anything-th" element of that array.

In C, the address of the zeroth element of an array:

```
&vals[0]
```

is the address of the start of the total array. But the array's name standing by itself *also* yields that beginning address. Thus:

```
vals
```

yields exactly the same address as does:

```
&vals[0]
```

Because the array's name itself yields the address of the array, it is a common mistake to think that an array name is a pointer name. It is not. Although the value of the name is an address, that address is a constant. The location of the array (its address) never changes. A pointer, on the other hand, is a *variable* whose value may be changed.

You also learned, in the last chapter, that array-handling functions need to declare their received arguments, when those arguments are arrays, as:

```
dumparray( ary )
int ary[];
{
    . . . .
```

However, you may also receive an array (address) as:

```
dumparray( ary )
int *ary;
{
    . . . .
```

In C, the two are almost interchangeable. Indeed, within the function *dumparray(),* you may access the elements of that array either as:

```
ary[5]
```

for example, or:

```
*(ary+5)
```

where the latter yields the value of what is stored in the address "(ary+5)".

The program called "afun.c" (Fig. 8–5) passes duplicate copies of the array *val's* address to the **dumparray()** function. The elements of that array are each then printed four times, illustrating the four different equivalences between pointers and arrays.

FIGURE 8-5 afun.c

```
/* afun.c: equivalence between pointers and array offsets */

#include <stdio.h>
#define MAX 3

main()
{
    static int vals[MAX] = { 1, 2, 3 };

    dumparray( vals, vals );
}

dumparray( ary, ptr )
int ary[];
int *ptr;
{
    int i;

    for( i = 0; i < MAX; i++ )
    {
        printf( "%d",     ary[i] );
        printf( "%d",     ptr[i] );
        printf( "%d", *(ary+i) );
        printf( "%d", *(ptr+i) );
        printf( "\n" );
    }
}
```

In **dumparray()**, the distinction between the two different forms of declaration is that:

```
int ary[];
```

declares **ary** as an array name and therefore a constant, whereas:

```
int *ptr;
```

declares **ptr** as a pointer and therefore a variable.

8.8 POINTER ARITHMETIC

Changing the Value of a Pointer   Because pointers are variables, their values can be changed. Like integers, you can increment and decrement them or add to and subtract from them. Since the values pointers contain are addresses, increasing or decreasing those values will change the addresses, and thereby where they point.

Unfortunately, this is of little use when dealing with pointers to ordinary variables. Assume *lookhere* is assigned the address of *data* with:

```
lookhere = &data;
```

and after that, *lookhere* is incremented (the address it contains is increased by 1):

```
lookhere++;
```

What does the new address point to? In C it points to nothing of any guaranteed use at all.

Arrays, on the other hand, are one of the few data types in C where changing a pointer's value produces a predictable result. Recall that array elements are arranged one after the other, end on end, in ascending order. This means that the *addresses* of array elements are *sequential*. The address of one may be changed and thereby made into the address of another, in a knowable and predictable way.

By way of example, examine the following declaration:

```
int *lookhere;      /* pointer to int */
int vals[3];        /* array of 3 ints */

lookhere = vals;
```

This first declares *lookhere* to be a **pointer to** type **int** and *vals* to be a three-element array of type **int.** The pointer *lookhere* is then assigned the address of that array (the array's name by itself yields its address). Since *lookhere* points to the zeroth element of *vals:*

```
*lookhere
```

will, of course, yield the value of that element. Incrementing *lookhere* by 1:

```
lookhere++;
```

will cause it to point to (change its value to the address of) the next element of the array because the address of that element is 1 more than the address of the previous element. So:

```
*lookhere
```

will *now* yield the value of *vals[1].* The following diagram illustrates this process:

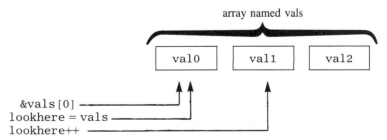

In Chapter 2, you learned that each type in C occupies a differing number of bytes. A **char** is 1 byte, and **int** 2 (or 4) bytes, and a **float** 4 (or more) bytes. Therefore, in an array of type **int,** where each element occupies 2 bytes, the address of each element is 2 bytes different from the addresses of its neighbors.

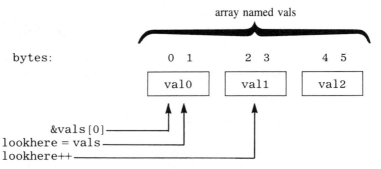

The beauty of C is that it knows how many bytes to add to an address so it points to the next element of the same type. Thus:

```
lookhere++;
```

will automatically increase the address value of **lookhere** by 1 byte if it is a **pointer to char,** by 2 (or 4) bytes if it is a **pointer to int,** and by 4 (or more) bytes if it is a **pointer to float.** This all happens invisibly to you, making use of pointers to array elements very simple.

The program "fish.c" demonstrates one application of this ability to change pointer values. Look at Fig. 8–6 and examine the function **putline().** In a loop, this function simply checks to see if what the pointer **line** points to has a value of 0. If not, it prints that value as a character. The pointer **line** is then incremented by 1, thus pointing to the next value in the array, and the loop continues.

The 0 was added to the end of the array *out* so that *putline()* would know

FIGURE 8-6 fish.c

```
/* fish.c: using a pointer to output an array of text */


main()
{
    static char out[11] = {
        'F', 'i', 's', 'h', ' ', 's', 'w', 'i', 'm', '\n', 0
    };

    putline( out );
}

putline( line )
char *line;
{
    while ( *line != 0 )    /* line points to out           */
    {
        putchar( *line );   /* print what line points to  */
        ++line;             /* then increment the pointer */
    }
}
```

when to stop. This was not an arbitrary selection. In C, strings are simply arrays of type **char,** whose last character is the value 0. The concept of strings will be discussed in greater detail in the next chapter.

The **putline**() function could also have been written using addition. Instead of incrementing the pointer, the constant 1 can be added to it each time in the loop with the same effect:

```
putline ( line )
char *line;
{
    while ( *line != 0 )
    {
        putchar ( *line );
        line = line + 1; /* replaces ++line */
    }
}
```

Another way to call **putline()** would be to pass it both the beginning address and ending address of the array. Here's an example:

```
putline ( out, &out [11] );
```

This requires **putline()** to declare two pointers and determine if it is done by comparing **line** to **end.** Remember that the addresses of array elements are always in ascending order, so **end** will always begin as a greater value than **line.**

```
putline ( line, end )
char *line, *end;
{
    while ( line < end )
        putchar ( line++ );
}
```

The advantage to using pointer arithmetic over offsets into arrays is mostly one of speed. Accessing an array element by use of an offset, as in:

```
vals [5]
```

where **vals** is an integer array, results in an add and a multiply being required to locate that element. Using a pointer as in:

```
* (ptr + 5)
```

requires merely an add. This makes pointer accessing of array elements much faster than offset accessing.[2]

In summary then, a pointer is a variable whose value is the address of another variable. Pointer values may be incremented and decremented; they may have integer values added to and subtracted from them; and they may be compared (for equality, greater than, less than, and so on). The real strength of pointer arithmetic lies in dealing with arrays, where C will always ensure that pointers will point to the correct element of an array regardless of the number of bytes occupied by a type.

---

[2]Imagine a problem in which *all* elements of a large array must be moved to some other array. Doing this by variable assignment requires as many assignments as there are elements to move (including offset calculations). Doing this by pointer assignment requires *one* pointer assignment, total!

9 · STRINGS

A Character Array Terminated with a Zero Value.

9.1 INTRODUCING STRINGS

A Convention Rather Than an a Actual Type   A string is nothing more than a group of letters and/or numbers. This sentence is a string. A word can be a string. This paragraph, indeed, this whole book could be a string. What defines a string is the way it is limited. By enclosing the string:

        "Bob"

in full quotation marks, for example, you are limiting it to the single word *Bob*.

The C language does not *directly* support strings or string types. Instead, the standard C library contains many functions that can be used for string manipulation. Those functions are all based on a common convention: A string is an array of type **char,** containing printable character values, and terminated with a value of 0. The character representation for that 0 value is the special notation '\0'. Thus the string "Bob", represented in memory as an array of characters, will appear as:

char	char	char	char
'B'	'o'	'b'	'\0'

Because this is a convention, rather than a type, methods to combine, truncate, compare, and measure strings must either be provided in the standard library or custom-created by you. Although this may seem a limitation, you will soon discover that it can be turned to your advantage.[1]

In this chapter you will learn how strings are limited, how they can be initialized, and how they are passed to functions. You will learn how to use and write functions that read, write, join, and compare strings.

9.2 INITIALIZING STRINGS

Some Shorthand and the Concept of String Constants   In Chapter 7, you learned that arrays of type **char** could be initialized at declaration time. For example:

```
char line[4] = { 'B', 'o', 'b', '\0' };
```

declares *line* to be an array of type **char** containing four elements. These elements are initialized by the compiler to be the letters *Bob* terminated by a character of value 0. Fortunately, C supports a handy shorthand for making this same initialization:

```
char line[] = "Bob";
```

Notice that the trailing 0 is not specified. Whenever a string is defined inside full quotation marks, the compiler supplies that terminating 0.

Any time you enclose a string between full quotation marks you are creating a character array. It is not necessary to give that array a name in order to use the string. When, for example, you pass a control string to *printf():*

```
printf ( "Bob" );
```

you are creating the array:

```
{ 'B', 'o', 'b', '\0' }
```

and passing the address of that array to *printf()*. Such quoted strings (strings not declared as named arrays) are called *string constants.*

At compile time, C stores string constants as unnamed character arrays and converts all references to them to address values. In the statement:

```
printf ( "Bob" );
```

it is the address of the character array *Bob* that actually gets passed to *printf()*, while the array (string) itself gets placed elsewhere in memory.

Because a string constant is handled as the address of an array, anywhere you have used quoted strings you may also use the addresses of character arrays themselves. It is perfectly legal to call *printf()* as:

```
static char name[] = "Bob";
printf ( name );
```

---

[1]String handlers built into other languages strictly define your usage. User-defined functions can, however, do almost anything, since they need not match convention.

Demonstrate this for yourself by compiling and running the program in Fig. 9–1, which is called "fishfly.c". Remember to make the arrays *string1* and *string2* **static** or **global.** Recall from Chapter 7 that your compiler will object loudly if they are **auto,** because **auto** arrays may not be initialized.

FIGURE 9-1 fishfly.c

```
/* fishfly.c:  illustrate passing addresses to printf() */

main()
{
    static char string1[] = "Birds gotta sing\n";
    static char string2[] = "Fish gotta fly....\n";

    printf( "All together now!\n" );

    printf( &string1[0] );

    printf( string2 );
}
```

9.3 STRING-HANDLING FUNCTIONS

An Overview of the General Techniques   As you have seen, a string in C is simply an array of characters terminated by a 0 value. This convention makes the design and understanding of string-handling functions relatively easy. As you learned in Chapter 7, all arrays must be passed by passing their addresses. This may either be done by passing the address of the zeroth element:

```
printf( &array[0] );
```

or by passing the name of the array itself, which also yields the array's address:

```
printf( array );
```

In the previous chapter, you learned that any function that receives an address as an argument must declare that argument as a type appropriate to receive an address. Declaring a variable as type **pointer to** satisfies this requirement. Since all strings are type **char,** any declaration such as:

```
char *line;
```

will do nicely, as it declares *line* to be a **pointer to char.** Pointers, you will recall, are variables whose value is the address of another variable.

Reexamine the function *putline()* from the last chapter. The function is shown in Fig. 9–2.

It is typical of most string-handling functions. The address of a zero-terminated character array is passed to it. A **pointer to char,** *line,* is assigned that address. Then, looping until the 0 value is found, the array element that the pointer points to is printed, and the pointer is incremented.

FIGURE 9-2   putline() (pointer version)

```
/*
** putline(): using a pointer to output an array of text
*/

putline( line )
char *line;
{
    while ( *line != 0 )    /* exit when 0 found          */
    {
        putchar( *line );   /* print what line points to  */
        ++line;             /* then increment the pointer */
    }
}
```

The ***putline()*** function could also have been written using array offsets. Compare the pointer version in Fig. 9–2 to the array version in Fig. 9–3.

FIGURE 9-3   putline() (array version)

```
/*
** putline(): rewritten to use offsets into an array
*/

putline( line )
char line[];
{
    int i = 0;

    while ( line[i] != 0 )  /* exit when 0 found    */
    {
        putchar( line[i] ); /* print i'th element   */
        ++i;                /* increment the offset */
    }
}
```

As we demonstrate and create string-handling functions throughout the remainder of this chapter, we will usually illustrate them by using both approaches. This will not only help you understand the general mechanisms, but it will also help you come to grips with pointers and pointer arithmetic.

9.4 STRING I/O

Introducing Puts() and Gets()   Two extremely useful library functions for handling string output and input are ***puts()*** and ***gets().*** The ***puts()*** function (pronounced "put s") prints a string to your standard output device (your video screen). The ***gets()*** function (prounounced "get s") reads a string from your standard input device (your terminal's keyboard).

The puts() Function

The *puts()* function can be called in any of several ways, all of which pass it a string to print. You may pass it a quoted string constant directly, as you would *printf()*:

```
puts ( "Bob" ) ;
```

Or you can declare a character array, then pass the address of that array:

```
static char name [] = "Bob";
puts ( name ) ;
```

Or you can assign the address of the array to a pointer, then pass that pointer:

```
static char name [] = "Bob";
char *ptr;

ptr = &name [0] ;
puts ( ptr ) ;
```

At first glance, *puts()* seems to do the same thing as *printf()*, but they differ in two key points. First, with *printf()*, the trailing newline ('\n') must be specified if it is to be printed, while with *puts()* a newline is printed at the end of *every* string. Specifying a newline, as:

```
puts ( "hello\n" ) ;
```

will cause two newlines to be printed.

The other difference is that *puts()* does no formatting. That is, it accepts only one argument, and ignores all % directives contained in that string. For example:

```
printf ( "x = %d\n", 2 ) ;
```

will print:

```
x = 2
```

while calling *puts()* with the same arguments will print:

```
x = %d
```

with an extra newline.

The program "fernbar.c", in Fig. 9–4, illustrates a few of the many possible ways to use *puts()*. Notice how the lines are printed in an unattractive manner. Ways to combine many strings into a single string will be covered later in this chapter.

As for how a *puts()* function can be written, recall in the last chapter that you wrote a function called *putline()*. That function can easily be converted to *puts()* by having it print a newline character '\n' before it returns. See Fig. 9–5.

Notice the expression:

```
* (ptr++)
```

in the call to *putchar()*. Such expressions are common in C. The parentheses say that the pointer itself will be incremented rather than the variable it points to. Be-

FIGURE 9-4 fernbar.c

```
/* fernbar.c:  demonstrates puts()  */

#include <stdio.h>

char Date[]  = "The date: early 1970's";
char Place[] = "The place: A fern bar, the Sunset district";
char Myname[] = "Bob";

main()
{
    char *who;

    puts( Date );
    puts( Place );
    puts( "-------------------------------------------");

    who = Myname;
    puts( "Hi good lookin'.  My name's" );
    puts( who );
    puts( "What's yours?" );
}
```

FIGURE 9-5 puts() (pointer version)

```
/*
** puts(): using a pointer to output a string
*/
puts( ptr )
char *ptr;
{
    while ( *ptr )              /* while true, ie != 0 */
        putchar( *(ptr++) );
    putchar( '\n' );           /* extra newline added */
}
```

cause the operator follows *ptr,* the value of what it points to will be used first, then the pointer will be incremented.

This function could also have been written without pointers, thus yielding a more understandable version with a slight sacrifice in efficiency. See Fig. 9–6.

The gets() Function

The *gets()* function is called by passing it one argument, the address of a buffer into which your input—what you type at your keyboard—will go. For example:

FIGURE 9-6 puts() (array version)

```
/*
** puts(): version using array offsets
*/
puts( array )
char array[];
{
    int i = 0;

    while ( array[i] )                  /* while true, ie != 0 */
    {
        putchar( array[i++] );
    }
    putchar( '\n' );                    /* extra newline added */
}
```

```
#define BUFSIZE 80
char inbuff [BUFSIZE];
gets( inbuff );
```

Here we have **#define'd** BUFSIZE so that the size of the buffer will be easy to modify if necessary. We then declared *inbuff* as a character array of BUFSIZE elements. Finally, we call *gets(),* passing the address of the buffer (the array *inbuff).*

The *gets()* function will then wait for you to type in a line of text. It will return when you type a newline character (the RETURN or ENTER key). The newline is converted to a '\0' that terminates the string in the buffer.

Be careful, though. The *gets()* function is not a well-designed one, and can cause the buffer to be overfilled. When using this function, always be sure to make your buffer large enough to hold the longest line you can reasonably expect.

A few libraries provide a *gets()* with ''smarts.'' In these, *gets()* is called this way:

```
gets( inbuff, BUFSIZE );
```

Again, it will return when you type a newline. As a bonus, however, it will also return if the buffer is full. If it returns because the buffer is full, a 0 value is added as the last character in the buffer. At most, BUFSIZE–1 characters will be placed into the buffer to ensure that room is always available for a terminating 0 value.

The following expanded version of ''fernbar.c'' (Fig. 9–7) features two similar approaches to calling *gets().*[2] The first passes the address of the buffer *inbuff* directly. The second passes a pointer whose value is that address. If your compiler doesn't support the BUFSIZE argument, just delete that argument from both calls.

A simplified version of *gets()* will serve to demonstrate how such a function may be written; it is shown in Fig. 9–8. We have included the BUFSIZE argument in its design to make it more robust. Note that the test for control characters must follow the tests for newline and backspace characters. Were it to precede them, these characters would never be found, because they are also control characters.

---

[2]This one assumes someone in the fernbar responds. Good luck.

FIGURE 9-7 fernbar.c (revision 1)

```
/* fernbar.c (revision 1):  demonstrates gets()  */

#include <stdio.h>
#define BUFSIZE 80                          /* size of buffer */

char Date[]  = "The date: early 1970's";
char Place[] = "The place: A fern bar, the Sunset district";
char Myname[] = "Bob";

main()
{
    char inbuff[BUFSIZE];                   /* buffer for gets() */
    char *inptr;

    puts( Date );
    puts( Place );
    puts( "-------------------------------------");

    puts( "Hi good lookin'.  My name's" );
    puts( Myname );
    puts( "What's yours?" );

    gets( inbuff, BUFSIZE );                   /* pass address */

    puts( "And what's your sign?" );

    inptr = inbuff;
    gets( inptr, BUFSIZE );                    /* pass pointer */
}
```

This is not the most compact, nor the most versatile version of a *gets()* function. The version supplied with most standard libraries allows you to cancel a line and delete characters. Your version may also allow some primitive editing, such as inserting characters or copying other text from the screen by moving the cursor over it.

9.5 STRING-MANIPULATING FUNCTIONS

Copy, Concatenate, Compare, and Measure Strings The standard library also contains functions for manipulating strings. Among these, the most common are *strcpy()*, *strcat()*, *strcmp()*, and *strlen()*. The *strcpy()* function is used to copy one string into another. The *strcat()* function is used to join two strings. The *strcmp()* function is used to compare two strings. And the *strlen()* function is used to find the number of characters in a string. Like *puts()* and *gets()*, these functions assume that a string is an array of type **char** terminated with a 0 value.

FIGURE 9-8 gets()

```
/*
** gets(): inputs a newline terminated string (or max-1
**         characters). Replaces newline or end with 0.
*/
gets( buf, max )
char *buf;
int max;
{
     int count = 1;

     while ( (*buf = getchar()) != '\n' )   /* exit on newline */
     {
         if (*buf == '\b')                      /* handle backspace */
         {
             if (count > 1)
             {
                 --count;
                 --buf;
             }
         }
         else if (*buf > (' '-1) )        /* reject control chars */
         {
             ++count;
             ++buf;
         }

         if (count == max)       /* exit if too many characters */
             break;
     }
     *buf = 0;                              /* make terminating zero */

}
```

The strcpy() Function

The *strcpy()* function is used to copy one string into another. Since strings are character arrays, it merely transfers the elements of one array into the corresponding elements of another.

It is passed two arguments. The first is the address of the array into which the characters of the second will be placed. The second is the address of the array from which the characters will be copied. For example:

```
strcpy( name, inbuff );
```

will copy the string in the array ***inbuff*** and place that copy into the array ***name***.

Suppose that in the program "fernbar.c" you wish to save the person's name for later use.[3] You can't keep it in the general input buffer because it will get

[3]Isn't it good to know you're getting practical, usable programs from this book?

clobbered when you fetch the person's sign. One solution is to transfer (copy) that
name into another buffer, thereby saving it for later use. This is demonstrated by the
program in Fig. 9–9.

FIGURE 9-9 fernbar.c (revision 2)

```
/* fernbar.c (revision 2):  demonstrates strcpy()  */

#include <stdio.h>
#define BUFFSIZE 80

char Date[]  = "The date: early 1970's";
char Place[] = "The place: A fern bar, the Sunset district";
char Myname[] = "Bob";

main()
{
    char inbuff[BUFFSIZE],      /* general input buffer */
         name[BUFFSIZE],        /* buffer to save name  */
         sign[BUFFSIZE];        /* buffer to save sign  */

    puts( Date );
    puts( Place );
    puts( "------------------------------------------" );

    puts( "Hi good lookin'.  My name's" );
    puts( Myname );
    puts( "What's yours?" );

    gets( inbuff, BUFFSIZE );        /* input name */
    strcpy( name, inbuff );          /* and save it */

    puts( "And what's your sign?" );

    gets( inbuff, BUFFSIZE );        /* input sign */
    strcpy( sign, inbuff );          /* and save it */

    puts( name );            /*  show we saved them */
    puts( sign );
}
```

The design of a *strcpy()* function is straightforward. The *strcpy()* function is
passed the addresses of two character arrays. The two pointers, *to* and *from,* begin
life with values that are the addresses of those arrays. Copying the second into the
first, the pointers are stepped along until the terminating 0 value is found in *from,* at
which point the function exits. See Fig. 9–10.

The **while** test in *strcpy()* may seem a bit subtle. First the value of what *from*
points to is assigned to the place where *to* points. The value of the assignment is

FIGURE 9-10 strcpy()

```
/*
** strcpy(): copies from to to.
**           No check for overflow of to.
*/
strcpy( to, from )
char *to, *from;
{
    while ( (*to = *from) != 0 )
    {
        ++to;
        ++from;
    }
}
```

then compared for inequality to 0. Since the comparison happens after the assignment, the entire string gets copied, including its 0 terminator.

The strcat() Function

The *strcat()* function joins (concatenates) two strings and places the combined result into the first. In "fernbar.c", for example, the person's astrological sign was saved in the array *sign,* and the person's name was saved in the array *name.* Suppose you wished to combine them with other text and print that composite as:

    "name the sign! Music to my ears. "

You can join them using *strcat(),* where *outbuff* is used to hold all the pieces:

```
strcpy( outbuff, name );      /* copy name into buffer */
strcat( outbuff, " the " );   /*    then add the pieces */
strcat( oubuff, sign );
strcat( outbuff, "! Music to my ears. " );
```

The process of *strcat()* is simply to join the second string to the end of the first string, leaving the result in the array that is the first string. Thus, if *name* contained "Betty" and *sign* contained "Pisces", *outbuff* would become:

    "Betty the Pisces! Music to my ears. "

Examine the revision of "fernbar.c" that is shown in Fig. 9–11. Note the way the output buffer *outbuff* is cleared. This works because a string is an array of characters terminated by a 0 value. If the 0 value is at the start, then the string contains no characters.

In the implementation of a *strcat()* function (Fig. 9–12), notice that the code for *strcpy()* is duplicated. First, the end of the string *to* is found by searching for the terminating 0. This leaves the address of that 0 in *to.* The string pointed to by *from*

FIGURE 9-11 fernbar.c (revision 3)

```
/* fernbar.c (revision 3):  demonstrates strcat()  */

#include <stdio.h>
#define BUFFSIZE 80

char Date[]  = "The date: early 1970's";
char Place[] = "The place: A fern bar, the Sunset district";
char Myname[] = "Bob";

main()
{
    char inbuff[BUFFSIZE], name[BUFFSIZE], sign[BUFFSIZE];
    char outbuff[BUFFSIZE];      /* general output buffer */

    puts( Date );
    puts( Place );
    puts( "-----------------------------------------" );

    puts( "Hi good lookin'.  My name's" );
    puts( Myname );
    puts( "What's yours?" );

    gets( inbuff, BUFFSIZE );
    strcpy( name, inbuff );

    puts( "And what's your sign?" );

    gets( inbuff, BUFFSIZE );
    strcpy( sign, inbuff );

    outbuff[0] = 0;                /*  clear output buffer */
    strcat( outbuff, name );       /*  then join the pieces */
    strcat( outbuff, " the " );
    strcat( outbuff, sign );
    strcat( outbuff, "! Music to my ears." );

    puts( outbuff );
}
```

is then simply copied over, beginning at that point. No check is made to see that the target array is, in fact, large enough to hold both strings.

The strcmp() Function

The *strcmp()* function compares two strings—one letter at a time—from left to right. If the strings are identical, the function returns 0. If they are not, it returns the difference between the values of the first nonmatching characters. Note that this difference could be negative, depending on the ASCII values of the letters.

FIGURE 9-12 strcat()

```
/*
** strcat(): join from to the end of to. No check to insure
** to is big enough to hold both strings.
*/
strcat( to, from )
char *to, *from;
{
    while ( *to != 0 )                /* find end of 1st string */
        ++to;

    while ( (*to = *from) != 0 )   /* then join 2nd to it */
    {
        ++to;
        ++from;
    }
}
```

The revision of "fernbar.c" that is shown in Fig. 9–13 illustrates one way *strcmp()* can be used to check a user's input for a match. Here the person's sign is compared to your sign.

As an exercise for you, we will leave it up to you to implement a version of *strcmp()*. Observe the basis of the comparison: If the first is alphabetically before the second, a negative value will be returned.

The strlen() Function

The last of these four string-manipulating functions, *strlen()*, simply returns the number of characters in a string. You pass it a single argument, a string, and it returns an **int** value that is that string's length. The 0 value terminating the string is not counted. Thus:

```
static char name[] = "Bob";
int boblen;

boblen = strlen( name );
```

will assign the value 3 to *boblen,* because there are three characters in the string "Bob".

The *strlen()* function is most useful for the file input/output functions we will be discussing later. It is also appropriate for applications such as checking a user's input for legal length and quickly locating the end of a string.

9.6 PUTTING IT TOGETHER

Carry on a Conversation with Your Computer [4]   The little conversationa l program shown in Fig. 9–14 affords a pleasant opportunity for you to test the functions

---

[4]It is faithful, will always talk to you, won't nag (unless programmed to do so), and leaves no messy droppings.

FIGURE 9-13   fernbar.c (revision 4)

```
/* fernbar.c (revision 4):   demonstrates strcmp()  */

#include <stdio.h>
#define BUFFSIZE 80

char Date[]  = "The date: early 1970's";
char Place[] = "The place: A fern bar, the Sunset district";
char Myname[] = "Hi good lookin', my name's Bob";
char Mysign[] = "scorpio";

main()
{
    char inbuff[BUFFSIZE], name[BUFFSIZE], sign[BUFFSIZE];
    char outbuff[BUFFSIZE];        /* general output buffer */

    puts( Date );
    puts( Place );
    puts( "----------------------------------------" );
    puts( Myname );

    puts( "What's yours?" );
    gets( inbuff, BUFFSIZE );
    strcpy( name, inbuff );

    puts( "And what's your sign?" );
    gets( inbuff, BUFFSIZE );
    strcpy( sign, inbuff );

    if( strcmp( sign, Mysign ) == 0 )
        puts( "Me too. We must be compatable!" );
    else
    {
        outbuff[0] = 0;
        strcat( outbuff, name );
        strcat( outbuff, " the " );
        strcat( outbuff, sign );
        strcat( outbuff, "! Music to my ears." );
        puts( outbuff );
    }
}
```

you've learned in this chapter. The important lesson here is in understanding what strings are and in learning how to use them.

Notice that *printf()* was used to print an assembly of strings, rather than *strcat()*. The %s directive tells *printf()* to insert a string at that place in its control string (Chapter 3). That directive expects an argument that is the address of a string.

FIGURE 9-14 fernbar.c (revision 5)

```
/* fernbar.c (revision 5):  putting it all together */

#include <stdio.h>
#define BUFFSIZE 80

char Myname[] = "Hi good looking, my name's Bob";
char Mysign[] = "scorpio";

main()
{
    char name[BUFFSIZE], sign[BUFFSIZE];

    puts( Myname );
    ask( "What's yours?", name );
    ask( "And what's your sign?", sign );

    if( strcmp( sign, Mysign ) == 0 )
        puts( "Me too. We must be compatible!" );
    else
    {
        printf( "%s the %s!\n", name, sign );
        puts( "Music to my ears." );
    }
}

ask( prompt, savebuff )
char *prompt, *savebuff;
{
    puts( prompt );
    gets( savebuff, BUFFSIZE );
}
```

9.7 INTRODUCING scanf()

Input's Answer to Printf()   The standard library contains a general-purpose input function called *scanf()*. It reads from the standard input (your terminal's keyboard) and places the results into variables. It uses the same % directives as *printf()* does. But it uses them to *read in* values, rather than print them. You may wish to review those directives (Chapter 3), as *scanf()* is best explained in terms of *printf()*.

Like *printf()*, you pass *scanf()* a control string followed by a list of arguments. Unlike *printf()*, however, those arguments must all be addresses or pointers. By way of example, to print an integer with *printf()*, you would:

```
printf( "%d", num );
```

but to input that number using *scanf()*, you must:

```
scanf( "%d", &num );
```

This tells *scanf()* to read an integer from the keyboard and place it into the **int** variable *num*, whose address is *&num*. The most common error encountered when using *scanf()* is to forget that its arguments *must* be addresses or pointers:

```
scanf ( "%c", &letter ) ;   /* read a char into letter */
scanf ( "%d", &num    ) ;   /* read an int into num    */
scanf ( "%f", &temp   ) ;   /* read a float into temp  */
                └── addresses
```

The *scanf()* function can also be used to read strings. Whereas *printf():*

```
printf ( "%s", string ) ;
```

prints a string totally, up to the terminating 0, *scanf()* considers only white space. It begins looking for a string at the first character that is not white space and stops at the first following character that is white space. Recall that white space characters are spaces, tabs, and newlines. Essentially, then, *scanf()* is best used for reading individual words. For example, if you were to request input with:

```
char buffer [80] ;

printf ( "Enter your first name: " ) ;
scanf ( "%s", buffer ) ;
```

and typed in response:

```
Bob Skinner
```

scanf() would place only ''Bob'' into *buffer*.

The loop in the following program, ''scanfdemo.c'' (Fig. 9–15), allows you to experiment with *scanf()*'s rules for interpreting your input.

FIGURE 9-15   scanfdemo.c

```
/* scanfdemo.c: experience scanf() first hand */

main()
{
    int number;
    char letter;
    char buffer[40];

    printf( "The great scanf() experience\n\n" );
    letter = 0;

    while( 1 )
    {
        printf( "Enter a number: " );
        scanf( "%d", &number );
        printf( "\nscanf got %d\n\n", number );
```

FIGURE 9-15 con't.

```
            printf( "Enter a letter (q to quit): " );
            scanf( "%c", &letter );
            if (letter == 'q')
                break;
            printf( "\nscanf got %c\n\n", letter );

            printf( "Enter a word: " );
            scanf( "%s", buffer );
            printf( "\nscanf got %s\n\n", buffer );
        }
        printf( "\nGoodbye\n" );
    }
```

As a final exercise, rewrite "fernbar.c", this time using only *printf()* and *scanf()*. Are there any string-manipulating functions that you can't replace? Don't forget that *scanf()* requires *all* its arguments to be pointers or addresses!

10 'ARGC, ARGV, AND REDIRECTION

Where I/O Goes, No Program Knows

10.1 PROGRAM INVOCATION

Passing Information to a Program Via the Command Line   Up to now we have only been able to read information into our programs with **getchar(), gets(),** or some other input-handling function. To refresh your memory, examine Fig. 10–1, a simplified version of the program "stars.c" from Chapter 6.

This program prints a line of *s, terminated with a newline. It determines how many *s to print by asking "How many stars?" When you execute the program by typing its name, "stars", it produces a session at your terminal that looks like this:

```
stars
How many stars? 20
********************
```

This program could, however, be rewritten in such a way that you could enter the number of stars when you run it—that is, as a part of the *command line*. The command line is the line you type at your terminal to execute the program. Its individual elements are called *command line arguments*. After "stars.c" is rewritten to accept command line arguments, the same session at your terminal will look like this:

```
stars 20
********************
```

However, before "stars.c" can be rewritten to use command line arguments, you must learn the mechanism for passing those arguments to a C program—the variables **argc** and **argv.**

FIGURE 10-1 stars.c (simplified)

```
/* stars.c (simplified): print a line of "*" characters */

#include <stdio.h>
#define DEFAULT 79

main()
{
    int howmany;

    printf( "How many stars? " );
    scanf( "%d", &howmany );

    if ( howmany <= 0 )          /* catch 0 and negative */
        howmany = DEFAULT;

    while ( howmany-- > 0)                    /* print the stars */
        putchar( '*' );

    putchar( '\n' );
}
```

10.2 THE VARIABLES argc AND argv

Passing Command Line Arguments Directly to Main()   Recall from Chapter 3 that the function named *main()* is a special one because it is where every C program begins execution. Just as with other functions, *main()* can have arguments passed to it. For *main()*, those arguments enable it to access the command line.

To access the individual command line arguments, every *main()* is told how many arguments there are and where to find them. The variables that receive this information are usually called *argc* (for argument count) and *argv* (for argument vector). Those variables must be declared by *main()*, and one common way to declare them is:

```
main( argc, argv )
int argc;
char *argv[];
{
        . . . . the rest of main goes here
```

Note, however, that you are not restricted to those names. We use *argc* and *argv* only because most other C programs use them. They are a convention rather than a rule, and we will abide by that convention because it helps to clarify what those variables do.

The int variable *argc* contains the *number* of arguments in the command line. Since every command line must contain the name of the program itself, *argc* will never have a value that is less than 1. Thus, given the command line:

average 10 45 32 98

argc would contain a value of 5.

The declaration for *argv:*

```
char *argv[];
```

is one you haven't seen before. It declares *argv* to be an array of pointers, each of which points to a string. Thus, given the same command line above:

```
argv[0] points to "average"
argv[1] points to "10"
argv[2] points to "45"
etc.
```

The program in Fig. 10–2, "showargs.c", illustrates the relationship between those variables, and a way to print the strings contained in *argv*. Notice that *argv[0]* is always the name that was used to execute the program and that the first *useful* argument passed to the program is always *argv[1].*

FIGURE 10-2 showargs.c

```
/* showargs.c: print the command line arguments */

#include <stdio.h>

main( argc, argv )
int   argc;
char *argv[];
{
    int i;

    printf( "argc = %d\n", argc );

    for ( i = 0; i < argc; i++ )
    {
        printf( "argv[%d] = %s\n", i, argv[i] );
    }
}
```

Running this program with the command line:

```
showargs a b c
```

will produce the output:

```
argc = 4
argv[0] = showargs
argv[1] = a
argv[2] = b
argv[3] = c
```

Now that you understand *argc* and *argv,* the program "stars.c" can be rewritten to take advantage of command line arguments. It can now be executed with a command line of the form:

```
stars 20
```

Notice, in the revision in Fig. 10–3, that we have introduced the library routine *atoi().* This function, when passed the address of a string, returns the integer value expressed by that string. You will find *atoi()* useful for processing command line arguments.

FIGURE 10-3 stars.c (revision 1)

```
/* stars.c (revision 1): revised to use argc & argv */

#include <stdio.h>
#define DEFAULT 79

main( argc, argv )
int   argc;
char *argv[];
{
    int howmany;

    if ( argc < 2 )                         /* no stars specified */
        howmany = DEFAULT;
    else
        howmany = atoi( argv[1] );          /* note: atoi()   */

    if ( howmany <= Ø )      /* catch illegal specification */
        howmany = DEFAULT;

    while ( howmany-- > Ø )
        putchar( '*' );

    putchar( '\n' );
}
```

10.3 THE exit() FUNCTION

The Art of a Graceful Egress[1]   One problem with both versions of "stars.c" is that they insist on printing 79 stars if the user neglects to tell them otherwise. One solution is to revise the program one more time, so it will inform the user that no stars were specified, then abort. The mechanism for achieving such an abort (suddenly quitting or exiting the program) is the library function *exit().*

Ordinarily, a program ends when there is nothing left to do in the function *main(),* but an early ending can be forced by calling the *exit()* function. This function can be used to exit a program from anywhere, and it is not limited to being called from *main().*

Generally, when *exit()* is called, it is passed a value that signifies whether the program's termination was due to an error. Such error notification can then be used by the operating system, for example, to abort a command file or shell script. By

[1]Or, leaving without regret.

convention, a value of 0 signifies a successful, nonerror condition. Nonzero values indicate the kind of error but vary from system to system. Passing a value to *exit()* is optional, but omitting that value is poor practice. We have chosen the value 0 to represent "success" and −1 to represent "some error," and we will use these values throughout the remainder of this book.

Revise "stars.c" once again, this time to civilize its behavior. Notice, in the listing in Fig. 10–4, if no number of stars is specified the program politely states its "usage," and then aborts. Notice, also, that the program's name is not assumed. Instead, *argv[0]* is printed. In this way, the "usage" and error messages will make sense, even if the program is run under a different name.

FIGURE 10-4   stars.c (revision 2)

```
/* stars.c (revision 2): revised to demonstrate exit() */

#include <stdio.h>
#define DEFAULT 79

main( argc, argv )
int  argc;
char *argv[];
{
    int howmany;

    if ( argc < 2 )
    {
        printf( "usage: %s count\n", argv[0] );    /* usage */
        exit( 0 );
    }
    else
        howmany = atoi( argv[1] );

    if ( howmany <= 0 )
    {
        printf( "%s: bad count\n", argv[1] );       /* error */
        exit( -1 );
    }

    while ( howmany-- )
        putchar( '*' );

    putchar( '\n' );
}
```

Another approach to stating "usage" and aborting is to call a separate "usage" function:

```
if (argc < 2)
    usage( argv[0] ) ;
```

The program will abort directly from within *usage()*, as:

```
usage ( progname )
char *progname;
{
    printf ("usage: %s count\n", progname );
    exit ( 0 );
}
```

This approach illustrates that the *exit()* function can be called from anywhere.[2] Even if it is called by a function other than *main()*, it will immediately abort the program.

10.4 REDIRECTION

I/O Revisions That Are Invisible to the Program   Many implementations of C language compilers and their corresponding environments allow for redirection of input and output. For example, instead of having your program's output printed to your video screen, you may *redirect* it to your printer. Because the rules for redirection can vary from system to system, we advise you to read this section with your documentation in hand.

Redirected Output

The term *standard output* usually refers to your terminal's video screen. This means that all output will go there (by default) unless the computer is told otherwise. You can redirect that output to disk files, or other devices, by entering the appropriate arguments in the command line.

To visualize this process, enter the following at your terminal. Observe that the program will be executed but no stars will be printed to the screen:

```
stars 20 >junkfile
```

Now look at your directory listing (with ls, CATALOG, DIR, or whatever). You should see that a new file named "junkfile" has been created. Using your editor or some other utility (like TYPE or cat), take a look at that file. It contains the line:

```
*******************
```

The symbol ">", followed by a place name, tells the operating system to redirect the standard output into that place name, in this case "junkfile". If "junkfile" did not exist, which it probably didn't, it is created. Had it already existed, it would have been overwritten (deleted and then recreated).

Now enter the command line:

```
stars 5 >>junkfile
```

[2]Building up a lot of small, easily understood functions with no side effects is important for good C programming.

The symbol ">>" again tells the operating system to redirect the standard output to "junkfile". But now it will append (add) that output to the end of "junkfile". Look at that file once again. It now contains an additional line—one with five stars:

```
********************
*****
```

But beware! On some systems, an error will be reported if you attempt to append to a file that doesn't exist. Even worse, some systems don't support the ">>" command at all. Using it, instead of causing an error, may cause a file named ">" to be created! Take a moment to see if, and how, your system handles the ">>" command.

In addition to disk files, the standard output can be redirected to other devices. The rules that govern this kind of redirection depend on your operating system. To send the standard output to a printer, for example:

Command	Operating System
stars 5 >/dev/lpr	Some Unix systems
starts 5 >lp0:	RSX with Software Tools
starts 5 >pr:	Aztec C, Apple II

Clearly, if you have need to send standard output somewhere other than to a disk file, you should consult your documentation or ask someone knowledgeable.

Redirected Input

The opposite of the standard output is the *standard input*. The standard input is your terminal's keyboard—the default means of entering information into your programs.

Look at the program in Fig. 10–5, "copy.c". We will be using it to illustrate redirection of the standard input. Take a moment to enter and compile it. Note that the variable *ch* is an **int.** This is one of those special cases mentioned in Chapter 4 where *getchar()* returns a value that will not fit into a **char.** The constant EOF, defined in "stdio.h", stands for *end-of-file* and is an **int** value.

FIGURE 10-5 copy.c

```
/* copy.c: copies standard input to standard output */

#include <stdio.h>

main()
{
    int ch;            /* int needed to hold EOF value */

    while ( (ch = getchar()) != EOF )
        putchar( ch );
}
```

When you run "copy", you will immediately notice that everything you type thereafter is echoed in your video screen. The program is taking its input from the standard input, your keyboard, and printing it to the standard output, your video screen. To terminate "copy", you must type the end-of-file (EOF) character for your system. Usually this is a CONTROL-D, although on some systems it is a CONTROL-Z or a CONTROL-@.

Once you've gotten "copy" to terminate, execute it again with the command line:

```
copy <junkfile
```

The "<" symbol tells the operating system to replace your keyboard with the file "junkfile" as the standard input into the program "copy". In other words, this redirects the standard input to come from "junkfile", and prints whatever "junkfile" contains to your video screen.

Redirection of both input and output can be combined within a single command line. For example, the command:

```
copy <junkfile >junk
```

sets "junkfile" as the input to "copy" and sets "junk" as the output. In this way, "copy" indeed copies "junkfile" to "junk".

10.5 PROGRAMS AS FILTERS

In One Ear and Out the Other   The program "copy.c" is one example of a *filter*. A filter neither knows nor cares where its input is coming from, nor where its output is going to. It merely handles the data that flows through it.

A filter of dubious value is the program "crunch.c". All this simpleminded program does is condense text by eliminating all spaces and tabs. The program is listed in Fig. 10–6.

FIGURE 10-6   crunch.c

```
/* crunch.c: filter spaces and tabs from stream */

#include <stdio.h>

main()
{
    int ch;

    while ( (ch = getchar()) != EOF )
    {
        if ( ch != ' '  &&  ch != '\t' )
            putchar( ch );
    }
}
```

Using "crunch" as:

```
crunch <crunch.c>crunched.c
```

creates a *crunched* version of "crunch.c". Try to compile that version. What spaces were necessary?

Don't let the program "crunch.c" fool you—most filters are very useful.[3] A revised version of "crunch.c", one that eliminates *extra* spaces or tabs, for example, could be very handy if you needed to send a C source file over a modem.

10.6 REDIRECTION AND argv

What Your Program Actually Sees Through All This   All redirection is completely invisible to a program. When the symbols "<", ">", and ">>" are found by the operating system, they, and the files they refer to, are handled and then stripped from the command line before it is passed to the program.

Rerun the program "showargs" to demonstrate this to yourself. Try:

```
showargs a b c d >junkargs
```

Looking at the file "junkargs" you will see:

```
argc = 5
argv[0] = showargs
argv[1] = a
argv[2] = b
argv[3] = c
argv[4] = d
```

Similarly:

```
showargs a b c d <junkfile
```

will ignore "junkfile" because "showargs" gets no information from the standard input.

---

[3]On Unix and Unix-like systems, filters can be fit together using "pipes" to create sophisticated processes from simple pieces. If yours is such a system, make it a point to investigate the exciting possibilities of combining filters with pipes.

11 · FILE INPUT/OUTPUT

Filing from Within a Program, Easy as Pie.

11.1 INTRODUCING FILE I/O

Files Can Be Opened, Read/Written, and Closed In the previous chapter, you learned that the output of a C program could be redirected *into* a file, and, similarly, that its input could be redirected to come *from* a file. In this chapter—a long but not difficult one—you will learn how to handle file input and output from within a program.

In general terms, file handling involves three distinct steps. Every file must first be opened so that reading/writing may occur. The file may be read from, or written to, a single character at a time or in large blocks. It can be read/written as text or raw data, sequentially or randomly. After that I/O is finished, the file must be closed.

When you open a file, you are telling the operating system to do a host of things you would otherwise have to do yourself:

1. Find the file. If it is being opened for writing and cannot be found, create it.
2. Make certain you have permission to use the file.
3. Set up a block of information necessary for the management of the file.
4. Preset where information will begin flowing to/from (either the beginning or end of the file).
5. Set aside a block of memory as a buffer, so the file can be read/written in large chunks (for efficiency).
6. Return to you a *file pointer,* so that you may easily refer to the opened file.

Once a file has been successfully opened, all you need to read from, or write to, that file is its file pointer, that is, a reference number used to access that file. After you are done reading/writing a file, that file must be closed to tidy up any unfinished business. Files can be closed individually with *fclose()* or all at once with *exit()*.

The C language *itself* contains no provisions for these file-handling commands.[1] Instead, you must either use functions provided in the standard C library or create your own file-handling functions. In this chapter we will discuss the functions found in the standard library.

As a final note of introduction, all the file-handling routines discussed in this chapter require that the line:

```
#include <stdio.h>
```

appear at the start of your program. That system-header file contains definitions for things like FILE, NULL, and EOF, which are used by all those routines.

11.2 fopen() AND THE FILE POINTER

The Art of Opening a File from Within a Program[2]   To open a file, call the *fopen()* function and pass it two arguments—the name of the file and the type of activity that will take place. Both arguments must be strings: either text within full quotation marks or the address of a zero-terminated character array. The general rule looks like this:

```
fopen( filename, mode );
```

where *filename* is any legal file name for your system, and *mode* is either ''r'' to open for reading, ''w'' to open for writing, or ''a'' to open for appending. Both ''r'' and ''w'' cause I/O to begin with the first character (zeroth character position) in the file. Opening with ''a'' causes writing to begin *just after* the last character in the file. Thus, to open the file ''myfile'' for reading, you would call *fopen()* as:

```
fopen( "myfile", "r" );
```

The value returned by *fopen()* is a ''pseudo'' type called a **file pointer.**[3] Before a file can be meaningfully opened, a variable to contain that ''pseudo'' type must be declared. After the file has been opened, that variable will then be used for all further interactions with the file.

Declaring a **file pointer** is exactly like declaring any other identifier of type **pointer to,** except that the type is specified by the word FILE. For example:

```
FILE *name;
```

---

[1]Strictly speaking, C *contains no I/O*. Since autistic programs are of limited utility, I/O libraries are almost always provided. Use the standard one and save yourself some grief.

[2]Some call it art. I call it being in the right place at the right time.

[3]This doesn't mean it's a type that doesn't work. It's ''pseudo'' because it's defined in ''stdio.h'' rather than in the language itself.

declares *name* to be a **pointer to** the type FILE, and thus declares *name* to be a **file pointer.** Every open file must have just such a **file pointer.** If you expect to have two open files (such as one for input and one for output) you must declare two different **file pointers:**

```
FILE *infp, *outfp;
```

We recommend you end **file pointer** names with the letters *fp* because this makes them easy to recognize in the body of your program.

The declaration of a **file pointer** combined with the call to *fopen()* will look like this:

```
#include <stdio.h>     /* always */
FILE *infp;
infp = fopen( "myfile", "r" );
```

First, the system-header file "stdio.h" is **#include'd** because it contains the definition for FILE. Then, the **file pointer** *infp* is declared. Finally, the call to *fopen()*, to open the file "myfile" for reading, yields a returned reference number for the opened file that is assigned to the **file pointer** *infp*. That **file pointer** will be used to access the file throughout the rest of the program.

It is also wise to include a test for errors when opening a file.[4] Checking for errors is easy because *fopen()* returns NULL (a 0 pointer value) when it encounters a file that doesn't exist or can't be opened. Thus, a test to see if a file has been successfully opened will look like this:

```
infp = fopen( "myfile", "r");
if ( infp == NULL )
{
     . . . . error-handling routine here
}
. . . . success, program continues
```

As a kind of shorthand, most C programs combine the call to *fopen()* with the test for NULL into the single statement:

```
if ( (infp = fopen( "myfile", "r" )) == NULL )
{
     . . . . error-handling routine here
}
. . . . success, program continues
```

This does the same thing: opens the file "myfile" for reading and assigns the returned **file pointer** to *infp*. The result of that assignment—the value of *infp*—is then compared for equality to NULL. Because this kind of shorthand is so common, we will use it in all the examples that follow.

The short program in Fig. 11–1, "files.c", illustrates the process of opening a file with error checking. Try executing it with various file names. If your system allows you to specify disk drives, try specifying files on different disks. You should

---

[4]Let me rephrase that. It's stupid *not to* include such a test.

FIGURE 11-1   files.c

```
/* files.c:   illustrate use of the fopen() function */

#include <stdio.h>        /* for FILE and NULL */

main( argc, argv )
int   argc;
char *argv[];
{
    FILE *infp;

    if ( argc != 2 )
    {
        printf( "usage: %s filename\n", argv[0] );
        exit( 0 );
    }

    if ( (infp = fopen( argv[1], "r")) == NULL )
    {
        printf( "\"%s\": can't open\n", argv[1] );
        exit( -1 );
    }
    else
        printf( "\"%s\": successfully opened\n", argv[1] );

    exit( 0 );
}
```

be able to specify a file name to the program no differently than you would normally do when entering file names as part of ordinary commands to your computer.

Again note that "stdio.h" must be **#include'd** because the type FILE and the value NULL are both defined in it. Like so many other things in C, they are not a part of the language itself. Since each is defined differently from machine to machine, they are placed in "stdio.h" so codes written on one machine will compile on another.[5]

11.3 READING AND WRITING

Single Character File Input and Output   Some new functions are needed if you are to read and write to the files you have opened. Two of these are *fgetc()*, for "get a character from a file," and *fputc()*, for "put a character into a file." Both require at least one argument, a **file pointer,** telling it which file to access. That **file pointer** is the reference number returned by *fopen()* when the file was opened.

---

[5]No programming language is *completely* portable between machines. Some of the worst machine dependencies, however, can be isolated in such header files as "stdio.h".

Reading with fgetc()

For *fgetc()* a **file pointer** is the only argument required. It is called as:

```
ch = fgetc ( infp ) ;
```

which causes the next character to be fetched from the file indicated by *infp* and assigns that character to the variable *ch.* If there are no more characters left in the file, *fgetc()* will return EOF for end-of-file. Thus, a call to *fgetc()* with a test for end-of-file will look like:

```
if ( (ch = fgetc ( infp )) != EOF )
{
        . . . . handle characters here
}
else
        . . . . handle end-of-file here
```

The program "files.c" may now be revised to use *fgetc().* A file is opened as before. Then, in a loop, the contents of that file are read one character at a time and printed to your video screen. Note that *ch* must be declared **int** because EOF is a special value that will not fit into a **char.** The revised program is in Fig. 11-2.

Writing with fputc()

To call *fputc(),* a function that writes a single character to a file, you must pass two arguments. They are the character you want placed into the file and a *file pointer* indicating which file to place that character into. Thus, a call to *fputc()* will look like:

```
fputc ( ch, outfp ) ;
```

This causes the character contained in the variable *ch* to be written to the file indicated by the **file pointer** *outfp.* If, for some reason, *fputc()* is unable to write the character, it will return EOF. A complete call, then, should test for success in writing, as:

```
if (fputc ( ch, outfp ) == EOF )
{
        . . . . error writing character here
}
else
        . . . . successful write here
```

Adding *fputc()* to the program "files.c" turns it into a file-copying program. The file is still opened as before, and the contents of that file are read in a loop. But now, instead of printing the read characters to the screen, they are "put" into a second file indicated by *outfp.* To clarify what this version of the program does, we have renamed it "fcopy.c", and it is listed in Fig. 11-3 on page 116.

FIGURE 11-2   files.c (revision 1)

```
/* files.c (revision 1):  expanded to demonstrate fgetc() */

#include <stdio.h>          /* for FILE and NULL */

main( argc, argv )
int   argc;
char *argv[];
{
    FILE *infp;
    int  ch;                /* added: ch declared */

    if ( argc != 2 )
    {
        printf( "usage: %s filename\n", argv[0] );
        exit( 0 );
    }

    if ( (infp = fopen( argv[1], "r")) == NULL )
    {
        printf( "\"%s\": can't open\n", argv[1] );
        exit( -1 );
    }

    /*
    ** in a loop, read and print all characters in file
    */
    while ( (ch = fgetc( infp )) != EOF )
    {
        putchar( ch );
    }

    exit( 0 );
```

By now you've noticed that all the versions of this program have ended with a call to the *exit()* function. All files must be closed before a program ends, and the *exit()* function not only aborts the program but also closes all open files.

11.4 CLOSING FILES

Gracefully Abandoning Files in Midprogram Closing files tidies up any unfinished business such as deallocating I/O buffers and marking the files themselves as no longer open. Additionally, when a file that was opened for writing (''w'') or appending (''a'') is closed, any data not yet actually written to that file is placed into it. It is very important that you close any files you have opened for writing or you may lose part of your data.

FIGURE 11-3 fcopy.c

```
/* fcopy.c (files.c modified): Copies file1 to file2 */          }

#include <stdio.h>

main( argc, argv )
int  argc;
char *argv[];
{
    FILE *infp,         /* input filepointer (file1)  */
         *outfp;        /* ouput filepointer (file2) */
    int  ch;

    if ( argc != 3 )            /* need 3 arguments now */
    {
        printf( "usage: %s file1 file2\n", argv[0] );
        exit( 0 );
    }

    if ( (infp = fopen( argv[1], "r" )) == NULL )
        quit( argv[1] );

    if ( (outfp = fopen( argv[2], "w" )) == NULL )
        quit( argv[2] );

    /*
    ** in a loop read from file1 and write to file2
    */
    while ( (ch = fgetc( infp )) != EOF )
        fputc( ch, outfp );

    exit( 0 );
}

quit( fname )
char *fname;
{
    printf( "\"%s\": can't open\n", fname );
    exit( -1 );
}
```

Closing with exit()

When a program is terminated with the *exit()* function, all open files are automatically closed. On many systems, all files are also closed when the program runs out of
things to do and ends. This is a risky business, however, and you should not count
on your files being properly closed without specific direction from you.[6] We recom-

---

[6]These programs are really quite unruly and need a short leash.

mend that you use *exit()* if you want to end or abort any program in which you have opened files.

The fflush() Function

When writing data to a file, you are sending that data to some file-handling routine within the computer. That routine is there to improve the efficiency of writing by buffering—collecting your data until it has gotten large enough to justify its placement into the file. This approach makes sense when you realize that most files are on disks, and writing to those disks (especially floppy disks!) takes a significant chunk of time. You wouldn't want that placement to occur for each character you write because that would cause your program to crawl at a snail's pace.

The improved efficiency of this system buffering, however, creates a small risk. The longer a user of your program goes without generating new data to be written, the greater the likelihood that some disaster will cause that data to be lost before it is ever placed into the file. A power failure is one possibility and, on small machines, the user might inadvertently switch floppy disks.

For those times when you need to *force immediate placement* of the buffered data into a file, the *fflush()* function is available. It causes system-buffered data to be placed (flushed) into a file immediately. The routine for calling *fflush()* is:

```
fflush( outfp );
```

This forces all system-buffered data that has been written to the file indicated by the **file pointer** *outfp* to be placed (flushed) into that file. If the attempt to flush a file is unsuccessful for some reason, *fflush()* will return EOF. The complete call to *fflush()*, then, including an error test, will look like:

```
if (fflush( outfp ) == EOF )
{
    .... handle problem flushing file here
}
.... success, continue program here
```

On large multiuser systems, ordinary text to your terminal's video screen is often buffered until a newline character is sent. In that circumstance, the *fflush()* function can be used to force printing of incomplete pieces of text. The concept of your screen being used as a file will be covered later in this chapter.

The fclose() Function

The *fclose()* function is used to close *individual* files while the program is still running. It flushes any written data to the file, marks that file as no longer open, and frees the **file pointer** for reuse. To call *fclose()*, pass it a single argument—a **file pointer** indicating which file is to be closed:

```
fclose( infp );
```

Just like *fgetc()* and *fputc()*, if a file cannot be closed, *fclose()* returns EOF. Otherwise, it returns 0. A complete call to *fclose()*, including an error test, might look like:

```
while ( fclose( infp ) == EOF )
{
        . . . . inform user of problem wait,
                and try again
}
        . . . . successful close, program continues
```

The *fclose()* function can also be called to free a **file pointer** for reuse. That **file pointer** may then be assigned to another file with *fopen()*.

To illustrate one application of *fclose()*, we will revise the program "files.c" (Fig. 11–3) and rename it "showfiles.c". By adding an outer loop, many files may now be specified in the command line. They will be read, one after the other, and printed to your video screen. Note that only one **file pointer,** *infp,* is needed because it is released for reuse by *fclose()* when each file is done. The program is in Fig. 11–4.

FIGURE 11-4   showfiles.c

```
/* showfiles.c: print a list of files by using fclose() */

#include <stdio.h>

main( argc, argv )
int   argc;
char *argv[];
{
    FILE *infp;              /* only one filepointer needed */
    int  ch, i;

    if ( argc == 1 )
    {
        printf( "usage: %s file(s)\n", argv[0] );
        exit( 0 );
    }

    for ( i = 1; i < argc; i++ )         /* for each file */
    {
        if ( (infp = fopen( argv[i], "r" )) == NULL )
        {
            printf( "%s: can't open\n", argv[i] );
            exit( -1 );
        }

        while ( (ch = fgetc( infp )) != EOF )
            putchar( ch );

        fclose( infp );              /* free the filepointer */
    }
}
```

Recall from the previous chapter that ***putchar()*** sends a single character to the standard output. Because this is usually (by default) your terminal's video screen, the output for ''showfiles'' is displayed on the screen. The standard output may, however, be redirected (using the ''>'' symbol as part of the command line) to go instead to a file or device. Thus, ''showfiles'' may be invoked with the command line:

```
showfiles file1 file2 >file3
```

This causes ''file1'' and then ''file2'' to be read and printed, but that printing, instead of going to your screen, will be redirected into ''file3''. This has the effect of joining the first two files together, creating a third.

11.5 stdin AND stdout

Redirectable Built-in Files and Their File Pointers   It may seem strange, but your keyboard and video screen can be opened just as if they were files. This is possible because all C's file-handling functions view files and devices as interchangeable.[7]

When any C program is executed, two files are always automatically opened. This happens invisibly to the user. One of these files is opened for reading and is the standard input or, by default, your keyboard. The other is opened for writing and is the standard output or, by default, your video screen.

The **file pointers** necessary to use those opened files are declared in the system header ''stdio.h''. The **file pointer** for the read file is called ***stdin*** for standard input. The **file pointer** for the write file is called ***stdout*** for standard output. All you need to do to use these **file pointers** is include the line:

```
#include <stdio.h>
```

at the beginning of your program so their declarations will become a part of it.

As far as your program is concerned, ***stdin*** is a **file pointer** associated with some automatically-opened file for reading, and that file just happens to be your keyboard. And ***stdout*** is a **file pointer** associated with some automatically-opened file for writing, and that file just happens to be your video screen.

Since ***stdin*** and ***stdout*** are both valid **file pointers,** the statement:

```
ch = fgetc ( stdin ) ;
```

can be used to read a single character from the standard input, or (by default) your keyboard. Similarly, the statement:

```
fputc ( stdout, ch ) ;
```

can be used to write a single character to the standard output, or (by default) your terminal's video screen.

Take a moment to review the program ''copy.c'' from the last chapter. It is listed again in Fig. 11–5.

---

[7]That is, the C library functions usually provided with a compiler.

FIGURE 11-5 copy.c

```
/* copy.c: copies standard input to standard output */

#include <stdio.h>

main()
{
    int ch;              /* int needed to hold EOF value */

    while ( (ch = getchar()) != EOF )
        putchar( ch );
}
```

Notice that *getchar()* is used to read from the standard input and *putchar()* is used to write to the standard output. Because the file pointers *stdin* and *stdout* are automatically available to you and accessible by **#include'ing** ''stdio.h'', that program can easily be rewritten using *fgetc()* and *fputc()*. See Fig. 11–6.

FIGURE 11-6 copy.c (revision 1)

```
/* copy.c (revision 1): revised to use stdin and stdout */

#include <stdio.h>            /* for needed definitions */

main()
{
    int ch;              /* int needed to hold EOF value */

    while ( (ch = fgetc( stdin )) != EOF )
        fputc( ch, stdout );
}
```

Take a moment to experiment with this revised version of ''copy''. Try:

    copy < copy.c > junk

which redirects the input to ''copy'' to come from the file ''copy.c'' and the output to go into the file ''junk''. You will find that this revision using *fgetc()* and *fputc()* behaves exactly as the original.

The stderr File Pointer

Rerun the program ''showfiles'' by typing:

    showfiles badfile > junk

where *badfile* is the name of a nonexistent file. When you look at the contents of the file ''junk'', you will discover that the error message was *also* redirected into it—

not a good situation because error messages should generally go to the video screen. Fortunately, C offers a solution.

In addition to *stdin* and *stdout,* every C program automatically opens another file and assigns it the **file pointer** *stderr.* That file is *always* your terminal's video screen no matter where the standard input and standard output may have been redirected. That output is called the *standard error output* and, on many systems, cannot be redirected.

Before you can apply *stderr* to a program, however, you need to learn about the file-handling versions of functions like *printf()* (to be covered in the next section) so you can easily print informative diagnostics to the screen. Trying to print error messages one character at a time with *fputc()* would prove to be a bit cumbersome.

11.6 FILE VERSIONS OF FUNCTIONS

Add an F and Presto! A File-Handling Function   All the input/output functions you learned about in previous chapters send their output to the standard output and get their input from the standard input. Those functions are:

printf()	prints formatted output to standard output
scanf()	takes converted input from standard input
puts()	puts (prints) a string to standard output
gets()	gets (reads) a string from standard input

Each of these functions has a file-oriented counterpart that allows information to flow to/from a place of your choice:

fprintf()	prints formatted output to a file
fscanf()	takes converted input from a file
fputs()	puts (prints) a string to a file
fgets()	gets (reads) a string from a file

The rules for calling each are the same as those for calling their nonfile counterparts, with one addition: A **file pointer** must be passed telling each which file to access.

The fprintf() Function

The way to call our old friend *printf()* is:

```
printf ( "control string", arg1, arg2, ... );
```

Similarly, the way to call its file-handling counterpart, *fprintf(),* is:

```
fprintf ( filepointer, "control string", arg1, arg2, ... );
```

The additional argument for *fprintf()* is a **file pointer** that specifies where (to which file or device) output is to go. Other than that extra argument, both functions are

exactly the same. But what a difference that argument makes! Where *printf()* always sends its output to the standard output, *fprintf()* can send its output anywhere.[8]
For example:

```
printf ( "Hello world\n" ) ;
```

will *always* print the string "Hello world\n" to the standard output, whereas:

```
fprintf ( outfp, "Hello world\n" ) ;
```

will print the string "Hello world\n" to the *file or device* indicated by the **file pointer** *outfp.*

Using *fprintf(),* we can now revise "showfiles.c" so that it will print its error messages to the video screen, *regardless* of how its output has otherwise been redirected. In the revision in Fig. 11–7, *fprintf()* has been substituted for *printf()* and the extra argument, a **file pointer,** added. That **file pointer** is *stderr* —one of the

FIGURE 11-7 showfiles.c (revision 1)

```
/* showfiles.c (revsion 1): uses fprintf() and stderr */

#include <stdio.h>

main( argc, argv )
int  argc;
char *argv[];
{
    FILE *infp;
    int  ch, i;

    if ( argc == 1 )
    {
        fprintf( stderr, "usage: %s file(s)\n", argv[0] );
        exit( 0 );
    }

    for ( i = 1; i < argc; i++ )
    {
        if ( (infp = fopen( argv[i], "r" )) == NULL )
        {
            fprintf( stderr, "%s: can't open\n", argv[i] );
            exit( -1 );
        }

        while ( (ch = fgetc( infp )) != EOF )
            putchar( ch );

        fclose( infp );
    }
}
```

[8]The standard output can, of course, also be sent anywhere via redirection.

three automatically defined **file pointers.** It connects to the standard error output, or your terminal's video screen.

Once again, try invoking this program with the command line:

```
showfiles badfile >junk
```

This time you will discover that the error message is printed on your screen, even though output was redirected into the file "junk".

The fscanf() Function

Like *scanf(),* the *fscanf()* function is used to read in text and convert that text to values. But, whereas *scanf() always* gets its input text from the standard input, *fscanf()* gets its input from wherever its additional argument, a **file pointer,** indicates.

To illustrate, since the **file pointer** *stdin* is automatically connected to the standard input, the expression:

```
scanf ( "%d", &num ) ;
```

and:

```
fscanf ( stdin, "%d", &num ) ;
```

both read a text representation of an integer from the standard input, convert it to an **int,** and place that value into the variable *num.*

Since *fscanf()* returns EOF when it reaches end-of-file, a complete statement using that function could appear as:

```
while (fscanf (infp, "%s", word) != EOF )
{
    .... process word here
}
fclose ( infp ) ;
```

In a loop, this reads whitespace-delimited strings from the file indicated by *infp,* placing them into the location *word,* until EOF is encountered. Then the file is closed.

The program "fwords.c" (Fig. 11–8) uses *fscanf()* to read a file and break it up into individual words. It prints those words to the standard output using *printf(),* so that output may be redirected to a file or printer.

The fputs() and fgets() Functions

For those times when you need to do simple string I/O, the functions *fputs()* and *fgets()* are available. In addition to needing a **file pointer,** these differ from their nonfile counterparts, *puts()* and *gets()* (Chapter 9) in one other way. The *puts()* function, when passed the address of a string, as:

```
puts ( string ) ;
```

FIGURE 11-8 fwords.c

```
/* fwords.c: read a file's words using fscanf() */

#include <stdio.h>

main( argc, argv )
int  argc;
char *argv[];
{
    FILE *infp;
    char word[128];            /* buffer to hold each word */

    if ( argc != 2 )
    {
        fprintf( stderr, "usage: %s file\n", argv[0] );
        exit( 0 );
    }
    if ( (infp = fopen( argv[1], "r" )) == NULL )
    {
        fprintf( stderr, "\"%s\": can't open\n", argv[1] );
        exit( -1 );
    }

    while ( fscanf( infp, "%s", word ) != EOF )
    {
        printf( "%s\n", word );
    }

    exit( 0 );
}
```

adds an extra terminating newline ('\n') to its output. Its file-handling counterpart
fputs(), called as:

> fputs(string, filepointer);

does not. Similarly, the *gets()* function, called as:

> gets(buffer);

strips the terminating newline ('\n') from the input placed into **buffer.** But its file-
handling version *fgets()*, called as:

> fgets(buffer, limit, filepointer);

includes the terminating newline ('\n') as part of its input.

By way of example, if the string in question is ''Bob'', then the difference in
output will be:

Expression	Output
puts(''Bob'');	''Bob\n''
fputs(''Bob'', outfp);	''Bob''

The difference in input, where you type "Bob" followed by a newline (the RE-TURN or ENTER key), will be:

Expression	Placed Into buff[MAX]
gets(buff, MAX);	'B', 'o', 'b', '\0'
fgets(buff, MAX, infp);	'B', 'o', 'b', '\n', '\0'

The chief application for *fgets()* and *fputs()* is in reading and writing newline-delimited strings to/from files or devices. The program "flines.c" uses *fgets()* to count the number of lines in the file specified in the command line. Note that, unlike the other file-reading functions you've learned so far, *fgets()* returns NULL upon encountering end-of-file. See Fig. 11–9.

FIGURE 11-9 flines.c

```
/* flines.c: counts number of lines in file using fgets() */

#include <stdio.h>
#define MAX 512                    /* maximum characters/line */

main( argc, argv )
int   argc;
char *argv[];
{
    FILE *infp;
    char buff[MAX];                /* buffer to hold each line */
    int linecount = 0;

    if ( argc != 2 )
    {
        fprintf( stderr, "usage: %s file\n", argv[0] );
        exit( 0 );
    }

    if ( (infp = fopen( argv[1], "r" )) == NULL )
    {
        fprintf( stderr, "\"%s\": can't open\n", argv[1] );
        exit( -1 );
    }

    while ( fgets( buff, MAX, infp ) != NULL )
        linecount++;

    printf( "\"%s\": %d lines\n", argv[1], linecount );

    exit( 0 );
}
```

Because *fgets()* and *fputs()* differ so much from their nonfile counterparts, indeed from the other file-reading functions, we recommend the following rule of thumb: If you ever need to process files on a line-by-line basis, think of *fgets()* and *fputs()*, then review both here and in your documentation how they are used and how they differ.

11.7 REASSIGNING stdin AND stdout

An Alternative to Exiting When the Unexpected Happens   Since both **stdin** and **stdout** are **file pointers,** it is legal to assign their values to **file pointers** of your own. For example, in the fragment:

```
if ( argc == 2)
{
    if ( (infp = fopen( argv[1], "r" )) == NULL )
        quit( "%s: can't open\n", argv[1] );
}
else
    infp = stdin;
```

a check is made to see if a file name was specified as a part of the command line. If one was, that file is opened. If not, the **file pointer** *infp* is assigned the value of *stdin,* thus attaching *infp* to the standard input.

The revised version of "fcopy.c" in Fig. 11–10 demonstrates how the ability to assign the value of one **file pointer** to another can make a program more robust. This revision acts like "fcopy.c" if both files are specified—that is, it copies the first into the second. If the second file name is missing from the command line, then the first is read and printed to the standard output. If both file names are missing, then the standard input is read and printed to the standard output.

This program may be executed in a number of ways. For example, entering the command line:

```
fcopy firstfile secondfile
```

will copy "firstfile" into "secondfile". Alternatively:

```
fcopy firstfile
```

will read "firstfile" and print it to your terminal's video screen. Or even:

```
filecopy <firstfile >secondfile
```

This will read the standard input, that is, "firstfile", because the standard input has been redirected "<" to come from that file. It will print to the standard output, that is, "secondfile", because the standard output has been redirected ">" to go to that file. The result is again that "firstfile" is copied into "secondfile".[9]

---

[9]You may wonder why a single program should have all these different ways to do file I/O. The point is that this frees the user from having to remember *exactly* how to use the program. That's a good idea.

FIGURE 11-10 fcopy.c (revision 1)

```
/* fcopy.c (revision 1):   modified to reassign stdin and stdout */

#include <stdio.h>

main( argc, argv )
int  argc;
char *argv[];
{
    FILE *infp, *outfp;
    int  ch;

    if ( argc > 3 )                  /* 3 arguments maximum */
    {
        fprintf(stderr, "usage: %s {{file1} file2}\n", argv[0]);
        exit( 0 );
    }

    if ( argc == 3 )
    {
        if ( (outfp = fopen( argv[2], "w" )) == NULL )
            quit( argv[2] );
    }
    else
        outfp = stdout;                /* reassign stdout */

    if ( argc == 2 )
    {
        if ( (infp = fopen( argv[1], "r" )) == NULL )
            quit( argv[1] );
    }
    else
        infp = stdin;                  /* reassign stdin  */

    while ( (ch = fgetc( infp )) != EOF )
        fputc( ch, outfp );

    exit( 0 );
}

quit( fname )
char *fname;
{
    fprintf( stderr, "\"%s\": can't open\n", fname );
    exit( -1 );
}
```

11.8 READING AND WRITING BLOCKS

The Art of File I/O Using Big Chunks   The standard library contains two functions for reading and writing large blocks of data. They are called *fread()*, for *read from a file*, and *fwrite()*, for *write to a file*.

Both functions require you to pass the address of a block of memory as the first argument. The simplest way of creating such a block is to declare a large array. For example:

```
#define MAX 512
static char buf[ MAX ];
```

This creates a 512-byte buffer, named *buf*, into which data may be read and from which data may be written. We will be using this buffer in the following examples as we discuss *fread()* and *fwrite()*.

The fread() Function

The rule for calling *fread()* is:

```
fread( buffer, size, count, filepointer );
```

where *buffer* is the address (location) of where the data will be placed. This may be an array name, the address of a variable yielded by the **&** operator, or a pointer. The *size* is the number of bytes in each "unit," where a "unit" is any meaningful division of the data. (For example, an array of type **int,** where each **int** is 2 bytes, could consider the unit to be a *size 2.*) The *count* is the number of those units to read. Finally, *filepointer* is a **file pointer** (reference number) for a file that has been opened for reading—that is, with a mode of "r".

An actual call to *fread()*, which looks like:

```
fread( buf, 1, MAX, infp );
```

is used to read 512 bytes (512 one-byte units) from the file indicated by *infp,* into the array *buf*.

The *fread()* function is not limited to reading large amounts of data. Assuming *ch* is a simple **char** variable, the expression:

```
fread( &ch, 1, 1, infp );
```

is just like:

```
ch = fgetc( infp );
```

in that it reads a single character from the file pointed to by *infp,* and places it into the one-byte buffer (variable) *ch*. The expression "&ch" is used because *fread()* expects its first argument to be an *address*.

The *fread()* function returns the number of units actually read. If end-of-file is reached, that number will be less than the number requested. If *fread()* is called again, after end-of-file was reached, it will return 0. Zero is also returned if any error occurred in reading. Thus, a complete call to *fread()*, including an error or end-of-file test, may appear as:

```
if ( (nbytes = fread(buf, 1, MAX, infp)) <= 0 )
{
    .... nothing left to read or error
}
.... use nbytes actually read here
```

The program ''fblock.c'' (Fig. 11–11) uses *fread()* to read a file in blocks of 512 bytes, and it reports the number of characters in the file based on the number of full and partial blocks read. Note that the buffer *buf* is only a temporary place into which blocks are read and is used over and over.

FIGURE 11-11 fblock.c

```
/* fblock.c: count chars by counting blocks with fread() */

#include <stdio.h>
#define MAX 512

static char buf[MAX];

main( argc, argv )
int   argc;
char *argv[];
{
    FILE *infp;
    int nbytes, chcnt = 0;

    if ( argc != 2 )
    {
        fprintf( stderr, "usage: %s filename\n", argv[0] );
        exit( 0 );
    }

    if ( (infp = fopen( argv[1], "r" )) == NULL )
    {
        fprintf( stderr, "\"%s\": can't open\n", argv[1] );
        exit( -1 );
    }

    while ( (nbytes = fread( buf, 1, MAX, infp)) > 0 )
        chcnt = chcnt + nbytes;

    fprintf( stderr, "\"%s\": %d chars\n", argv[1], chcnt );

    exit( 0 );
}
```

The fwrite() function

The rules for calling *fwrite()* are the same as those for calling *fread()*:

```
fwrite( buffer, size, count, filepointer );
```

The difference is that *fread()* reads from a file into the buffer, and *fwrite()* writes from the buffer into a file. Both functions return the number of units actually read or written. If that actual number differs from what you requested, then you have either reached the end-of-file or encountered a write error.

Adding *fwrite()* to "fblock.c" converts it to yet another file-copy program. Notice that the buffer size has been increased to 16000 bytes to minimize the number of passes—that is, to reduce the number of reads and writes. See Fig. 11–12.

FIGURE 11-12 fblock.c (revision 1)

```
/* fblock.c (revision 1): fwrite() added. copy file1 to file2  */

#include <stdio.h>
#define MAX 16000

static char buf[MAX];

main( argc, argv )
int   argc;
char *argv[];
{
    FILE *infp, *outfp;
    int nbytes;

    if ( argc != 3 )
    {
        fprintf( stderr, "usage: %s file1 file2\n", argv[0] );
        exit( 0 );
    }

    infp  = fopen( argv[1], "r" );
    outfp = fopen( argv[2], "w" );
    if ( infp == NULL || outfp == NULL )
    {
        fprintf( stderr, "can't copy\n" );
        exit( -1 );
    }

    while ( (nbytes = fread( buf, 1, MAX, infp)) > 0 )
        fwrite( buf, 1, nbytes, outfp );

    exit( 0 );
}
```

11.9 ERROR HANDLING

A Graceful Egress in the Midst of Trouble   The standard library contains several functions designed to handle file I/O problems that may occur from time to time. They are: *feof(),* which reports if end-of-file has been reached; *ferror(),* which reports if a file error has occurred; *clearerr(),* to undo error status and try again; and *perror(),* to print what kind of error occurred without having to determine the cause on your own.

The feof() Function

The *feof()* function can be called to test for an end-of-file condition. For example, the fragment:

```
if ( feof ( filepointer ) )
{
    . . . . handle end-of-file here
}
```

can be used to test the file indicated by *filepointer* to see if you are at the end of that file.

Some file-handling functions, like *fgetc(),* return EOF when end-of-file has been reached *or* when there is a read error. The *feof()* function can be used to determine why that EOF was returned. A complete call to *fgetc(),* including a test to differentiate end-of-file from read errors, will look like this:

```
if ( (ch = fgetc ( infp )) == EOF )
{
    if ( feof ( inpf ) )
    {
        . . . . really was end-of-file here
    }
    else
        . . . . must have been a read error
}
```

Here, EOF signals some end to the data. A check is made using *feof()* to see if that end is due to having reached the end of the file. If *feof()* returns 0, for *not* EOF, then that end must have been caused by some read error.

The ferror() Function

A handy companion to *feof()* is the *ferror()* function. You call it to see if *any* error has occurred while handling a file. Like *feof(),* it is passed a single argument, which is a **file pointer.** If there was no error, a 0 is returned. If an error occurred, a nonzero value is returned. A typical call to *ferror()* looks like:

```
if ( ferror ( filepointer ) )
{
        . . . . handle error here
}
```

This tests to see if any error occurred while handling the file pointed to by *filepointer*.

A common application for *ferror()* is in delaying all error checking until the end of a chunk of code. Suppose you wanted to write three values to the beginning of some file—the file's length, start address, and revision number. Such a section of code could be written as:

```
fwrite ( &len, 2, 1, outfp );    /* file's length  */
fwrite ( &adr, 2, 1, outfp );    /*        address  */
fwrite ( &rev, 2, 1, outfp );    /*    revision #   */

if ( ferror ( outfp ) )
{
        . . . . oops, some error while writing
}
```

Here, three calls to *fwrite()* were made on the assumption that all was going well. Only *after* all three calls were made is a check done to see if there were any errors while writing to that file.

The clearerr() Function

Once an error has occurred while handling a file, that error condition will continue to exist until it is cleared. The *clearerr()* function is used to clear any error condition associated with a file. It is called by passing it a single argument, which is a **file pointer**.

Generally, *clearerr()* is used to repeatedly prompt a user to rectify some abnormal condition—an error while writing because the door on the disk drive had been left open, for example. The code to handle that situation might appear as:

```
while ( fputc ( ch, outfp ) == EOF )
{
      . . . error message here
      . . . and pause while user fixes problem
    clearerr ( oufp ) ;
}
```

Note the need to pause and give the user time to rectify whatever is wrong. This could be as simple a thing such as printing:

```
"file": error writing < RETURN > to continue
```

then waiting for the user to press the RETURN or ENTER key, or returning to some main menu.

The perror() Function

Some standard libraries contain a function that prints an appropriate diagnostic message for any given error in a file. Called *perror()*, it is passed one argument—a string, the file's name you want printed.

By way of example, suppose you detected some error while writing to a file named "junk". A call to *perror()*,

```
perror ( "junk" );
```

will cause a message to be printed that details the kind of error that occurred. That message will have the form:

```
junk: disk full
```

Certainly, this is more informative than a simple "can't write" message!

The following program, called "errs.c", provides an exercise in writing robust or "idiot-proof" code. It combines all the error-handling functions we've outlined in this chapter and applies them to the task of catching and reporting any and all errors. If your standard library does not contain the *perror()* function, substitute a print statement. The new program is in Fig. 11–13.

11.10 REPOSITIONING WITHIN A FILE

The Basis for Random-Access Files   Recall that there are only three ways to open a file: "r" and "w" open it for reading and writing at the *beginning* of the file; "a" opens it for writing at the *end* of the file. There are times, however, when you will want to read or write at places other than the beginning or end. A *random-access file* is one example. This kind of file is divided into *records,* each of which is the same size and each of which can be accessed in any order. To create an use files like random-access files, the standard library supplies a pair of functions called *ftell()* and *fseek().*

The ftell() Function

The *ftell()* function, when passed a **file pointer,** returns a value, which is your current position within that file. Your position within a file is measured in bytes offset from the beginning of the file. Thus, a position of 0 would mean you are at the beginning of the file. That position indicates where the next byte will be read from or written to.

Generally, *ftell()* is used to determine if you are where you expect to be. It is called with a statement like:

```
offset = ftell ( filepointer );
```

where *offset* is a new type called **long** (covered in the next chapter[10]).

---

[10]I'll give you a hint—it's a kind of integer that's generally longer than "short." If you don't know what that means, I guess you'll have to wait until the next chapter.

FIGURE 11-13 errs.c

```
/* errs.c: copy file1 to file2. error trapping added */

#include <stdio.h>
#define MAX 16000

static char buf[MAX];

main( argc, argv )
int  argc;
char *argv[];
{
    FILE *infp, *outfp;
    int nbytes;

    if ( argc != 3 )
    {
        fprintf( stderr, "usage: %s file1 file2\n", argv[0] );
        exit( 0 );
    }

    if ( (infp  = fopen( argv[1], "r" )) == NULL )
        quit( argv[1] );                    /*  open error */
    if ( (outfp = fopen( argv[2], "w" )) == NULL )
        quit( argv[2] );                    /*  open error */

    while ( (nbytes = fread( buf, 1, MAX, infp)) == MAX )
        if( fwrite( buf, 1, MAX, outfp ) != MAX )
            quit( argv[2] );                /* write error */

    if ( ferror( infp ) )
        quit( argv[1] );                    /*  read error */
    else
        if( fwrite( buf, 1, nbytes, outfp ) != nbytes )
            quit( argv[2] );                /* write error */
    exit( 0 );
}

quit( fname )
char *fname;
{
    perror( fname );
    exit( -1 );
}
```

The fseek() Function

The *fseek()* function is used to move to a new position within a file. It is passed three arguments:

```
fseek( filepointer, offset, how );
```

where the *filepointer* indicates which file; *offset* is the number of bytes to move; and *how* a value stating how that *offset* is to be used. If the value of **how** is 0, then the *offset* is from the beginning of the file. If it is 1, then the *offset* is relative to the current position (for example, an *offset* of −1 moves back one byte, 1 moves forward one byte). If **how** is 2, then the *offset* is backward from the end of the file and *offset* must be negative.

If a file is divided into many records, each of length 100 bytes, for example, then one way to begin reading at record 20 would be:

```
recsize = 100L;     /* size of each record   */
recnum = 20L;       /* record number sought */

fseek( infp, recsize * recnum, 0 );
```

Here the last argument (0) indicates that the new position will be *recsize* times *recnum* bytes from the *beginning* of the file. This marks where the next byte will be read from or written to. The *L* following the two constants (100L and 20L) indicates the new type called **long,** which you will learn about in the next chapter.

12.'MORE ABOUT TYPES

Variations on Previous Types Come Rolling Into View.

12.1 THE sizeof KEYWORD

How to Measure a Type in Bytes   Up to now, we have managed to write all our sample programs using only the types **char, int,** and **float.** As you will recall, these represent the most common divisions of the computer's memory. Typically a **char** occupies a single byte, an **int** two (or four) bytes and a **float** four (or more). The precise number of bytes required depends on the specifics of your computer hardware. If you have a 64k microcomputer, for example, your **int** will most likely occupy two bytes. If, on the other hand, you are working on a large, multiuser machine, like a VAX, your *int* will likely occupy four bytes.[1]

You might expect this variation in the number of bytes for a given type to make it difficult to transport programs from one machine to another. Fortunately, C contains an operator called **sizeof** that yields the "size of" things, and can yield the number of bytes used by types. The **sizeof** operator makes it possible to build a test to determine if your types are the right size for your needs and make adjustments if they aren't.

When applied to **int,** for example, as:

```
sizeof (int)
```

---

[1]There is an incredible variety in the integer word lengths for all the different computers made. The current trend for larger microcomputers and minicomputers, however, is to have 32-bit (4-byte) integers.

it yields the number of bytes an **int** occupies. That value may then be assigned directly to a variable, as:

```
numbytes = sizeof (int);
```

or passed directly to a function, as:

```
printf ( "int is %d bytes\n", sizeof (int) );
```

The **sizeof** operator may also be applied to expressions like variables and arrays. For example:

```
int num, numbytes;
numbytes = sizeof (num);
```

will assign the number of bytes occupied by the variable ***num*** to ***numbytes***. And:

```
int ary [123];
numbytes = sizeof (ary);
```

will assign to ***numbytes*** the total number of bytes in the array ***ary***.

The rule for **sizeof** is that keywords for types (such as **int, char,** etc.) *must* be within parentheses:

```
sizeof (int)
```

For expressions (such as variables, array names, and computation) the parentheses are optional. Thus, for the variable ***num:***

```
sizeof num
sizeof (num)
```

are both legal.

Compile the short program "mysizes.c", which is listed in Fig. 12–1. This program will be revised several times throughout this chapter as you learn about other types and variations on types.

12.2 THE TYPES short AND long

Smaller and Larger Versions of Type Int   The type **int** comes in three varieties. If you wish to use fewer bytes than the normal **int** to hold an integer value (to save memory, for example), the type **short int** is available. Conversely, to allocate more bytes, you may use the type **long int.**

As explained in Chapter 2, the number of bytes reserved for a type determines the range of values it may hold. In the case of integers:

Bytes	*Range of Possible Values*	
1 byte	+127 to	−128
2 bytes	+32,767 to	−32,768
4 bytes	+2,147,483,647 to	−2,147,483,648

FIGURE 12-1 mysizes.c

```
/* mysizes.c: displays the size in bytes of several types */

#include <stdio.h>

main()
{
    printf( "Table of sizes for my machine and compiler:\n\n" );

    showsize( "char",   sizeof (char)  );
    showsize( "int",    sizeof (int)   );
    showsize( "float",  sizeof (float) );
}

showsize( typename, bytes )
char *typename;
int  bytes;
{
    printf( "%s\t is %d bytes\n", typename, bytes );
}
```

Depending on your computer, **int** may be the same as **short**, or **int** may be the same as **long**. So before continuing, we will revise the program "mysizes.c" to see what range of values these new types make available on your machine. See Fig. 12–2.

Notice that the types **long int** and **short int** may be declared as **long** and **short**, respectively. Thus, for brevity, they may be used as:

```
short sname;
long lname;
```

or for clarity as:

```
short int sname;
long int lname;
```

Both declare the variable *sname* to be a **short int** and *lname* to be a **long int**.

You must append the letter *L* to an integer constant when you want the compiler to treat it as a **long**:

```
long name = 6543210L;
```

This forces the compiler to treat the constant 6543210 as a **long** integer.

Similarly, the functions *printf()*, *fprintf()*, *scanf()*, and *fscanf()* all require that the integer format string "%d" be written "%ld" when dealing with **long** integers. For example:

```
scanf( "%ld", &biginteger );
```

tells *scanf()* to convert its input into a **long** and place that **long** value into *biginteger*.[2] The *l* in the "%" directive may be optional on machines that have **ints** and **longs** that are the same number of bytes. To ensure portability, however, always use *l* for **long**.

FIGURE 12-2 mysizes.c (revision 1)

```
/* mysizes.c (revision 1): the sizes of some new types */

#include <stdio.h>

main()
{
    printf( "Table of sizes for my machine and compiler:\n\n" );

    showsize( "char",   sizeof (char)  );
    showsize( "short",  sizeof (short) );
    showsize( "int",    sizeof (int)   );
    showsize( "long",   sizeof (long)  );
    showsize( "float",  sizeof (float) );
}

showsize( typename, bytes )
char *typename;
int  bytes;
{
    printf( "%s\t is %d bytes\n", typename, bytes );
}
```

The program called "skip.c", in Fig. 12–3, illustrates the type **long** through its application to the function *fseek()*. Recall, from the last chapter, that *fseek()* is used to change your position in a file and that its second argument must be the type **long**. This program prompts for a file name and an offset, then prints the file beginning at that offset.

To review, the type **long** is used to represent integer values of a greater range than that of a normal **int**. The type **short** provides a way of representing small integer values when program size is a problem. Depending on your machine, however, either **long** or **short** may actually be the same number of bytes as an **int**.[3]

12.3 THE TYPE unsigned

Double the Positive Range of an Integer   Thus far, we have dealt only with integers that have a range of values extending (roughly) equally in both the positive and negative directions. But there will be times when you will want an integer variable to represent positive values only. The keyword for accomplishing this is **unsigned.** As an added bonus, **unsigned** almost doubles the positive range of values that can be held by an integer.

---

[2]The format string "%lo" will format a long as an octal number, and "%lx" will format a long as a hexadecimal number. These formats will be dealt with in detail in Chapter 19.

[3]For example, on a VAX, **short** is 2 bytes and both **int** and **long** are 4 bytes. On an Apple II, using the Aztec C compiler, both **short** and **int** are 2 bytes, and **long** is 4 bytes.

FIGURE 12-3 skip.c

```c
/* skip.c: Print a file starting part way in. Uses fseek() */

#include <stdio.h>
#define MAX 80

main()
{
    FILE *infp;
    long offset;
    char filename[MAX];
    int  ch;

    fprintf( stderr, "File: " );
    gets( filename, MAX );

    if ( (infp = fopen( filename, "r" )) == NULL )
    {
        fprintf( stderr, "%s: can't open\n", filename );
        exit( -1 );
    }

    fprintf( stderr, "Starting at: " );
    scanf( "%ld", &offset );

    if ( fseek( infp, offset, 0 ) < 0 )
    {
        fprintf( stderr, "Improper seek value\n" );
        exit( -1 );
    }

    while( (ch = fgetc( infp )) != EOF )
        putchar( ch );

    exit( 0 );
}
```

Assuming **char** is one byte, **short** and **int** are two bytes, and **long** is four bytes, then:

The Type	Can Represent a Range of Values	
char	$+127$ to	-128
unsigned char	0 to	$+255$
short int	$+32,767$ to	$-32,768$
unsigned short int	0 to	$+65,535$
int	$+32,767$ to	$-32,768$
unsigned int	0 to	$+65,535$
long int	$+2,147,483,647$ to	$-2,147,483,648$
unsigned long int	0 to	$+4,294,967,295$

Beware, however. Not all compilers support **unsigned** for the types **char, short,** or **long.** Check your documentation.

Again, for brevity, the type declaration:

    unsigned int name;

may also be written:

    unsigned name;

Both declare the variable *name* to be an **unsigned int** with no change in meaning or number of bytes allocated. Note that **unsigned** must be accompanied by **char, short,** or **long** to make those types **unsigned.**

Another advantage of **unsigned** is its aid to readability. By declaring an integer to be **unsigned,** for example, you are telling anyone reading your source text that the integer is never expected to hold a negative value.[4]

There are no hard and fast rules governing where and when these variations on **int** should be used. As we have seen, **long** gives integers a greater range, and **short** can be used to make programs smaller. **Unsigned** should be used when negative values are not needed and the extended range gained by using positive values will be of benefit.

Since one of the strengths of C is its portability, you should beware the consequences of selecting particular types simply to enhance the performance of your machine. What is faster or smaller on your computer may be slower or larger on another. When optimization is needed, try to restrict that trade-off between performance and portability to short or isolated routines in which the benefits are high.[5]

12.4 THE TYPE double

An Extended Float for Greater Precision   Just as **long** extends the *range* of **int,** **double** extends the *precision* of **float.** A variable of type **float,** on many machines, represents seven digits of precision. For example, the number:

    0.12345678987654321

when stored in a **float** variable, would be stored as:

    0.1234568

with the last digit rounded.

The type **double** more than doubles this precision. On those same machines, a **double** variable will represent 16 decimal digits of precision, or:

    0.1234567898765432

The declaration that a variable is to be of type **double** can take either of two forms:

---

[4]It had better not!

[5]Most of a program's execution time is frequently spent in a small fraction of the code. Find such sections before going out of your way to make your program ugly and unportable, then do your optimization in those limited regions.

```
double name;
long float name;
```

Both declare the variable *name* to be of type **double.**

Revise the program "mysizes.c" once again to show the number of bytes that are used to represent these new types on your system. See Fig. 12–4.

FIGURE 12-4 mysizes.c (revision 2)

```
/* mysizes.c (revion 2): The size of some new types */

#include <stdio.h>

main()
{
    printf( "Table of sizes for my machine and compiler:\n\n" );

    showsize( "char",      sizeof (char)     );
    showsize( "short",     sizeof (short)    );
    showsize( "int",       sizeof (int)      );
    showsize( "unsigned",  sizeof (unsigned) );
    showsize( "long",      sizeof (long)     );
    showsize( "float",     sizeof (float)    );
    showsize( "double",    sizeof (double)   );
}

showsize( typename, bytes )
char *typename;
int  bytes;
{
    printf( "%s\t is %d bytes\n", typename, bytes );
}
```

The type **double** is useful for scientific and engineering calculations. Its extended precision provides for greater accuracy and minimal error, although the price paid for this accuracy depends on your machine. Microcomputers generally perform double-precision arithmetic more slowly than integer arithmetic.[6] Floating-point computations, whether **float** or **double,** require special floating-point hardware if they are to be done quickly.

Again, the types **float** and **double** are not strictly necessary to learn the language.[7] Since some compilers require special procedures to use these types, our

---

[6]Some micros use special purpose chips, like the 8087, which does away with this imbalance.

[7]If you're learning C for use in scientific and engineering applications, you certainly need floating point. If you're in this category, you will find that arrays and variables of type **float** are much like Fortran's REAL*4 and that double is much like REAL*8. Further, pointer arithmetic with floats and doubles can *greatly* speed up computation over array accesses. For this reason alone, C is *preferable* to Fortran for many computationally intensive engineering applications *if* the compiler comes with the proper library support.

sample programs will continue to use only variations of the types **int** and **char,** wherever reasonable.

12.5 CASTS

How to Use the Value of One Type as Though It's Another Type When a value of one type needs to be converted to a different type, it may be *cast*. If, for example, *num* is the type **int,** then:

        (float) num

yields the value of *num* as a floating-point value. That is, the integer value has been cast as a **float.** This conversion in no way affects the type of *num* itself, which remains **int.** The cast merely converts a *copy* of *num's* value to the type **float** for the purpose of computation.

    Casts must be in parentheses, and must be one of the keywords for declaring a type. Thus:

Cast	*Converts to*
(float) num	value of num as a float
(char) num	value of num as a char
(char *) num	value of num as a pointer to char
(unsigned) num	value of num as an unsigned int

One common application for casts is to obtain a **float** result when dividing two **ints.** Ordinarily, when two **ints:**

```
int num1, num2;
float answer;
num1 = 1;
num2 = 2;
```

are divided as:

```
answer = num1 / num2;
```

the result is of type **int** because an **int** over an **int** yields an **int** result. Since the result of 1 over 2 is 0.5, the value assigned to *answer* will be 0, because all integer computations throw away the fractional part. The value assigned to *answer* will be 0 no matter what the type of *answer,* because the division takes place before and independently of the assignment. To get the desired **float** result from this division, the two **ints** should be cast to **floats,** as:

```
answer = (float)num1 / (float)num2;
```

This works because a **float** over a **float** yields a **float** result.[8]

---

[8]If you have one of the shoddy compilers that doesn't do this correctly, send it back in smelly fish wrap.

A rule in C is that any operation on two different types will first *promote* the smaller type to the same type as the larger. If you divide a **float** by an **int,** for example, the **int** will be promoted (automatically cast) to a **float** before that division takes place and the result will be a **float.** Because of this rule, the above example may be written:

```
answer = (float)num1 / num2;
```

and will also yield the correct **float** result.

The test program "casts.c" illustrates these relationships. It is listed in Fig. 12–5. Some compilers do not correctly handle casts, and this program may be used to see if yours is one of these.

FIGURE 12-5 casts.c

```
/* casts.c: Detects compiler mishandling of casts */
/*          Note: Uses float                       */

main()
{
    int    num1, num2;
    float answer;

    num1 = 1;
    num2 = 2;

    answer = num1 / num2;
    printf( "Without casts answer = %f\n" , answer );

    answer = (float)num1 / (float)num2;
    printf( "Casting num1 & num2:   %f\n" , answer );

    answer = (float)num1 / num2;
    printf( "Casting num1 only:     %f\n" , answer );
}
```

Another application for casts is to pass an argument of the correct type to a function. Recall that *fseek()* is called as:

```
fseek( filepointer, offset, how );
```

where *offset* must be a **long.** If you need to pass an **int** variable as *offset,* you may cast it to a **long** as part of the function call:

```
fseek( filepointer, (long)offset, how );
```

Although C tends to be forgiving about the mixing of types, there are times when you must be specific. The cast operation allows you to mix types with a clear conscience and with the assurance the compiler will not misunderstand your intent.

12.6 FUNCTION TYPES

Functions Can Return Values of Types Other Than int   Just as functions may be passed arguments of different types, they may also return them. By default, all functions return values of type **int** unless told to do otherwise. For example:

```
somefunct()
{
    return ( someval );
}
```

returns an **int** value to the function that called it.

To declare the type a function will return, simply place a type declaration directly before its name. If you design a function that needs to return a **long** value, for example, you would declare it as:

```
long somefunct()
{
    return ( someval );
}
```

This tells the compiler that the function *somefunct()* will be returning a value of type **long.**

Review the function *getd()* in Chapter 5, which we will revise once again. Because it now returns a **long,** we have renamed it *getl().* See Fig. 12–6.

FIGURE 12-6 getl()

```
/*
** getl(): Read digits from the keyboard and return
**         them as a single long value.  Non-digits ignored.
*/
long getl()
{
    int ch, sign;
    long num;

    num = 0L;
    sign = 1;
    while ( (ch = getchar()) != '\n' )
    {
        if ( ch == '-' )      /* minus sign makes negative */
            sign = -sign;

        ch = ch - '0';          /* convert to correct value */

        if ( ch >= 0 && ch <= 9 )  /* ignore non-digits */
            num = (num * 10L) + (long)ch;
    }
    return ( num );
}
```

Before *getl()* can be called from another function, that calling function must let the compiler know that the call will be returning a **long.** This is done by declaring the called function as though it were a local variable and adding empty parentheses to the end of its name. Thus:

```
main()
{
    long getl();
    .... rest of main here
}
```

tells the compiler that *main()* will be calling *getl(),* and that *getl()* will be returning the type **long.**

We can now write a program that tests *getl().* Called ''oddeven.c'', it asks you to enter a number, then tells you if that number is odd or even. The program is in Fig. 12–7.

FIGURE 12-7 oddeven.c

```
/* oddeven.c: test getl() by reporting num as odd or even */

#include <stdio.h>

main()
{
    long num, getl();

    while( 1 )
    {
        fprintf( stderr, "Enter number (Ø to quit): " );

        if ( (num = getl()) == ØL )
            break;

        if ( (num % 2L) == 1 )
            fprintf( stderr, "%ld is odd\n", num );
        else
            fprintf( stderr, "%ld is even\n", num );
    }
}

/** the getl() function goes here **/
```

Whenever you call a function that returns a value other than **int,** you should declare the type of the called function locally, as we have done above. Omitting that declaration says that the function will, by default, return a value of type **int.** Some compilers are forgiving and allow those local type declarations to be omitted. But, even if yours is forgiving, make it a habit to declare all calls to non-int functions. This will help to ensure that your code will be as portable as possible.

13° SWITCH-CASE AND GOTO

Ways to Control the Flow of Your Program.

13.1 CHOICES, AN EXAMPLE

Creating the Basis for a Selection   A frequent need in programming is to select one from many possible alternatives, then perform actions based on that selection. Suppose you wished to develop a program that provided some simple file-management tools. The menu presented by that program might look like this:

```
The File Helper < version 1 >

Select from this menu:

     [c] Copy a file
     [j] Join two files
     [v] View a file
     [h] Help (this menu)
     [q] Quit this program
Choice:
```

Here the user is presented with several choices and asked to press a key to indicate which action to take.

Before examining how to handle that choice, take a moment to enter ''filehelp.c'', the program in Fig. 13–1. It is the beginning of a program we will expand throughout this chapter. The instructions to generate the above menu are divided into three functions: *showtitle(),* which is only called to print the title of the program; *showmenu(),* which lists the choices and will be called again if an 'h' is selected: and *prompt,* which is called to elicit user input.

147

FIGURE 13-1 filehelp.c

```c
/* filehelp.c: beginning of a menu driven file utility */

#include <stdio.h>

main()
{
    int choice;

    showtitle();
    showmenu();
    choice = prompt();
}

showtitle()
{
    fprintf( stderr, "The File Helper -- version 1\n" );
}

showmenu()
{
    fprintf( stderr, "\nSelect from this menu:\n\n" );
    fprintf( stderr, "\t[c] Copy a file\n" );
    fprintf( stderr, "\t[j] Join two files\n" );
    fprintf( stderr, "\t[v] View a file\n" );
    fprintf( stderr, "\t[q] Quit this program\n" );
    fprintf( stderr, "\t[h] Help (this menu)\n" );
}

prompt()
{
    int ch;

    fprintf( stderr, "\nChoice: " );

    while ( (ch = getchar()) == '\n' )
        continue;

    return ( ch );
}
```

This program provides a beginning framework by allowing you to put a menu on the screen and prompt the user to pick one of the alternatives. Next, we must determine what the user's choice is and take appropriate actions based on it. One way to approach this problem is with a series of **if-else** statements:

```
if ( choice == 'q' )
    exit( 0 );
else if ( choice == 'c' )
{
     . . . . do copy stuff here
}
else if (choice == 'j' )
{
     . . . . do join stuff here
}
. . . . etc., etc., etc.
else
{
     . . . . invalid choice stuff here
}
```

There is nothing wrong with this approach—it gets the job done. However, C provides a way to make this code more compact and choices being handled more apparent: the **switch-case** statement.

13.2 THE switch-case STATEMENT

Like a Railroad Switching Yard   The **switch-case** statement provides a handy way to select one alternative from a number of different ones. It is composed of two parts. The first part is the **switch** command followed by an integer value in parentheses that is the basis of the selection:

```
switch ( choice )
```

After this command comes a series of integer constants that form alternatives against which the selection is compared. Each such constant is preceded by the keyword **case** and followed by a colon:

```
case 'q':
```

For the choices in "filehelp.c", **switch** and **case** may be used as:

```
switch ( choice )
{
  case 'c':
          . . . . copy stuff here
          break;
  case 'j':
          . . . . join stuff here
          break:
  . . . . etc., etc., etc.
  default:
          . . . . no-match stuff here
}
. . . . break lands here
```

Note that the **case** tests and the single **default** statement are all contained in a curly-brace pair following the **switch.** That curly-brace pair is mandatory. The general rule for **switch-case,** then, looks like:

```
switch ( value )
{      case constant:
              .... do these if value == constant
            break;
       case nextconstant:
              .... do these if value == nextconstant
            break;
       default:
              .... do these if no match was found
}
    .... break lands here
```

The **switch-case** statement can handle only integers of type **int** for the *value* being tested and the **constant** cases. In the **switch** command itself, the **value** (choice) may either be a variable, a value derived from calculation, or the value returned by a function (as long as it is of type **int**). For example:

```
switch ( choice )           a variable of type int
switch ( (int)fltval )      a float cast to int
switch ( getd() )           value returned by int function
switch ( num = --*ptr )     value of a computation
```

are all legal because each tests a **value** that is of type **int.**

The **case** statements in **switch-case** must test against an integer constant. Remember that integer constants are numeric (123) or character ('v'), and note that the constant is always followed by a colon. Thus:

```
case 123:
case 'v':
```

are examples of legal integer constant test **cases.** A noninteger constant, like 123.45, will produce an error. A variable or function call is similarly illegal.

No two **case** test constants may be the same in a given *switch-case* statement. That is, if you test for 'v' at the start, you may not test for it again:

```
case 'v':
case 'a':
case 'v': ◄—— error
```

When a **case** is tested and no match is found, the flow skips to the next *case* test. When a match is found, the instructions following the colon are executed. When **case** tests are stacked—that is, when more than one test can trigger the same instructions:

```
case 'Q':      no instructions here
case 'q':
              .... instructions for both cases here
```

the instructions following the colon of the *last* **case** are executed if *any* of the **cases** match. Thus, for:

```
case 'Q':      no instructions here
case 'q':
          . . . . do quit stuff here
        break;
```

the ''do quit stuff here'' instructions will be executed if *choice* matches *either* 'Q' or 'q'. There is no limit to the number of **case** tests that may be stacked in this way. For:

```
case 'Q':
case 'q':
case 'X':
case 'x':
case '0':
          . . . . do quit stuff here
        break;
```

the ''do quit stuff here'' instructions will be executed if *choice* matches any of 'Q', 'q', 'X', 'x', or '0'.

A common application for stacking **case** tests is to make a program more ''user proof.'' In ''filehelp.c'', for example, stacking can be used to protect against the user entering an uppercase character by mistake:

```
switch ( choice )
{
  case 'C':
  case 'c':
          . . . . do if choice is 'C' or 'c'
          break;
  case 'J':
  case 'j':
          . . . . do if choice is 'J' or 'j'
          break;
  . . . . etc., etc., etc.
  default:
          . . . . no-match stuff here
}
. . . . break lands here
```

The **break** instructions causes the flow to immediately exit the *entire* **switch-case** statement. When **break** is omitted, as:

```
case 'q':
          . . . . do quit stuff, and
              fall through to ────────┐
case 'c':                             │
          . . . . do copy stuff ◄─────┘
        break;
```

the flow following the executed instructions falls through to the next instruction and *skips* any further **case** tests! That is, within a **switch-case** statement, only one successful **case** match will be found, and after it is found, all further *case* tests will be ignored. The **break** statement, then, is a necessary terminator for each **case.** Without it, the **case** consequences cease to be isolated from each other.

The **default** keyword specifies the instructions to be taken should *none* of the **case** tests yield a match. That is, the progression within **switch-case** is to first test all the **cases,** then, if there was no match, to execute the instructions following the **default** statement. The program's flow arrives at **default** only after all the **cases** have been checked and rejected—regardless of where **default** is placed. There may be only one **default** in any **switch-case** statement, and it is optional. Without it, **switch-case** performs all the tests, then quietly exits if there was no match. Generally, **default** will be placed last, following all the **case** tests, for clarity.[1]

Combined into a diagram, the preceding rules can be pictured as:

```
switch ( choice )
{
  case 'Q':
  case 'q':
        . . . . do quit stuff
                and fall through to ◄─────────────┐
  case 'C':                                        │
  case 'c':                                        │
        . . . do copy stuff  ────────────────┘
┌──────────────break;
│   . . . . etc., etc., etc.
│   default:
│         . . . . do this if no case matches
│  }
└──►. . . . break lands here
```

The program "filehelp.c" can now be expanded to include *switch-case* as a mechanism for selecting from the menu. The actual routines for handling files were covered earlier in Chapter 11. If you wish to make this program do something, you might adapt those routines for use here. The program is listed in Fig. 13–2.

13.3 COMMAND LINE FLAGS

A Method for Bypassing the Need for a Menu Another way to pass choices to a program is to indicate them as part of the command line (Chapter 10). After using "filehelp" for a while, you might wish to skip the menu and directly access some function. For example, to join two files and then view the result, you could simply type:

```
filehelp -j -v
```

The dash is one traditional means of indicating command line flags. Thus, "−j" is a flag telling the program to skip directly to the join function.

The **switch-case** mechanism provides a handy means of parcing these flags from the command line. Examine the revision of "filehelp.c" that is shown in Fig.

---

[1]Even the best programmers must occasionally resort to clarity.

FIGURE 13-2 filehelp.c (revision 1)

```c
/* filehelp.c (revision 1): demonstrate switch-case */

#include <stdio.h>

main()
{
    int choice;

    showtitle();
    showmenu();

    while ( 1 )
    {
        switch ( choice = prompt() )
        {
          case 'C':
          case 'c':
                fprintf( stderr, "\ncalling copyfile()\n" );
                break;
          case 'J':
          case 'j':
                fprintf( stderr, "\ncalling joinfile()\n" );
                break;
          case 'V':
          case 'v':
                fprintf( stderr, "\ncalling viewfile()\n" );
                break;
          case 'Q':
          case 'q':
                fprintf( stderr, "\naborting program\n" );
                exit( 0 );
          case 'H':
          case 'h':
          case '?':
                showmenu();
                break;
          default:
                fprintf( stderr, "\n?huh?\n" );
        }
    }
}
/* showtitle(), showmenu(), & prompt() here */
```

13-3. Note how command line flags can cause the menu to be skipped and the appropriate functions to be called instead.

In summation, **switch-case** provides a handy mechanism for determining what a program will do next. It provides for the grouping of **case tests,** for an easy exit with **break,** and a means to match anything with **default.** Along with **if-else,**

FIGURE 13-3 filehelp.c (revision 2)

```
/* filehelp.c (revision 2): handles command line flags */

#include <stdio.h>

#define USAGE "usage: %s {-c -j -v}\n"

main( argc, argv )
int   argc;
char *argv[];
{
    int i;

    if ( argc == 1 )           /* no args, do menu version */
        menu();
    else for ( i = 1; i < argc; i++ )
    {
        if ( *(argv[i]) == '-' )
        {
            switch ( *(argv[i]+1) )
            {
              case 'c':
                    fprintf( stderr, "calling copyfile()\n" );
                    break;
              case 'j':
                    fprintf( stderr, "calling joinfile()\n" );
                    break;
              case 'v':
                    fprintf( stderr, "calling viewfile()\n" );
                    break;
              default:
                fprintf( stderr, "%s: bad flag\n", argv[i] );
                fprintf( stderr, USAGE, argv[0]);
            }
        }
        else
        {
            fprintf( stderr, "%s not a valid argument\n" );
            exit( -1 );
        }
    }
}

/* previous main() renamed menu(), & rest of functions here */
```

switch-case is used to control the flow of your program. The strength of both these methods is their clarity. At a glance, it is possible to tell where a program will go next and how it will respond to conditions.

13.4 LABELS AND goto

An Occasionally Useful Flow-Control Mechanism   C provides a means of leaping suddenly and directly from one part of a function to another: the **goto** statement. Note, however, that we recommend you use **goto** only when there is *absolutely* no "clean" way of getting from one place in a function to another.[2] Overuse of **goto** makes programs messy and hard to follow.[3]

The rule for using **goto** is simple:

```
goto label;
```

where *label* is a name following the same rules as the names of variables.

The *label* tells **goto** where to go. A separate statement of the form:

```
label:
```

elsewhere in the function identifies the place in the function where the flow will continue after the **goto** is encountered. We recommend that all labels be placed at the left margin in your source text for clarity.

When encountering a **goto,** the program's flow immediately diverts to the next instruction following the label. That label may appear before or after the **goto.** Both, however, *must* be within the *same* function. Thus, the action of **goto** can be illustrated as:

```
        somefunct()
        {
                 . . . .
                 goto label;
                 . . . .
                 . . . .
        label:
                 . . . . goto lands here
        }
```

or:

```
        anotherfunct()
        {
        label:
                 . . . . goto lands here
                 . . . .
                 . . . .
                 goto label;
        }
```

but *not*:

---

[2]You might ask why C provides a feature that nearly all C programmers will (conceptually anyway) boo and hiss at. The reason is that C represents *freedom* for the programmer. You are free to write rotten code if you want. Please don't.

[3]Take a look at some older Fortran engineering code sometime, commonly referred to as "spaghetti." The flow is hopelessly tangled between all the ***goto's.*** It's nice to know where you're going and why.

```
somefunct()
{
    goto label:  ◄────────can't goto another function
}
anotherfunct()
{
label:
}
```

The **goto** command can be used to escape from deeply nested loops. In the event of some disastrous error, the following code can provide a means of recovery:

```
while ( .... )
{
    for ( .... )
    {
        for ( .... )
        {
            while ( .... )
            {
                ....
                if ( disaster )
                    goto ERROR;
                ....
            }
            ....
        }
    }
    ....
ERROR:
    .... error recovery stuff here
```

A **break** would not do in this situation. It would only exit the innermost loop—not the whole mess. The **goto** command may not be the preferred way out. Depending on the program, *exit()* or **return** may be better and cleaner. Often when *goto* seems like the only answer, a simple modification, such as adding a flag, will provide an alternative. For example:

```
switch ( .... )
{
  case 1:
          .... stuff
          break;
  case 2:
          .... stuff
          if ( badnews )
              goto BAD;
          break;
  case 3:
          .... stuff
          break;
}
.... good stuff here
BAD:
    .... bad stuff here
```

with the addition of a simple flag, can be rewritten:

```
flag = 0;
switch ( .... )
{
  case 1:
          .... stuff
        break;
  case 2:
          .... stuff
        if ( badnews )
            flag = 1;
        break;
  case 3:
          .... stuff
        break;
}
if ( !flag )
        .... good stuff here
else
        .... bad stuff here
```

13.5 THE null STATEMENT

When the Computer Must Sit on Its Hands A bit of shorthand related to program flow is the **null** statement. A semicolon (;) all by itself, is the *null.* It tells the computer to do nothing at all.

An example of where the null can be handy is in the following self-contained **while** test. Here, a pointer to a string is moved forward until a space character is found:

```
while ( *(++str) != ' ' )
     ;
```

Although the null is a legal, self-contained, do-nothing statement, it may be often replaced altogether with *continue.* Thus:

```
while ( *(++str) != ' ' )
     continue;
```

does exactly the same thing, and results in a 100% increase in clarity.

But beware! Because the **null** is a legal statement, extra or unintentional semicolons may be accepted by the compiler. These can result in bugs that are difficult to locate. Witness:

```
if ( big < 100 );
     big++;              semicolon added by mistake
```

The **null** following the **if** test mistakenly tells the program to do nothing if *big* is less than 100. Since the intention here, as indicated by indenting, is that *big* should be incremented when it is less than 100, the extra semicolon is a bug. A simple rearrangement shows this error more clearly:

```
if ( big < 100 )
    ;  ◄──────────────── do nothing (null)
big++;
```

Like **goto,** the null statement should be used sparingly. When it is necessary, place it on a line by itself, and indent it one tab position. Wherever you can replace it with **continue,** do so.

14. MULTIDIMENSIONED ARRAYS

Groups of Groups of Groups of. . .

14.1 ARRAYS REVIEWED

How to Use and Initialize Arrays of Other Types   In Chapters 7 through 9, you were introduced to the concepts of arrays, pointers to arrays, and strings as arrays of type **char.** Recall that an array is generally declared as:

```
class type name[SIZE];
```

where *class* is, by default or specification, either **static** or **auto;** *type* defines the storage type of what will be stored in each element of the array; *name* is any legal identifier name; and SIZE specifies the size of the array (number of elements) and must be a constant value.

Recall, too, the rules for initializing arrays. Arrays that are **static**—by default when **external** or **global,** or by declaration when inside functions—can be initialized when they are declared. When arrays are initialized using the empty square-brace pair ([])the number of elements reserved is determined by the number of initializers. In the case of:

```
static int nums[] = { 1, 2, 3, 4, 5 };
```

the array *nums* is created with enough storage space for the five items listed. This is akin to specifying:

```
static int nums[5];
```

and assigning the initial values later.

Of course, it is perfectly legal to specify both the size of the array and initialize it, too. Just be sure the array is large enough to hold the data. Thus:

```
static int nums[5] = { 1, 2, 3 };
```

fills the first three elements of **nums** with the values 1, 2, and 3, and leaves the remaining two elements set to 0.

Arrays of type **char** that are used to represent strings can be initialized in two different ways. Either:

```
static char inputname[] = { 'b', 'o', 'b', '\0' };
```

or the shorthand initialization:

```
static char inputname[] = "bob";
```

both of which reserve four items, three for the characters and a fourth for the terminating 0. Both create the same size array as would:

```
static char inputname[4];
```

When initializing arrays containing numeric quantities, however, there is no shorthand. Each value must be listed individually and separated from the others by commas.

In Chapter 12, you were introduced to a whole raft of new types, and arrays can be created using any of them. The declaration rules don't change. For example:

```
static double results[];      array of double
unsigned int Mph[];           array of unsigned
short int flags []            array of short
```

For all arrays, the number of elements declared between the square braces must be an integer constant expression. Any attempt to set the size of an array with a variable, or an expression containing a variable, will cause a compile-time error.

Recall that an array name by itself yields the address of the array. This means that when you call a function that expects an address, you may pass the array name. For example:

```
int secs = 5;
static char msg[] = "Please wait %d seconds. \n";

printf( msg, secs );
```

Although an array name may be passed just as a pointer can, it is not a pointer—it is an address. A pointer is a variable whose value is an address, whereas an array name *yields* an address that is a *constant*. Arithmetic that is legal for a pointer is illegal for an array name:

```
char msg[];  msg++;  is illegal
char *msg;   msg++;  is legal
```

Because of this distinction, never use an array name as though it were a pointer. If you absolutely need to perform arithmetic on an address constant, assign that address to a pointer. For example:

```
static char hex[] = "0123456789abcdef";
char *hexptr;
hexptr = hex;     /* assign address constant to pointer */
while( *hexptr++ != index )
    . . . .
```

Finally, recall the remarkable way that pointers get changed. When you increment a pointer, for example, it is always changed to point to the next element of an array regardless of the number of bytes occupied by that element. Thus:

```
sometype hex[SIZE], *hexptr;
hexptr = hex;
hexptr++;
```

will cause **hexptr** to point to **hex[1],** regardless of the type of the array **hex.**

14.2 TWO DIMENSIONS

How to Use and Initialize Arrays of Arrays   There are times when a single, linear array won't do the job. Suppose, for example, you wanted to create a list of five names. You know that a name is represented as an array of characters, but rather than creating a separate array for each name, it is more efficient to group them all under one roof—in a two-dimensional array.

An array all by itself is one dimensional (or linear) because it has length only. A two-dimensional array is an array whose elements are other arrays. By using a two-dimensional array, we can store the five names (each an array) as a single unit. This can be pictured as:

```
                    columns
         name1    B  o  b  0  .  .  .  .
         name2    M  a  r  y  0  .  .  .
rows     name3    N  e  l  s  o  n  0  .
         name4    J  o  e  0  .  .  .  .
         name5    R  e  b  e  c  c  a  0
```

Here each name is a linear array that forms one row of the larger unit, a two-dimensional array.

The rule for declaring a two-dimensional array is:

```
class type name[ rows ][ columns ];
```

For our list of names, a reasonable declaration would be:

```
#define MAXNAMES 5  /* maximum number of names */
#define NAMELEN 8   /* max length each name    */

char namelist[ MAXNAMES ][ NAMELEN ];
```

This two-dimensional array, **namelist,** has five rows of eight items each. As with all two-dimensional arrays, it declares the number of rows first, then the number of columns. This declaration creates, as a single unit, a two-dimensional array that looks like this:

```
                          columns
                  0   1   2   3   4   5   6   7
        row0  →   .   .   .   .   .   .   .   .
        row1  →   .   .   .   .   .   .   .   .
        row2  →   .   .   .   .   .   .   .   .
        row3  →   .   .   .   .   .   .   .   .
        row4  →   .   .   .   .   .   .   .   .
```

As with linear arrays, both rows and columns are numbered from element 0 and count up from there.

To access a value stored at a certain place in a two-dimensional array, you must specify the row and column where that value is stored. Thus:

```
namelist[0][0]
```

will yield the value stored in the zeroth row and the zeroth element (column) of that row. Similarly:

```
namelist[4][7]
```

yields the value stored in row 4, column 7.

The address of a two-dimensional array can be passed in the same fashion as that of a singly dimensioned array:

```
somefunction( namelist );
```

and is the address of the beginning of the entire array. To pass the address of a row, pass the address of the zeroth element of the required row:

```
&nameslist[row][0]
```

Another way to pass the address of a row is with the shorthand:

```
namelist[row]
```

Referencing a two-dimensional array by the row offset sans the column always yields the address of that row. For clarity, however, we prefer the former method, as it better shows that an address is being obtained or passed.

Compile the short program "addnames.c" (Fig. 14–1) that demonstrates ways to manipulate this two-dimensional array. Note that the array has been made larger to more realistically store common names.

Initializing Two-Dimensional Arrays

The rule for initializing two-dimensional arrays is the same as that for their singly dimensioned counterparts. The initializing values, however, fill the array row by row, starting with the zeroth row. By way of example, consider the 3×3 array named **box:**

```
int box[3][3];
```

FIGURE 14-1 addnames.c

```
/* addnames.c: illustrating two dimensional arrays */

#include <stdio.h>
#define MAXN 10     /* max names        */
#define MAXL 20     /* max name length */

main()
{
    int numnames, i;
    char names[MAXN][MAXL];

    numnames = 0;

    do
    {
        printf( "-> Enter name to add: " );

        if ( gets( &names[numnames][0], MAXL ) == EOF )
            exit( 0 );

        if ( names[numnames][0] == 0 )
            exit( 0 );

        numnames++;

        puts( "Names in list:" );

        for ( i = 0; i < numnames; i++ )
            puts( &names[i][0] );

    } while ( numnames < MAXN );

    printf( "\nSorry, no more room for names\n" );
}
```

Initializing it with nine values:

    int box[3] [3] = { 1, 2, 3, 4, 5, 6, 7, 8, 9 };

Fills it row by row and yields:

```
                    columns
                  0    1    2
    row 0   →     1    2    3
    row 1   →     4    5    6
    row 2   →     7    8    9
```

It is preferable, however, to specify the rows by enclosing their values in yet another set of curly braces. Observe how:

```
int box [3] [3] = { {1, 2, 3,}, {4, 5, 6}, {7, 8, 9} };
```

more clearly indicates the row assignments. This technique is also handy if you wish, for example, to initialize only the first two elements of each row. The declaration:

```
int box [3] [3] = { {1, 2} , {3, 4}, {5, 6} };
```

will fill the first two elements of each row, and yield:

```
            columns
          0   1   2
row 0  →  1   2   0
row 1  →  3   4   0
row 2  →  5   6   0
```

Since you can only initialize arrays that are **global** or **static,** the unspecified elements will be set to the default value 0.

A similar approach is used when initializing two-dimensional arrays of strings:

```
static char names [3] [6] = { "bob", "ted", "alice"};
```

This creates a two-dimensional array with three rows, each of which contains a zero-terminated string. Examine the program "addnames.c", which has been revised (Fig. 14–2) to demonstrate this initialization. The program begins with two names already in the list (initialized), and new names are added beginning with the third row.

When initializing rows, it is good form to arrange them one above the other for clarity. Compare:

```
float Nums [3] [2] = { {1.0, 3.2}, {4.9, 1.2}, {6.0, 0.0} };
```

to the much clearer declaration:

```
float Nums [3] [2] = {
      {  1.0,    3.2 },
      {  4.9,    1.2 },
      {  6.0,    0.0 }
};
```

One possible source of compile-time errors is that of placing a comma after the last item in an initialization list. This happens most often when creating a long list of initializers:

```
static char fruits [ MAXF ] [ MAXL ] = {
   "apple",
   "orange",
   "pear",
   "mango",
   "lime",
   "lemon",          ←extra comma
};
```

FIGURE 14-2 addnames.c (revision 1)

```
/* addnames.c (revision 1):  revised to initialize array */

#include <stdio.h>
#define MAXN 10      /* max names           */
#define MAXL 20      /* max name length */

main()
{
    int numnames, i;
    static char names[ MAXN ][ MAXL ] = {
        "Flipper",
        "Jenny"              /* initialization added */
    };

    numnames = 2;            /* 2 names already in list */

    do
    {
        printf( "-> Enter name to add: " );

        if ( gets( &names[numnames][0], MAXL ) == EOF )
            exit( 0 );

        if ( names[numnames][0] == 0 )
            exit( 0 );

        numnames++;

        puts( "Names in list:" );

        for ( i = 0; i < numnames; i++ )
            puts( &names[i][0] );

    } while ( numnames < MAXN );

    printf( "\nSorry, no more room for names\n" );
}
```

Although this extra comma is legal, some compilers freak-out hopelessly if it's there.

14.3 MORE DIMENSIONS

A Cube of Data and Other Diversions   You have already seen that array items may themselves be arrays. Taking this a step further, it is perfectly possible to create an array, each element of which is a two-dimensional array. The rule for such a construction is:

```
class type name [depth] [rows] [columns];
```

Look at this simple example of a three-dimensional array of integers:

number of two-dimensional arrays (depth)

size of each two-dimensional array

```
int nums [3] [3] [3];
```

This is an array of 3 two-dimensional arrays, where each of those two-dimensional arrays has three rows and three columns. This is best visualized as a cube, with each of the two-dimensional arrays pictured as a plane. See Fig. 14–3.

FIGURE 14-3   3-dimensional array (empty)

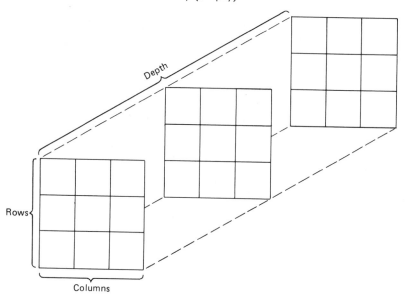

When you initialize a three-dimensional array, the rows and columns of each two-dimensional plane are filled row by row, as you learned earlier, beginning with the first plane, and continuing until all the planes are filled. For example, the declaration:

```
int nums [3] [3] [3] = {
     1, 2, 3, 4, 5, 6, 7, 8, 9, 10, 11, 12, 13, 14,
     15, 16, 17, 18, 19, 20, 21, 22, 23, 24
};
```

will fill the cube with values as diagrammed in Fig. 14–4.

For clarity, however, you should specify the values for each plane by isolating them with additional curly braces:

FIGURE 14-4 3-dimensional array (initialized)

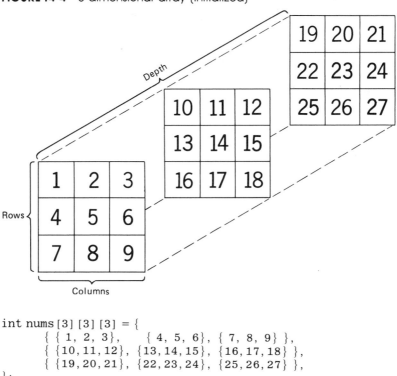

```
int nums [3] [3] [3] = {
        { { 1, 2, 3},    { 4, 5, 6}, { 7, 8, 9} },
        { {10, 11, 12}, {13, 14, 15}, {16, 17, 18} },
        { {19, 20, 21}, {22, 23, 24}, {25, 26, 27} },
};
```

All the rules that apply to two-dimensional arrays apply to three-dimensional arrays and arrays of larger dimensions. By way of example, the following declarations are perfectly legal:

```
char soup [12] [13] [23] [10];        4 dimensions
int nuts [1] [2] [3] [4] [5];          5 dimensions
```

The program in Fig. 14–5, "arraydemo.c", illustrates some ways to use the data stored in two-dimensional arrays. These same techniques can be extended to encompass arrays of any number of dimensions.[1]

14.4 FUNCTIONS AND MULTIDIMENSIONS

Passing and Receiving Arrays of Arrays In Chapter 8, you learned that an array could only be passed to a function by passing its address. As a consequence, any effect a function has on that array changes the array itself, not a *copy* of the array. The same is true for multidimensioned arrays.

---

[1]As in other respects, C provides maximum freedom here so you should strive to exercise self-restraint. If you have 10 control loops nested or 10-dimensional arrays, you should probably try to simplify your algorithm.

FIGURE 14-5 *arraydemo.c*

```c
/* arraydemo.c: illustrating operations on array elements */

#include <stdio.h>
#define ROW 10      /* number of rows    */
#define COL 10      /* number of columns */

main()
{
    int i, j;
    int array[ ROW ][ COL ];

    printf( "Filling the array....\n" );

    for ( i = 0; i < ROW; i++ )
    {
        for ( j = 0; j < COL; j++ )
        {
            array[i][j] = i + j;
        }
    }

    printf( "The array now contains the values:\n" );

    for ( i = 0; i < ROW; i++ )
    {
        for ( j = 0; j < COL; j++ )
        {
            printf( "%3d", array[i][j] );
        }
        printf( "\n" );
    }
}
```

Examine the first half of the program "sortdemo.c", shown in Fig. 14–6. Note that the actual list of names will be sorted, not a copy of the list.

The sort routine itself, ***bubble()*** (Fig. 14–7), uses a method called a *bubble sort*. In a bubble sort, a pass is made through the list, from the bottom to the top, in which adjacent pairs of names are compared. If a pair is out of order, they are switched. This way, after one pass, the highest has been moved (progressively switched or "bubbled") to the top of the list.[2] A second pass is done, this time excluding the top (bottom to top − 1). When it is done, the second-highest name has been moved to the position just below the top. This process continues, each time "bubbling" up to one position lower, until a pass consists of only the bottom two

---

[2]This is not the world's fastest sort technique, but it is conceptually simple, and has a great name.

FIGURE 14-6 sortdemo.c

```
/* sortdemo.c: first half of bubble sort demo program */

#include <stdio.h>
#define NUMR 10       /* number of rows of names */
#define NUMC 20       /* max length each name     */

static char Names[NUMR][NUMC] = {
    "Bryan",
    "Nelson",
    "George",
    "Beatrice",
    "Zephyr",
    "Geri",
    "Ben",
    "Soma",
    "Tigr",
    "Jim"
};

main()
{
    int i;

    printf( "unsorted list:\n" );

    for ( i = 0; i < NUMR; i++ )
        printf( "\t%s\n", &Names[i][0] );

    bubble( Names );    /* call the sort routine */

    printf( "\nsorted list:\n" );

    for ( i = 0; i < NUMR; i++ )
        printf( "\t%s\n", &Names[i][0] );
}

/* the function bubble() goes here */
```

names. They are compared and reversed if necessary, and the sort is done. See Fig. 14–7.

Notice in **bubble()** that the received array argument is declared as:

```
char list[] [NUMC] ;
```

When a function receives an array, you *must* specify the size of all dimensions except the first, which is optional. Thus:

FIGURE 14-7 bubble()

```
#define NUMR 10      /* number of rows of names */
#define NUMC 20      /* max length each name    */

/*
** bubble( list ): Uses strcmp() from standard library
*/
bubble( list )
char list[][NUMC];
{
    int rows, i;
    char temp[NUMC];

    for ( rows = NUMR - 1; rows > 0; rows-- )
    {
        for ( i = 0; i < rows; i++ )
        {
            if ( strcmp( &list[i][0], &list[i+1][0] ) > 0 )
            {
                /*
                ** swap the names
                */
                strcpy( &temp[0],      &list[i+1][0] );
                strcpy( &list[i+1][0], &list[i][0]   );
                strcpy( &list[i][0],   &temp[0]      );
            }
        }
    }
}
```

```
char list [NUMR] [NUMC] ;
char list [] [NUMC] ;
```

are both legal as declarations of a function's array arguments.

14.5 ARRAYS OF POINTERS

Exchanging Pointers Speeds Up a Sort   It is perfectly legal for an array to have pointers as its elements. In declaration:

```
int *nums [ SIZE ] ;
```

nums is an array of SIZE elements, each of which is a **pointer to** an **int.** This declaration should look familiar. You have been using something similar all along whenever *main()* expected command line arguments:

```
main( argc, argv )
int argc;
char *argv [] ;     ◄──── array of pointers
{
    . . . .
```

Here *argv* is declared as an array of pointers, each of which **points to** a **char.** Recall that the number of rows is optional in the receiving function, hence its legal omission from *argv.*

The initialization of an array of pointers:

```
static char *names[] = {
    "fairy",
    "godmother"
};
```

looks similar to the initialization of a two-dimensional array:

```
static char names[][10] = {
    "fairy", "godmother"
};
```

In both cases, the number of rows is filled in by the compiler when it counts the actual number of initializers. The difference lies in how the two are represented in memory. The doubly dimensioned declaration:

```
static char names[][10]
```

creates a "regular" array, the kind we are familiar with:

```
                            columns
            0   1   2   3   4   5   6   7   8   9
names[0]    f   a   i   r   y   0   0   0   0   0
names[1]    g   o   d   m   o   t   h   e   r   0
```

But the array of pointers

```
static char *names[]
```

creates an irregular array:

```
names[0] points to  f a i r y 0
names[1] points to  g o d m o t h e r 0
```

that more efficiently allocates space.

Another advantage to using arrays of pointers lies in increased execution speed. The *bubble()* function has been exchanging names by copying each string in its entirety. If those exchanges were done by swapping pointers, far fewer bytes need to be moved for each exchange.

Take a moment to rewrite "sortdemo.c" and *bubble()* (Figs. 14–8 and 14–9), this time taking advantage of the improved efficiency of pointers. The speed improvement for sorting 10 names will not likely be apparent. But in the next chapter, you will learn how to sort thousands of lines of text from a file, and we will dramatically demonstrate this increased speed.

14.6 POINTERS TO POINTERS

An Alternative to Using Array Subscripts   One additional step can be taken to turn an array of arrays into an array of pointers. The declaration:

```
char **argv;
```

FIGURE 14-8 sortdemo.c (revision 1)

```
/* sortdemo.c (revision 1): Names as an array of pointers */

#include <stdio.h>
#define NUMR 10                   /* number of rows of names */

static char *Names[] = {          /* array of pointers */
    "Bryan",
    "Nelson",
    "George",
    "Beatrice",
    "Zephyr",
    "Geri",
    "Ben",
    "Soma",
    "Tigr",
    "Jim"
};

main()
{
    int i;

    printf( "unsorted list:\n" );

    for ( i = 0; i < NUMR; i++ )
        printf( "\t%s\n", Names[i] );

    bubble( Names );   /* call the sort routine */

    printf( "\nsorted list:\n" );

    for ( i = 0; i < NUMR; i++ )
        printf( "\t%s\n", Names[i] );
}
```

declares *argv* to be a **pointer to** a pointer. That is, *argv* **points to** the zeroth element of an array that is itself a pointer. Since **argv* yields that pointer, ***argv* will yield the value that **argv* points to. Thus, the expression:

```
**argv
```

yields the same value

```
argv[0] [0]
```

yields, or the first letter of the name of the program. (Recall from Chapter 10 that *argv[0]* is the zeroth argument of the command line). It follows, then, that the expression:

```
*argv
```

FIGURE 14-9 bubble() (revision 1)

```
/*
** bubble() (revision 1): an application of pointers
*/
bubble( list )
char *list[];               /* make list an array of pointers */
{
    int rows, i;
    char *temp;                         /* make temp a pointer */

    for ( rows = NUMR - 1; rows > 0; rows-- )
    {
        for ( i = 0; i < rows; i++ )
        {
            /*
            ** compare using pointers
            */
            if ( strcmp( list[i], list[i+1] ) > 0 )
            {
                /*
                ** swap the pointers
                */
                temp      = list[i+1];
                list[i+1] = list[i];
                list[i]   = temp;
            }
        }
    }
}
```

is the same as:

> argv[0]

which is the same as:

> &argv[0][0]

or the address of the zeroth argument (a string).

By declaring a variable to be a **pointer to** a pointer, rather than a two-dimensional array, you become free to perform arithmetic on it.[3] As an example of this, examine the following common approach for handling command line arguments:

---

[3]In scientific calculations, speed can sometimes be *greatly* improved by using pointers rather than arrays. Moving rows of matrices can be done by pointer exchanges, thereby avoiding the multiplications and adds required to access array elements. Given floating-point hardware, these operations can be dominant. Caveat: If a function is *not* time-critical, two-dimensional arrays are easier to read and understand than pointers to pointers, or arrays of pointers.

```
while ( --argc > 0 )
{
    switch ( **argv )
    {
      case '-':
            switch ( *(*argv+1) )
            {
                .... case stuff
            }
            break;
        default:
            fprintf ( stderr, "bad flag\n" );
    }
    ++argv; /* increment a pointer to pointer */
}
```

Here, the expression

```
++argv;
```

is legal because **argv** was declared as a pointer rather than an array. Because it is a **pointer to** a pointer, incrementing it causes it to point to the next pointer, which in turn points to the next argument of the command line.

Arrays and pointers are so closely intertwined that constructions like:

```
*(*argv+1)
```

can be rewritten as:

```
argv[i][1]
```

with much the same result. Indeed, for the beginning programmer, arrays are best handled as arrays (that is, by specifying specific rows and columns in square braces). The advantage to using pointers lies in their ability to speed up many processes and is further demonstrated in the next chapter.

15. MEMORY MANAGEMENT

There's More to Memory Than Meets the Eye

15.1 MEMORY ALLOCATION

What's Where and How to Use the Leftovers   The time has come to look at how memory is organized in a typical computer and how your compiled program fits into it. To begin, examine the short program "donothing.c", listed in Fig. 15–1.

FIGURE 15-1   donothing.c

```
/* donothing.c: memory allocation example */

#define DONOTHING

static int   num     = 1;
static char  word[]  = "one";
static int   array[2] = { 1, 2 };

main()
{
    int var;

    DONOTHING;
}
```

When compiled, the executable version of this program will load into memory at some location where it can be run. For the sake of simplicity, assume that place is the bottom of memory. A diagram of how the program occupied that memory might look like:

	Memory	Program Segment	Contents	
1.	bottom	static variables	num	(an int)
			word	(a string)
			array	(of two ints)
2.		main()	executable code	
3.		runtime stack	var	(auto int)
		end of program		
		UNUSED MEMORY	"free memory"	
	top	end of memory		

The precise way a program uses memory varies from machine to machine, but as a general principle, memory usage in C is determined by three things:

1. All variables of class **static,** including string constants, require a fixed chunk of memory.
2. The executable code, including all your functions and any library functions, requires another piece of memory.
3. Finally, a *runtime stack* is required. This is a block of memory used to house **auto** variables and the information needed for function calls to return.

These three taken together comprise the "size" of your executable program. Unless you write a monster of a program, this size will usually be less than the available memory in your machine.[1]

Memory not occupied by your executable program is called *free memory*. Depending on your specific computer, this free memory could be anything from a few thousand bytes to a few million bytes. Whatever its size, it is available for your use. You need only ask.

15.2 THE malloc() AND free() FUNCTIONS

How to Obtain Some Free Memory, Then Give It Back   The standard library contains a handy function for grabbing chunks of free memory. It is called ***malloc(),*** for *memory allocate*. To use it, simply pass it the number of bytes you want, and it will return a **pointer to** the first byte of a chunk that size. If your request is too large, *malloc()* will return NULL.

```
char *ptr, *malloc();  /* returns pointer to char */
if ( (ptr = malloc( NUMBYTES )) == NULL )
      .... didn't get it.
```

[1]If you don't have virtual memory (which gives a larger program space than physical memory) there's not much point in writing such monsters.

A simple routine for getting the most memory you can involves a loop of diminishing requests. Ask for a lot, get refused, ask for less, and so on:

```
char *ptr, *malloc();
int want;
want = 32000;
while( (ptr = malloc( want )) == NULL )
{
    want = want - 1000;
    if ( want == 0 )
        . . . . couldn't get anything.
}
. . . . here you have ptr pointing to want bytes.
```

The way to give back what you've gotten with *malloc()* is with the function *free()*. Simply pass *free()* a **pointer to** the memory you are giving back. That memory will be returned to the *free memory pool.* The pointer you pass must be the same value that you received from *malloc().* Thus:

```
free( ptr );
```

releases the memory previously allocated by *malloc()* to *ptr.*

On many microcomputers the runtime stack—needed for **auto's** and function returns—occupies free memory. Because of this, especially on small machines, it is wise to avoid snatching all of free memory. The function *mostmem()* demonstrates a way to get as much as you can, then give back a little. See Fig. 15–2.

Take a moment to test this function by writing a short program to incorporate it. That program should report how much memory *mostmem()* was able to get.

15.3 THE calloc() FUNCTION

How to Obtain Even More Free Memory   To provide for larger memory allocations, the standard library has a companion function called *calloc(),* for *calculated allocate.* The arguments passed to *calloc()* are the number of items you need space for and the size in bytes of each item. These are both of type **unsigned.** Thus, a call of:

```
unsigned numitems = 3;
unsigned itemsize = 5;

calloc (numitems, itemsize );
```

would allocate 15 bytes total (3 items of 5 bytes each), returning a *pointer to* the first byte.

The function *mostmem()* can be revised to use *calloc()* so that it starts by asking for one million bytes. Note that *size* has been made into an **unsigned int** (Fig. 15–3).

FIGURE 15-2 mostmem()

```c
#include <stdio.h>

/*
** mostmem(): Returns a pointer to the largest chunk
**      of memory it can get. 32000 maximum, 1000
**      minimum.  Returns NULL if unsuccessful.  Leaves
**      1000 bytes free for runtime stack.
** Note: effects size directly.
**
** Call as:    #include <stdio.h>
**             int size;
**             char *ptr, *mostmem();
**
**             if ( (ptr = mostmem( &size )) == NULL )
**                 ....process error here
*/
char *mostmem( size )
int *size;
{
    char *fptr, *malloc();

    *size = 32000;
    while ( (fptr = malloc( *size )) == NULL )
    {
        *size = *size - 1000;
        if ( *size == 0 )
            return ( NULL );
    }

    free( fptr );

    *size = *size - 1000;   /* for stack */
    if ( *size == 0 )
        return ( NULL );

    fptr = malloc( *size );
    return ( fptr );
}
```

Dynamic memory allocation can be handy for file I/O routines. It is much faster, for example, to read in an entire file all at once rather than to read it in a line or a character at a time. The program "linecount.c" illustrates this process (Fig. 15–4). It uses *mostmem()* to allocate a large chunk of memory, reads the file into that memory all at once, and then counts the lines.

You might wish to expand this program into a truly useful tool by adding the ability to count words and characters. Try to make it more versatile by having it read excessively large files in several small chunks.

FIGURE 15-3 mostmem() (revision 1)

```
#include <stdio.h>

/*
** mostmem(): Revised to call calloc()
**
** Call as:    #include <stdio.h>
**             unsigned size;
**             char *ptr, *mostmem();
**
**             if ( (ptr = mostmem( &size )) == NULL )
**                 ....process error here
*/
char *mostmem( size )
unsigned *size;
{
    char *fptr, *calloc();
    unsigned item = 1000;

    *size = 1000;
    while ( (fptr = calloc( item, *size )) == NULL )
    {
        --*size;
        if ( *size == 0 )
            return ( NULL );
    }

    free( fptr );

    --*size;                /* for stack */
    if ( *size == 0 )
        return ( NULL );

    fptr = calloc( item, *size );

    *size = *size * item;

    return ( fptr );
}
```

15.4 DYNAMIC ARRAYS

Make an Array Out of Free Memory   In the previous chapter, you learned how to add names to a list of names contained in a two-dimensional character array. The number of names was limited by the number of rows the array was declared to have. If you ever have need to, it is possible to add rows "on the fly." Indeed, you may begin with no rows, then create an array completely from scratch.

FIGURE 15-4 linecount.c

```
/* linecount.c: counts the number of lines in a file of text */

#include <stdio.h>

main( argc, argv )
int   argc;
char *argv[];
{
    int numbytes, numread, count;
    char *start, *end, *mostmem();
    FILE *fp;

    if ( argc != 2 )
        quit( "usage: %s file\n", argv[0] );

    if ( (start = mostmem( &numbytes )) == NULL )
        quit( "%s: no free memory\n", argv[0] );

    if ( (fp = fopen( argv[1], "r" )) == NULL )
        quit( "%s: can't open\n", argv[1] );

    numread = fread( start, 1, numbytes, fp );

    if ( numread == numbytes )
        quit( "%s: file too big\n", argv[1] );

    end = start + numread;

    for ( count = 0; start <= end; start++ )
    {
        if ( *start == '\n' || *start == '\r')
            count++;
    }
    printf( "%d lines\n", count );
    exit( 0 );
}

quit( str, arg )
char *str, *arg;
{
    fprintf( stderr, str, arg );
    exit( -1 );
}

/* mostmem() ( malloc() version ) goes here */
```

The technique is to declare a buffer into which the names will first be placed and give this buffer a chunk of free memory with *malloc()*. Then, declare an array of pointers to strings:

```
char *ptr[];
```

Again, space will be allocated with *malloc()*.

Examine "newaddnames.c", which is listed in Fig. 15–5. In a loop, each name is read into a buffer and its length found using the standard library routine *strlen()*. Then *len* bytes (plus one for the zero terminator) are allocated by *malloc()*, the name is copied into that allocated space, and the *pointer to* that space is assigned to the next element of *ptr*.

FIGURE 15-5   newaddnames.c

```
/* newaddnames.c: creating an array on the fly */

#include <stdio.h>
#define MAXN 80
#define MAXPTR  1000


main()
{
    int len, numnames, i;
    char *ptr[MAXPTR], *buffer, *malloc();

    buffer = malloc( MAXN );

    numnames = 0;
    while ( 1 )
    {
        if ( numnames )
        {
            puts( "names in list:" );
            for ( i = 0; i < numnames; i++ )
                puts( ptr[i] );
        }
        printf( "\nname to add: " );

        if ( gets( buffer, MAXN ) == 0  ||  buffer[0] == 0 )
            break;

        len = strlen( buffer ) + 1; /* one extra for '\0' */

        if ( (ptr[numnames] = malloc( len )) == NULL )
        {
            puts( "out of memory... aborted\n" );
            break;
        }
        strcpy( ptr[numnames], buffer );
        ++numnames;
    }
}
```

The chief advantage to this dynamic array storage is that each entry uses only as many bytes as it needs. When using a fixed-size array, on the other hand, you must make the columns big enough to hold all possible entries. Given an array of [rows][80], an entry like "Bob" would occupy only 4 bytes of a row, leaving the other 76 wasted.

Clearly, the dynamic allocation of array storage provides the best means of packing the most possible into limited memory. Rather than having the compiler lock you into a predetermined amount of memory, you are able to grab pieces of memory while the program is running. Hence, dynamic allocation is also called *runtime memory allocation.*

15.5 SORTING A FILE

Sort Using Pointers Into Free Memory   In the last chapter, you learned how to sort using an array of **pointers to** names. Recall that those names and the **pointers to** them were declared as a **static** array of strings:

```
static char *namelist[] = {
    "Rebecca",
    "Bob",
    .... etc.
};
```

Using **malloc()**, it is now possible to sort names and other text based on pointers into free memory.

First, we need to revise the **bubble()** routine from the previous chapter. This time, in addition to the array of pointers to be sorted, it is also passed the number of lines. That single added argument makes it into a more general-purpose subroutine called **bubsort()** that can be attached to many different programs. See Fig. 15–6.

The program that calls **bubsort()** is a revision of "linecount.c" called "filesort.c". (See Fig. 15–7.) It begins by allocating a large chunk of memory with **mostmem()** and reading a file into that memory in its entirety, rather than character by character.

An array of **pointers to** the individual lines is then created. The first pointer is clearly the start of the allocated memory. The program then scans forward looking for '\n' characters. When one is found, it is replaced with a '\0' to mark the end-of-string (EOS). Moving forward one more place, the address of the next string is noted. This process is repeated until the end of the file is reached.

The **bubsort()** routine is then called. When the array has been sorted, the result is printed to the standard output. The order in which the lines are printed is determined by the sorted array of pointers.

THE index() AND blockmv() ROUTINES

How to Find and Move Things Around in Memory   The first **for** loop in "filesort.c" is used to increment the pointer **start.** For each new value of this pointer, a check is made to see if the value it points to is '\n'. As it happens, the

FIGURE 15-6 bubsort()

```
/*
** bubsort(): Passed the number of lines to sort and
**      a pointer to the start of an array of pointers,
**      it sorts by exchanging those pointers.
**      Returns nothing.
*/
bubsort( lines, ptr )
int  lines;
char *ptr[];
{
    int  i;
    char *temp;

    if ( lines < 2 )           /* nothing to sort */
        return;


    while ( --lines )
    {
        for ( i = 0; i < lines; i++ )
        {
            if ( strcmp( ptr[i], ptr[i+1] ) > 0 )
            {
                temp     = ptr[i];
                ptr[i]   = ptr[i+1];
                ptr[i+1] = temp;
            }
        }
    }
}
```

standard library contains a function that does much the same thing.

Called *index(),* this function searches a string looking for a specified character. If that character is found, it returns a **pointer to** that character; otherwise, it returns NULL. In the fragment:

```
char *ptr, *str, *index();
char c;
if ( (ptr = index( str, c )) == NULL )
    .... not found stuff
```

index() is used to search for the character *c* in the string *str.* If that character is found, its address is assigned to *ptr;* otherwise, NULL is assigned to *ptr.*

The *index()* function can also be used to search allocated memory. Be sure to make the last byte of that memory '\0', to prevent *index()* from running off the deep end:

```
start = malloc( size );
start[size - 1] = '\0'
```

FIGURE 15-7 filesort.c

```
/* filesort.c: sort file by lines to standard output */

#include <stdio.h>
#define MAXLINES 1000  /* should be enough */

main( argc, argv )
int  argc;
char *argv[];
{
    int i, numbytes, numread, count;
    static char *ptr[MAXLINES];
    char *start, *end, *mostmem();
    FILE *fp;

    if ( argc != 2 )
        quit( "usage: %s file {> output}\n", argv[0] );

    if ( (start = mostmem( &numbytes )) == NULL )
        quit( "%s: no free memory\n", argv[0] );

    if ( (fp = fopen( argv[1], "r" )) == NULL )
        quit( "%s: can't open\n", argv[1] );

    numread = fread( start, 1, numbytes, fp );

    end = start + numread;
    ptr[0] = start;
    for ( count = 1; start <= end; start++ )
    {
        if ( *start == '\n' || *start == '\r' )
        {
            *start = '\0';
            ptr[ count ] = start + 1;
            if( ++count == MAXLINES )
                quit( "too many lines to sort\n", "" );
        }
    }

    *start = '\0';

    bubsort( count, ptr );                          /* sort */
    for ( i = 0; i < count; i++ )                   /* print */
        puts( ptr[i] );
}
/* quit(), mostmem() and bubsort() here */
```

Another handy function for dealing with memory is ***blockmv()*** for *block memory move*.[2] To use it, simply specify the destination (a pointer), the address of the first byte to be moved to the destination (a pointer), and the number of bytes to move:

```
char *dest, *source;
int count;
blockmv( dest, source, count );
```

Several situations for which ***blockmv()*** is a natural occur in a word-processing or text-editor program (for example, the need to insert and delete words, copy lines, and move blocks of text). Here it will be used to insert a word into a text buffer.

The routine in Fig. 15–8, ***insword()***, is passed two arguments—the word (a string) to be inserted, and a **pointer to** where in the text that word is to be placed. This function also needs to know where the current text ends. That end-of-text is provided in the **global** variable ***Endtxt***. Using ***blockmv()***, first a ''hole'' is made for the word by moving all text from the insert point to end-of text up by ***strlen(word)*** number of bytes. Then ***blockmv()*** is called again to move the ***word*** into that ''hole.''

FIGURE 15-8 insword()

```
/*
** insword(): Inserts word at spot. Endtxt is
**          presumed to be a global pointer to
**          the end of text.  No check is made
**          for buffer overflow, nor for correctness
**          of space placed after word.
*/
insword( word, spot )
char *word, *spot;
{
    int movlen, wrdlen;
    char *dest;

    strcat( word, " " );     /* add a space to word */

    wrdlen = strlen( word );
    movlen = Endtxt - spot;
    dest = spot + wrdlen;
    Endtxt = Endtxt + wrdlen;

    blockmv( dest, spot, movlen );  /* make a hole */
    blockmv( spot, word, wrdlen );  /* fill hole   */
}
```

[2]Some installations have replaced the ***blockmv()*** function with one called ***bcopy()***. Check your documentation.

The program "fillme.c" demonstrates the use of ***insword(), blockmv(),*** and ***index().*** It should not only prove instructive, but entertaining to boot.[3] Beginning with the sentence "fill me." (Fig. 15–9), it asks you to enter words to build a longer sentence. It has some very strange rules. If the first letter of your word begins with a letter that is already in the sentence, your word is inserted just before that letter. Otherwise, it is inserted at the start of the sentence. An empty input line terminates the program.

FIGURE 15-9   fillme.c

```
/* fillme.c: a silly game of filling a sentence */

#include <stdio.h>
#define LIMIT 1000
#define MAXWORD 80

static char *Endtxt;
static char line[LIMIT] = "fill me";

main()
{
    char *spot, word[80], *index();

    Endtxt = line + strlen( line ) + 1;

    while( 1 )
    {
        printf( "%s\n", line );
        printf( "enter word: " );

        if ( gets( word, MAXWORD ) == EOF )
            break;

        if ( word[0] == 0 )
            break;

        if ( (spot = index( line, *word )) == NULL )
            spot = line;

        insword( word, spot );
    }
}

/*** insword() goes here ***/
```

---

[3]Depending on how easily you're entertained.

16. STRUCTURE AND UNION

Different Types Together, or One at a Time

INTRODUCING struct

Strange Bedfellows in a Strange Bed Arrays are the means of organizing many variables of the *same* type under a single name. There are times when you will want to organize *different* types under one name. Take the case of a personal check. The important information regarding a check is the check number, the date, who it was written to, and its amount. The variables to hold these pieces of information could be separately declared as:

```
unsigned checknum;
short    month, day, year;
char     towhom[MAXTO];
float    amount;
```

They all relate to the same concept, that of a check, but are of different types. We can, however, organize them under a single name by means of a *structure*. A structure is a special kind of array that contains variables of *different* types as its elements. For a structure, however, those elements are called *members* and are accessed by names rather than by offsets.

Patterns and struct

Before you can declare a structure (special array), you must define a pattern of variables—the members that will be used by that structure—and give that pattern a name. One way to define a pattern named ''check'' is:

```
                                    ──────────── name of pattern
struct check  {
    unsigned  checknum;
    short     month, day, year;         ⎫    members of
    char      towhom[MAXTO];            ⎬    pattern
    float     amount;                   ⎭
};
```

Here we have only defined a *pattern* of variables—the members our structures (special arrays) will contain—and given that pattern the name (or tag) **check.** No memory has been allocated, as yet. The keyword **struct** indicates that this is a pattern for a structure, as opposed to a **union** (to be covered later).

Before we can use the pattern "check", we must declare which structures (special arrays) are of that type—that is, which will contain the members (variables) defined by that pattern:

```
                        variable          variable          variable
          type          name              name              name

          ───────       ──────────        ──────────        ──────────
        struct check    rentcheck,        gascheck,         bedcheck;
```

Here the keyword **struct,** combined with the pattern name "check", can be thought of as a new type. That type, ***struct check,*** is used to declare three structures (***rentcheck,*** etc.). Each will contain as its members the variables defined by the pattern "check". This declaration also allocates memory storage for each of those structures.

Structure Members

To access the *members* (variables) within structures, use the form:

```
structname.membername
```

That is, use the name of the structure, a dot, then the name of the member of that structure. To access and print the amount of your rent check, for example, you could use the expression:

```
printf( "%d", rentcheck.amount );
```

where ***rentcheck*** is the structure name and ***amount*** the member name.

To enter values into all the members of ***rentcheck,*** you could use the following fragment of code. Note how "Olympic Realty" is copied into the member ***towhom*** using the ***strcpy()*** routine from Chapter 9:

```
rentcheck.checknum = 101;
rentcheck.month    = 6;
rentcheck.day      = 31;
rentcheck.year     = 87;
strcpy( rentcheck.towhom, "Olympic Realty" );
rentcheck.amount = 138.50;
```

Structure *members* can be manipulated in the same way as ordinary variables are. They follow the same rules for arithmetic, comparisons, assignments, and so forth. The only restriction is that each member must be referenced by the name of the structure containing it, a dot, and then its name.

Although structure members are ordinary variables, structures themselves are not. You may not perform arithmetic, comparisons, or assignments on them.[1] These operations can be done only on *members* of structures. All you can do with a structure is take its address or pass it as an argument to a function. Illegal operations on structures are a common source of errors. Just remember that the *members* are the variables and the structure is just a convenient means of grouping them together.[2]

Other Ways to Define a Pattern

Remember that the members are defined when you define the pattern:

```
                    ┌─────────────────── name of pattern
                    ▼
struct check        {
    unsigned        checknum;
    short           month, day, year;      ⎫
    char            towhom[MAXTO];         ⎬  members of
    float           amount;                ⎭  pattern
};
```

But before those members can be accessed, you must separately declare structures that are of that pattern by using the new type **struct check:**

```
              variable          variable          variable
    type       name              name              name
  ‿‿‿‿‿‿     ‿‿‿‿‿‿‿         ‿‿‿‿‿‿‿         ‿‿‿‿‿‿‿

struct check    rentcheck,       gascheck,       bedcheck;
```

It is also possible to define a pattern and declare a structure to be of that pattern all at once. The structures **rentcheck** and **gascheck,** for example, may be declared at the same time as the pattern is defined:

```
                    ┌─────────────────── name of pattern
                    ▼
struct check        {
    unsigned        checknum;
    short           month, day, year;
    char            towhom[MAXTO];
    float           amount;
} rentcheck, gascheck;
    ▲         ▲
    └─────────┴──────────────────────── structures having this pattern
```

[1] Some new compilers allow structure assignments.

[2] A structure is like a shopping bag and the members like the groceries.

When structures are defined in this way, the name of the pattern becomes optional and can be omitted:

```
                      ┌─────── name of pattern omitted
       struct {
           unsigned      checknum;
           short         month, day, year;
           char          towhom[MAXTO];
           float         amount;
       } rentcheck, gascheck;
```

In this case, no name is given to the pattern. A name (or tag) is only needed if the shorthand declaration:

struct check bedcheck;

will later be used. The name (tag) of a pattern provides a convenient means to declare many structures of that pattern, and obviates the need to spell out, in detail, what a pattern contains each time.

The following program, "structdemo.c", demonstrates one use of a structure. (See Fig. 16–1.) Notice that the pattern *check* is declared outside and before all functions. This makes that definition globally accessible to all functions. Had this not been done, you would have to redefine it locally inside each function.

FIGURE 16-1   structdemo.c

```c
/* structdemo.c: using members of a structure */

#include <stdio.h>
#define MAXTO 30

struct check {                      /* pattern declared globally */
    unsigned checknum;
    short    month, day, year;
    char     towhom[MAXTO];
    float    amount;
};

main()
{
    struct check rentcheck;      /* structure of pattern check */

    rentcheck.checknum = 1;

    printf( "This is check number %d\n", rentcheck.checknum );

    rentcheck.checknum = rentcheck.checknum + 5;

    printf( "The check number is now %d\n", rentcheck.checknum );

}
```

16.2 PASSING STRUCTURES TO FUNCTIONS

When Passed by Value, Members Are Insulated from Change   Some compilers allow structures to be passed directly to functions. When this can be done, only a copy of that structure and its members are passed. This is the same as passing a simple variable in that any changes made to the copy do not affect the original.

The program in Fig. 16–2, "checkbook.c", demonstrates how to pass a structure to a function for compilers that allow this. Note that the structure definition for **check** is again **global** to simplify declaration of the argument **item** in **showcheck()**. Since the structure **item** is a copy of the structure **chk1**, **showcheck()** makes no attempt to change the values of any of the members. It would be unable to do so even if we wanted it to, because it is dealing with a copy.

FIGURE 16-2   checkbook.c

```
/* checkbook.c: pass a copy of a structure to a function */

#include <stdio.h>
#define MAXTO 30

struct check {                    /* pattern declared globally */
    unsigned checknum;
    short    month, day, year;
    char     towhom[MAXTO];
    float    amount;
};

main()
{
    struct check chk1;         /* structure of pattern check */

    printf( "check number: " );
    scanf( "%d", &chk1.checknum );
    printf( "date (as mm dd yy): " );
    scanf( "%d%d%d", &chk1.month, &chk1.day, &chk1.year );
    printf( "written to: " );
    gets( chk1.towhom, MAXTO );
    printf( "amount $" );
    scanf( "%f", &chk1.amount );

    showcheck( chk1 );
}

showcheck( item )
struct check item;             /* argument of pattern check */
{
    printf( "%03d ", item.checknum );
    printf( "%02d/%02d/%2d ", item.month, item.day, item.year );
    printf( "%30s ", item.towhom );
    printf( "$%9.2f\n", item.amount );
}
```

16.3 POINTERS TO STRUCTURES

How to Affect the Members Themselves   For most compilers, a structure can have only its *address* passed to functions. Like arrays, this allows you to affect the structure's members directly, rather than affect a copy of those members.[3]

In "checkbook.c" the **&** operator was used to pass *scanf()* the address of the structure's members. Thus:

```
&structure.member
```

yields the address of *member*. Similarly, the expression:

```
&structure
```

yields the address of the structure itself. To pass the address of a structure to a function, then:

```
fillchecks( &rentcheck );
```

Recall that a function that *receives* an address as an argument must declare that argument as a suitable type. In the case of a structure's address, this requires the type **pointer to struct.** To declare a variable to be a **pointer to** a structure the same rule is used as for **pointers to** ordinary variables. For example:

```
struct check *item;
```

declares *item* to be a **pointer to** a structure of type **struct check.**

Since *fillcheck()* will be receiving the address of a structure as its argument, you must declare:

```
fillcheck ( item )
struct check *item;
{
    . . . .
```

This says that *fillcheck()* will be receiving as its single argument the address of a structure defined by the pattern "check". The pointer *item* is a **pointer to** a structure of that pattern and will contain that structure's address.

Within *fillcheck()*, to access the members of a structure using a pointer requires a "->" instead of the dot. That odd-looking symbol is composed of a minus sign (or hyphen) and a greater-than symbol and resembles an arrow. Thus, in the case of:

```
struct check rentcheck, *item;
item = &rentcheck;
```

Both of the following:

```
rentcheck.checknum
item->checknum
```

yield the same thing—the value of the member *checknum.*

---

[3]Since all compilers allow the address to be passed, and only a few allow a copy to be passed, we recommend you stick to the address method outlined here, for the sake of portability.

FIGURE 16-3 fillcheck()

```
/*
** fillcheck(): Receives a pointer to a structure of
**          type struct check.  Prompts for and places
**          entries into that structure. No checking is
**          for, or correction made of input errors.
*/
fillcheck( item )
struct check *item;              /* pointer to structure */
{
    printf( "Enter check number: " );
    scanf( "%d", &item->checknum );

    printf( "Enter date (as mm dd yy): " );
    scanf( "%d", &item->month );
    scanf( "%d", &item->day );
    scanf( "%d", &item->year );

    printf( "Check written to: " );
    gets( item->towhom, MAXTO );

    printf( "Amount of check $" );
    scanf( "%f", &item->amount );
}
```

Examine the following implementation of *fillcheck()*. Note how the "->" is used in the same way as the "." was used in "checkbook.c". See Fig. 16–3.

Compare the pointer accessing of members used here with the nonpointer method in the preceding version of "checkbook" (Fig. 16–3). For example, assume that the member *checknum* is the variable whose value we are interested in. In "checkbook", *chk1* is a structure of type **struct check.** In *fillcheck(),* **item** is a **pointer to** a structure of type **struct check.** It follows, then, that:

> chk1.checknum   and   item->checknum

will both yield the *value* of the member *checknum.* And both:

> &chk1.checknum   and   &item->checknum

will yield the *address of the member checknum.*

The program "checkbook.c" can now be revised to use the function *fillcheck().* This revision is in Fig. 16–4. Because that function uses a **pointer to** a structure, it affects the referenced argument itself rather than a copy. Note that the program's *main()* has become much shorter and cleaner, and we can now conveniently handle multiple checks.

If your compiler is one of those that can *only* pass the address of a structure, you should take the time now to rewrite the function *showcheck().* Just make *item* a pointer:

FIGURE 16-4 checkbook.c (revision 1)

```
/* checkbook.c (revision 1): pass a pointer to a structure */

#include <stdio.h>
#define MAXTO 30

struct check {                 /* pattern declared globally */
    unsigned checknum;
    short    month, day, year;
    char     towhom[MAXTO];
    float    amount;
};

main()
{
    struct check chk1, chk2;    /* variables of pattern check */

    printf( "First check entry:\n----------------\n" );

    fillcheck( &chk1 );         /* pass address of structure */

    printf( "Second check entry:\n----------------\n" );
    fillcheck( &chk2 );

    printf( "\nSummary of checks entered:\n" );
    showcheck( chk1 );
    showcheck( chk2 );          /* pass copy of structure */
}

/** place showcheck() and fillcheck() here **/
```

```
            struct check *item;
```

and substitute the ''->'' operator for all occurrences of the ''.'' operator.

16.4 ARRAYS OF STRUCTURES

A Simple Data Base Using Structures Even with our improvements, ''checkbook.c'' will become unmanageable if even a dozen checks have to be processed. A solution to this lies in C's ability to group many structures into an array of structures.

Arrays of structures are created and used just like arrays of ordinary variables. The declaration:

```
struct check book[MAXCHECKS];
```

declares **book** to be an array that can contain at most **MAXCHECKS** number of items, each of which is a structure of type **struct check**. To access a particular member of any of these structures, simply state which structure (that is, which array element), a dot, and the name of the member sought. To find out to whom the sixth check was written, for example, state:

    book[5].towhom

Similarly, to yield the *address* of a particular member, state:

    &book[5].amount

Likewise, to yield a particular structure itself:

    book[5]

And to get the address of that structure use the **&** operator, as:

    &book[5]

By the addition of an array, the program "checkbook" may now be rewritten as a more powerful tool. The revision is in Fig. 16–5. The trivial *menu()* function is left to the reader.

Ideas for Expanding checkbook.c

From this humble beginning, you can build a powerful data base for your checks by creating new functions and expanding the menu. You need not limit this approach to checks. Structures are handy for organizing all sorts of things from complex numbers to library cards to players in a computer baseball game. For now, we will stick to checks to illustrate the ins and outs of creating new functions to handle arrays of structures.

One way to improve the "checkbook" program is by giving it the ability to read and write its array of checks to and from a file. This is a situation in which the two arguments *size* and *count* in the standard library functions *fread()* and *fwrite()* (Chapter 11) can be used to good advantage. Recall that *size* is the number of bytes occupied by each unit and *count* is the number of those units. You can then use:

    fwrite(book, sizeof struct check, count, fp);

to write your array of checks to a file, and:

    count = 0;
    while (fread(book[count], sizeof struct check, 1, fp) != 0)
        count++;

to read them back in. It is necessary to use the **sizeof** operator because the number of bytes a structure occupies will vary from machine to machine. (Remember that an **int** on one machine will be two bytes, while on another it may be four bytes.)

Another way to improve the "checkbook.c" program is by giving it the ability to delete and insert checks. Although this will seldom be used for a real checkbook, it is a need common to most other data-base programs.[4] The following frag-

---

[4]Unless you keep two sets of books.

FIGURE 16-5 checkbook.c (revision 2)

```
/* checkbook.c (revision 2): a menu driven check register */

#include <stdio.h>
#define MAXTO 30
#define MAXCHECKS 25

struct check {                        /* pattern declared globally */
    unsigned checknum;
    short    month, day, year;
    char     towhom[MAXTO];
    float    amount;
};

main()
{
    struct check book[MAXCHECKS];   /* array of structures */
    int count, choice, i;

    count = 0;                          /* start with no checks */

    while ( (choice = menu() ) != 'q' )
    {
        switch ( choice )
        {
          case 'a':                             /* add a check */
            fillcheck( &book[count] );
            count++;
            break;

          case 'v':                            /* view all checks */
            for ( i = 0; i < count; i++ )
                showcheck( book[i] );
            break;
        }
    }
}

/** place showcheck(), fillcheck() and menu() here **/
```

ment illustrates one approach. In it, we delete an element from an array of structures by copying all the higher array elements (structures) down by one position to fill its place.

```
        --count;
        for (i = delnumber; i < count; i++ )
        {
            book[i].checknum = book[i+1].checknum;
            book[i].month    = book[i+1].month;
            book[i].day      = book[i+1].day;
```

```
book[i].year     = book[1+1].year
strcpy( book[i].towhom, book[i+1].towhom );
book[i].amount   = book[i+1].amount;
}
```

Inserting an entry is just the opposite. First move all the array elements up by one, beginning at the insert point. Then copy the new entry into that "hole."[5]

Other functions you might want to add to your data base would be the abilities to sort, total amounts, search, and print out. You might also want to add members to the pattern "check", say, to indicate if a check has cleared the bank or to specify what a check was for.

16.5 STRUCTURE NESTING

Unraveling the Spaghetti   You've seen that arrays may contain structures, but structures themselves may also contain structures. As an extreme example, look at a structure called ***ourchecks:***

```
struct {
    unsigned mynum;
    struct check mybook[MAXCHECKS];
    unsigned yournum;
    struct check yourbook[MAXCHECKS]; } ourchecks;
```

With this arrangment, you could look at *my first* check's amount by saying:

```
ourchecks.mybook[0].amount
```

and you could look at *your last* check's amount with:

```
ourchecks.yourbook[ ourchecks.yournum − 1 ].amount
```

Notice that each statement proceeds left to right, from the outermost structure name to the relevent innermost member name.

Just to convey their legality, look at some statements from programs that use structures within structures within . . .

```
*vp = mp->dirq.filn[i].nextp;
fp = fopen( year[curyear].day[today].msgfname, "r" )
while( (++(tnod->bnod)->leaf = getchar()) != EOF )
    continue;
```

What may seem confusing at first glance is actually quite straightforward. Follow along as we unravel the first example. In it, some value will be assigned to where *vp* points. That value is found by evaluating left to right. First, *mp* points to a structure that has a member *dirg*, but *dirg* is also a structure that has as a member *filn*, which is an array of structures. The i'th element of that array is a structure, whose member *nextp* contains the value sought.

---

[5]This could be done much more quickly using pointers rather than exchanging all elements. However, then it wouldn't be as clear an example.

Take the time to unravel the last two examples yourself.[6] Remember that in an expression such as:

```
tnode->bnode
```

the "->" means that *tnode* is a pointer to a structure.

16.6 INITIALIZING STRUCTURES

Assign Values to a Structure When It Is Declared   Structures can be initialized only if they are either declared **static** or are **global**—like arrays. It is illegal to initialize a structure of class **auto.** The initializing values are assigned from within curly braces proceeding from the first member to the last member, left to right. For example, the declaration:

```
static struct check renttemp = {
    0, 0, 0, 0,
    "Mr Landlord",
    132.50
};
```

assigns the value 0 to *rentcheck's* members *checknum, month, day,* and *year.* It also assigns the string "Mr. Landlord" to the member *towhom,* and the value 132.50 to the member *amount.*

When fewer initializing values are specified than there are members, the last members are assigned a default value of 0. For example:

```
static struct check datetemp = { 0, 6, 20, 87 };
```

gives the members *towhom* and *amount* each the default value 0.

An array within a structure may be partially initialized by enclosing it within an inner pair of curly braces. Thus:

```
struct check temp = { 0, 0, 0, 0, {'M', 'r', 0} };
```

initializes the member *towhom* as the string "Mr", and sets all the other members to a beginning value of 0.

16.7 LINKED LISTS

Another Approach to Handling Data   Structures can be made up of any type variables, including structures and **pointers to** structures. If a structure is defined to contain a **pointer to** another structure of its same type, then the basis of a linked list is created.[7]

---

[6]Since it does take time to unravel such code, try to not use it unless really necessary.

[7]Linked lists are a basic data structure and can be implemented without structures. However, structures are a convenient way of grouping the data with pointers connecting that data.

```
struct link {
    char string[MAX]
    struct link *nextlink};
```

Here a pattern of type ***struct link*** is defined. It contains two members: ***string***, a character array that will be used to hold a string, and ***nextlink***, a **pointer to** another structure of type **struct link.**

To illustrate how this pattern can be used to create a linked list, we will first declare three structures as:

```
struct list first, second, third;
```

and then assign some strings to the ***string*** member of each:

```
strcpy( first.string,   "I am first"  };
strcpy( second.string,  "I am second" };
strcpy( third.string,   "I am third"  };
```

and finally, link them together:

```
first.nextlink  = &second;
second.nextlink = &third;
third.nextlink  = NULL;
```

The following diagram illustrates the result:

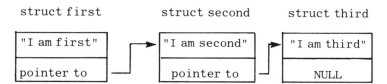

One of the chief advantages of linked lists is that the data they contain can be accessed without needing to know the number of links. That should be clear from the diagram. Another advantage is that links may easily be inserted and removed by reconnecting pointers. The next two diagrams illustrate the deletion of struct ***second*** and its replacement with:

```
struct link new;
strcpy( new.string, "I am new" );
```

First, to delete ***second:***

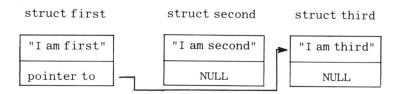

change *first.nextlink* to point to *third* and change *second.nextlink* to a NULL. The NULL is used to prevent its being mistaken for an active link. In practice, that may not be necessary.

Inserting a new link is just as easy. By changing two pointers, the link *struct new* is inserted into the list:

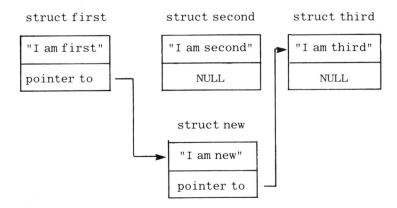

The program "linkdemo.c"(Fig. 16–6) further illustrates this process of manipulating linked lists. Notice that much of the work is done using the address of the start of the list.

16.8 INTRODUCING union

Many Variables Share One Space, One at a Time   The keyword *union* provides a way of allowing different types to share the same space in memory. A **union** can have only a single value at any one time, but the type of that value may be any one of several. A **union** is primarily used in such projects as symbol-table management, compiler writing, complex system design, and similar advanced projects. It does not find much use in day-to-day programming. However, you must understand **union** if you are to understand the language as a whole.

A **union** is declared and initialized very much like a structure. It is defined by the keyword **union,** an optional name (or tag) for the pattern, and a list of possible member types enclosed by curly braces. For example:

```
union number {
      char alpha[MAXNUML];
      int decimal;
} sample;
```

defines the type **union number,** which can be used to hold either an array of type **char,** or an integer of type **int.** It also declares *sample* to be a variable of the type **union number.**

FIGURE 16-6 linkdemo.c

```
/* linkdemo.c: demonatrate linked list using structures */

#include <stdio.h>

struct link {
    char        *string;
    struct link *nextlink;
};

struct link new      = { "I am new",    NULL    };
struct link third    = { "I am third",  NULL    };
struct link second   = { "I am second", &third  };
struct link first    = { "I am first",  &second };

main()
{
    puts( "The original list:" );
    showlinks( &first );

    puts( "Deleting second:" );
    first.nextlink = first.nextlink->nextlink;
    showlinks( &first );

    puts( "Inserting new:" );
    new.nextlink = first.nextlink;
    first.nextlink = &new;
    showlinks( &first );
}

showlinks( linkptr )
struct link *linkptr;
{
    while( linkptr != NULL )
    {
        puts( linkptr->string );
        linkptr = linkptr->nextlink;
    }
    putchar( '\n' );
}
```

The accessing, assigning, and passing of **unions** is identical to that of structures. For example:

```
strcpy( sample.alpha, "fifty" );
```

places a value into *sample* that is the character string ''fifty''. And:

```
sample.decimal = 50;
```

treats *sample* as if it were an integer variable, placing the **int** value 50 there.

Pointers to **unions** also access their member type with the "->" operator, just like structures:

```
union number *sampointer;

sampointer = &sample;
sampointer->decimal = 150;
```

A **union** may be defined to contain as many members as you desire. The compiler will set aside enough room to accommodate the largest member. You can, of course, create arrays of **unions,** or structures with members that are **unions.**

The program in Fig. 16–7, "dumpfi.c", prints the contents of a file as either integer or floating-point values. Serving as an example of one application for **union,** it expects a flag telling it the type and a file name. That file is printed as either a series of integers or floating-point numbers, depending on the flag specified as part of the command line.

In large, complex programs it is possible to lose track of what type is stored in a given **union** at a given time. One solution to this problem is to make the **union** a member of a structure:

```
struct {
    short ifflag;
    union {
        float fval;
        int ival;
    } uval;
}iorfnum ;
```

Thereafter, you need only check:

```
iorfnum.ifflag
```

to discover what type is currently stored in the **union.**

FIGURE 16-7 dumpfi.c

```
/* dumpfi.c: dump a file as either int or float values */

#include <stdio.h>

main( argc, argv )
int  argc;
char *argv[];
{
    FILE *fp;
    union {
      int i;
      float f;
    } type ;

    if ( argc != 3  || (*argv[1] != 'i' && *argv[1] != 'f' ))
    {
        fprintf( stderr, "usage: dumpfi [fi] filename\n" );
        exit( 0 );
    }

    if ( (fp = fopen( argv[2], "r" )) == NULL )
    {
        fprintf( stderr, "\"%s\": can't open\n", argv[2] );
        exit( -1 );
    }

    while( 1 )
    {
        switch( *argv[1] )
        {
          case 'i':
            if ( fread( &(type.i), sizeof (int), 1, fp ) <= 0 )
                goto QUIT;
            printf( "%d\n", type.i );
            break;

          case 'f':
            if ( fread( &(type.f), sizeof (float), 1, fp ) <= 0 )
                goto QUIT;
            printf( "%f\n", type.f );
            break;
        }
    }
QUIT:
    exit( 0 );
}
```

17 · MODULAR AND CONDITIONAL PROGRAMMING

Construct a Unified Whole from Modular Pieces.

17.1 LINKING

Combine Many Small Files to Create a Large Program   In Chapter 1, you learned that the standard library must be included at *link* time for your program to use the functions found in it. The *linker,* however, can do more than join functions from a library to your program. It can also join together *object* files that are not part of a library.

Object files are intermediate files created as one of the steps in compiling a program. If you have been using an all-in-one "cc" command to compile your programs (or a shell script or submit file), you may never have seen any object files listed in your directory. Those all-in-one commands often delete any object files after having successfully compiled a self-contained program, that is, a program that contains a *main()* and for which all called functions are either a part of it or can be found in a library. If a program is *not* self-contained, compiling aborts during linking—in which case, an executable file is not created but an *object* file is left behind.

Demonstrate this by compiling the partial program "readopen.c", which contains the single function *readopen()*. This function attempts to open a file for reading and exits if that file can't be opened. It is in Fig. 17–1.

Attempting to compile this file will cause the linker to issue an error message such as:

```
link: undefined "main"
```

The exact message will vary, but the idea is that the function *main()* is missing.

FIGURE 17-1   readopen.c

```
/* readopen.c: file contains the single function readopen() */

#include <stdio.h>

/*
** readopen():   Opens fname for reading and returns a
**               filepointer for that file. Any error
**               aborts with a diagnostic message.
**
** call as:  FILE *fp, *readopen();
**           fp = readopen( "filename" );
*/
FILE *readopen( fname )
char *fname;
{
    FILE *fptr;

    if ( (fptr = fopen( fname, "r" )) == NULL )
    {
        fprintf( stderr, "\"%s\": can't open\n", fname );
        exit( -1 );
    }

    return ( fptr );
}
```

Now look at your directory of files and you will find that the linker has left behind an object file for "readopen" called "readopen.obj".[1]

Next, compile the program "head.c", which is in Fig. 17–2. This program simply reads in and prints the first 15 lines of any file. Notice that it contains a call to ***readopen()***.

Again, the linker will abort with an error, this time something similar to:

```
link: undefined "readopen"
```

Now you have two object files, named "readopen.obj" and "head.obj". We will link them, together and to the standard library, to create a single executable program. To do so, you must specify all three files to the linker. The method for doing this varies from machine to machine, so you may wish to review the general techniques outlined in Chapter 1. Reexamine the way you link a self-contained program, like "world.obj", to the standard library. For example:

---

[1]Depending on your compiler and operating system, this object file may be called "readopen.o" or "readopen.rel" or may have any of a number of other tags or endings. Review your documentation if you have any doubt.

FIGURE 17-2 head.c

```
/* head.c: print the first 15 lines of a file */

#include <stdio.h>
#define WIDTH 80          /* screen width */

main( argc, argv )
int   argc;
char *argv[];
{
    FILE *fp, *readopen();
    int i;
    char line[WIDTH];

    if ( argc == 1 )
    {
        fprintf( stderr, "usage: head filename\n" );
        exit( 0 );
    }

    fp = readopen( argv[1] );

    for ( i = 0; i < 15; i++ )
    {
        if ( fgets( line, WIDTH, fp ) != 0 )
            fputs( line, stdout );
        else
            break;
    }

    exit( 0 );
}
```

  tkb world/cp=world, lb: [1, 1] c/lb (for Decus C, PDP/11)

or

  ln world.rel sh65.lib (for Aztec C65, Apple II)

Linking three things together follows the same pattern. To link "head" and "readopen", together and to the standard library, expand the "link" command as:

        object file names
  tkb head/cp=head, readopen, lb: [1, 1] c/lb

or

        object file names
  ln =o head head.rel readopen.rel sh65.lib

The result will be an executable program called "head".

This example illustrates the general method for combining separate, modular files into a whole. This way you can break a program up into bite-sized pieces. More important, this technique opens the door to a form of modular programming.

17.2 MODULAR PROGRAMMING

Grouping Related Functions Into Discrete Files   Modular programming is the technique of writing programs in which individual tasks are given to individual functions. One function normally performs a task that is done many times throughout the program as a whole. Basically, this is what we have done all along in this book.

With the linker, it is possible to group functions that perform tasks relating to a common *aspect* of the program into a single *file*. A good example is the file "readopen". An object file could be created containing useful functions that deal with file-handling problems:

```
/* filetools.c
 *
 *    readopen():   open a file for reading.
 *    writeopen():  open a file for writing.
 *    apopen():     open a file in append mode.
 *    badread():    print read error and exit.
 *    badwrite():   print write error and exit.
 *    quitfile():   abandon and delete file.
 */
```

Such a file, having been written once, would always be available to be linked to any new programs you produce. It would form one *module* of a modularized program.

By grouping related functions into separate files and making each as general in purpose as possible, you will reap a host of benefits:

- Saved labor: not having to type in the same lines of code over and over with each new program
- Simplified debugging: writing and debugging a module once and thereafter having it available and bug free[2]
- Clarified logic: making it is easier to understand how a program operates by grouping related functions together
- Improved portability: isolating unusual or machine dependent functions in a single file, making them easier to find and alter should the program be compiled on another machine
- Faster compiling: not having to recompile proven modules, as you would if they were all in the same file

---

[2]The only good thing you can say about the bugs is that they won't increase if you leave the code alone.

17.3 THE extern KEYWORD

Variables Made Global Among Many Files   In Chapter 7, you learned that variables declared outside of, and before, all functions in a file become *globally* available to all the functions *in that file*. As it happens, they are also globally available to functions in *other* files:

```
/* file starts here */
int Foo;          /* global to all files */
main()
.... rest of functions in this file follow
```

Before a function in another file can access such a variable, a declaration must be made stating that it will be found externally. The keyword *extern* conveys that meaning:

```
/* another file */
extern int Foo;   /* found elsewhere */
```

The keyword **extern** does not create the variable, nor does it allocate any memory. It merely tells the compiler that the variable exists in *some other* file.

But beware! When a **global** variable is *declared* **static,** it is **global** only to the file in which it is declared. That is, it is local to that file and **global** only within that file. For example:

```
/* file starts here */
static int Foo;   /* global to this file only! */
main()
.... rest of functions follow
```

If you want to restrict a **global** variable to a single file just declare it as **static.** Omitting the keyword **static** will cause that variable to become accessible to all functions in all files that additionally declare it as *extern.*[3]

The following three-file example illustrates all of these concepts:

```
static int Num1;          /* global to this file only */
int Num2;                 /* global to all files */

dummy ()
{
    static int num3;      /* available to dummy only */
    int num4;             /* available to dummy only */
}
```

file1.c

---

[3]Some C compilers for micros have bizarre conventions for *externals,* *globals,* and so forth. Check your documentation carefully on this point.

```
extern int Num2;          /* found elsewhere and available
                           * to boffo.
                           */
boffo ()
{
     int num5;             /* available to boffo only */
}
```

file2.c

```
fuzzy ()
{
     extern int Num2;      /* found elsewhere and
                            * available to fuzzy only.
                            */
}
```

file3.c

A variable **global** to all files can be declared and initialized only once. Any other files or functions that need to access that variable must identify it with the keyword **extern.** When identifying arrays as **extern,** you must show the number of dimensions for that array and give the size of each dimension, except the first, which is optional:

optional

```
extern int Scores [ GAMES ] [ PLAYERS ] [ INNINGS ];
```

The type stated in the *extern* declaration must, of course, agree with the type in the original **global** declaration.

Just as you were cautioned against the overuse of **global** variables within a file, you are doubly cautioned against their use across file boundaries. **Global** variables provide communication links between functions. Where such links are needed, and no better alternative is available, **global** variables should be used and are preferable to excessively long function argument lists. The overuse of *global* variables, however, can make a program unreadable and difficult to modify or debug.[4]

---

[4]You may never know the full extent of program changes and their side effects when *global* or "common" variables are extensively used.

17.4 STYLE

Uniformity of Style Enhances Communication   One good reason to split a program into modules is to allow two people or a whole team to work on it at the same time.[5] Modular programming is also good for an individual working on a large project over many weekends. Whatever the case, modularity enables parts of a program to be written and tested independently of the rest of the program. With the advantages of such modularity, however, there comes a responsibility. The more spread out and disconnected a program becomes, the more it needs a consistent, well-documented style and a common uniformity of conventions. It won't do, for example, for one programmer to write:

```
/* create the root node from the header file */
if ( cnode( file, 1) == 0) {
    cnode( NULL, 1);
    nodes++;
}
```

and for another to write the same thing, but in a different style and with a different understanding of the order in which arguments will be passed:

```
/*
** create the root node from the header file
*/
if ( cnode( 1, file) == FALSE)
{
    cnode( 1, NULL );
    ++nodes;
}
```

Each is perfectly readable in its own right. Yet, when combined as part of a single program, the concept quickly becomes muddled. Does 0 mean FALSE? Which is the correct way to call *cnode()?* Whether helping to develop a style with a team, or simply setting your own standards, there are several questions to be answered before beginning:

1. In what order will arguments be passed? Will, for example, all be (fp, buff) or (buff, fp)?

2. Which names are always uppercase? Which have the first letter capitalized? Which begin with an underscore?

3. When, where, and how should a program be commented? Will comments indicating revisions carry a name and date or initials or a number?

4. Where will curly braces be placed and indented? Are there exceptions for structures and the like?

---

[5]If at all possible, avoid this altogether. It's hard enough to understand your own methods, much less communicate them to others.

5. What is the standard for spacing generally, and within parentheses and square brackets?

6. How will modules be grouped?[6]

17.5 MORE ABOUT #include

Including Personal Headers and Other Files   Another tool for dealing with both single and multiple-file programs is the C preprocessor. Thus far you have seen it used to include the standard C input/output header file:

```
#include <stdio.h>
```

and to perform simple substitutions:

```
#define MAXELEN 80
```

In addition to these straightforward abilities, the preprocessor provides for the inclusion of personal header files into your program.

When you tell the preprocessor to:

```
#include <stdio.h>
```

the angled braces "<>"signal that it should look in a special, system-dependent place to find the file named "stdio.h". Finding it, the preprocessor will then read from that file, as though it were a part of your program. In addition to signaling file inclusion with angled braces, you can specify a file between full quotation marks:

```
#include "myfile.h"
```

This tells the preprocessor to look for that file in the current directory. You can specify a drive or another directory as part of the file name:

```
#include "b:myfile.h"      (cp/m)
#include "myfile.h,d1"      (Apple)
#include "[1,1]myfile.h"    (rsx)
#include "/hd/myfile.h"     (Unix)
```

and the preprocessor will then look for that file in that place.

You will find it convenient, when dealing with a program that has been broken up among many files, to be able to group all common **#define** statements and **structure/union** definitions into a single **#include'd** file. Suppose, for example, you declared MAX with:

```
#define MAX 1000
```

and then used MAX in several files. By placing that definition into a common

---

[6]You should decide on a general strategy for **global** versus **local** variables as part of an overall choice of data structures. If the data structures are consistent among modules, the individual algorithms may vary with little impact.

header file, you would only have to change a single instance if you later decide to make MAX 2000.[7]

Your personal header files should normally be the last of the **#include** files. If you **#include** several personal headers, their order should generally be the same in all files.

```
#include <stdio.h>              system headers first
#include <ctypes.h>
#include "myfile.h"             then personal headers
#include "other.h"
```

Another possible use for your own header files is to collect all **extern** declarations into a single place. The following list presents one approach to accomplishing this. Remember: Variables that are **global** to other files may be declared and initialized only *once* among all the files.

extern.h	*main.c*	*subs.c*
extern int Cols;	#include <stdio.h>	#include <stdio.h>
extern int Lines;	int Cols = 80;	#include "extern.h"
	int Lines = 24;	

It is best to avoid the kind of file nesting where included files **#include** other files.

Another use for personal (or in this case "user specified") **#include'd** files is as a means to bypass the linker. Earlier in this chapter, you learned that two object files could be joined with a "linker" command such as:

```
link file1.o file2.o
```

As an alternative, the two source files (which precede those object files) could be combined into a *single* object file by **#include'ing** the second as a part of the first:

```
/* this is file1.c */
```

. . . . body of file here

```
#include "file2.c"
```

This is the usual technique used by compiler systems that do not provide a linker.

17.6 CONDITIONAL COMPILATION

Preprocessor Directives Create Many Programs from One   The preprocessor also has the ability to cause part of your source text to be ignored by the compiler and another part to be compiled. This can be done by using special directives. Those

---

[7]To put it another way, if you have the same definition in multiple files, you will probably forget to change some of them, leading to bugs.

directives base the decision to ignore or compile on external conditions you are able to affect.

The conditional directives are:

```
#ifdef TOKEN          is TOKEN #define'd?
#ifndef TOKEN         is TOKEN not #define'd?
#endif                conclude #ifdef, #ifndef, and #if
#else                 else for #ifdef, #ifndef, and #if
#undef TOKEN          un-#define's TOKEN
#if (expression)      is (expression) true?
```

The **#ifdef** and **#ifndef** directives deal with whether a token has been **#define'd.** The **#ifdef** directive asks if the token has been **#define'd,** and if so, the source text following it is compiled. The **#ifndef** directive asks if the token has *not* been **#define'd,** and if it has *not,* the source text following it is compiled. The range of source text affected, in both cases, is terminated by the **#endif** directive. Additionally, both may have an *else* section, indicated by the **#else** directive. For example:

```
#define FOO
#ifdef FOO . . . is Foo #defined?
        . . . . yes, all the code here will be compiled
#else
        . . . . and all the code here will be skipped
#endif
#ifndef FOO . . . is FOO not #defined?
        . . . . no (it is defined), skip this stuff
#else
        . . . . and the code here will be compiled
#endif
```

The preprocessor on many compilers *predefines* selected tokens. That is, the preprocessor acts as though the line:

```
#define token
```

had been found in your program. These predefined tokens fall into three classes. Generally, the machine the compiler is running on is defined, as *vax, pdp1,* and so forth. The operating system is also usually predefined, as *rsx, unix, msdos,* and so forth. And finally, such useful goodies as the date and source program name are defined, as for example, ''__DATE__'' and ''__FILE__''.

The program ''predefined.c'', in Fig. 17–3, can be used to see what tokens have been predefined in your environment. You should, of course, replace the tokens it checks for with ones that make sense for your system.

The main use for conditional compilation directives is to enable the creation of a single source file that can be compiled for any of several target environments. Even if the necessary token was not predefined for your needs, you can always **#define** it yourself.

Another application for the conditional directives is to create multiple versions of a program for a single environment. You might, for example, make a program overly verbose during program development by inserting lots of print state-

FIGURE 17-3 predefined.c

```
/* predefined.c: any tokens predefined here? */

#include <stdio.h>

main()
{

#ifdef pdp11
    puts( "yes pdp11" );
#endif

#ifdef rsx
    puts( "yes rsx" );
#endif

#ifdef decus
    puts( "yes decus" );
#endif

#ifdef _DATE_
    printf( "Today is %s\n", _DATE_ );
#endif

}
```

ments to aid in debugging. Then, once you have the program working correctly, remove the VERBOSE token. All those portions of the program formerly compiled by:

```
#ifdef VERBOSE
```

will then be eliminated from the final version.

The **#undef** directive is less useful generally, but very handy when needed. It un-**#define's** a token previously **#define'd.** You might, for example, want to compile a program on a vax as though it will run on an IBM PC:

```
#ifdef vax
#undef vax
#endif
#ifndef pc
#define pc
#endif
```

Or you might wish to redefine some token partway through your program:

```
#define MAX 30
      . . . . . . code here uses MAX at 30
#undef MAX
#define MAX 10
      . . . . . . code here uses MAX at 10
```

The last conditional directive is **#if.** This directive evaluates a *constant expression* following it and processes source text based on the truth of that expression. If the constant expression evaluates to zero, it is false and the source text is skipped. If it evaluates to non-zero, it is true and the source text is compiled. The **#endif** directive is again used to terminate the range of the source text affected:

```
#define MAXCASE 5
    switch( c )
    {
#if (MAXCASE > 3)
        case 3:
#endif
#if (MAXCASE > 4)
        case 4:
#endif
#if (MAXCASE > 5)
        case 5:
#endif
        . . . . stuff
    default:
        . . . . stuff
    }
```

All preprocessor conditionals can be nested. Just be sure there is a matching **#endif** for each. Excessive nesting is not recommended. A typical nesting is:

```
#ifdef pdp11
#ifdef rsx
    . . . . stuff
#endif
#ifdef venix
    . . . . stuff
#endif
#endif
```

One problem with this directive nesting is that the preprocessor is uncharacteristically (for C) inflexible about where directives must start. The "#" symbol (on most compilers) must start at the leftmost margin of your source text. The previous fragment would be much clearer if we could have indented it as:

```
#ifdef pdp11
    #ifdef rsx
        . . . . stuff
    #endif
    #ifdef venix
        . . . . stuff
    #endif
#endif
```

If yours is one of a handful of compilers that allow this, you should nonetheless avoid such indenting, as it is not portable.

17.7 LIBRARIES

Create Your Own Personal Library of Functions   Eventually, you will develop a group of functions you use often. The problem with collecting them into a *single* object file is that they will *all* be linked to your program, regardless of whether it needs them. Fortunately, many compiler environments provide the means for creating a library. Each function in a library is a single object file. When you link to a library, only those functions actually called by your program are linked to it. Obviously, this is more efficient, especially on small machines where program size is limited.

The means of creating, adding to, and modifying libraries are as many as there are environments. Take the time now, before the need arises, to review your documentation about libraries. If you are on a multiuser machine, try

        help lib

or

        man –k library

or, as a last resort, ask someone knowledgeable.

18·SHORTER AND/OR FASTER

Techniques to Improve a Program's Winning Performance.

18.1 THE ?: OPERATORS

Shorthand for Simple if Tests   As you saw in Chapter 4, a common programming situation is the need to obtain one of two alternative values based on the "truth" of a third. For example, the statement:

```
if ( X )
    return ( A );
else
    return ( B );
```

will return *A* if *X* is "true" (that is, not equal to zero) and *B* if *X* is "false" (that is, equal to zero). As another example, consider the following fragment. In it, ***result*** will be set to whichever of the two values, ***num1*** or ***num2,*** is greater:

```
if ( num1 >= num2)
    result = num1;
else
    result = num2;
```

This is a long piece of code for such a simple need. Fortunately, C provides a shorthand pair of operators for handling this common situation: **?** and **:**. An expression placed to the left of the **?** is tested for truth. The **:** separates two values, one of which will be yielded as a result of that test:

test ? value if test true : value if test false

This *entire expression* yields one of two possible values based on the "truth" of the test to the left of the **?**. Using these operators, the preceding code fragment can be rewritten more compactly as:

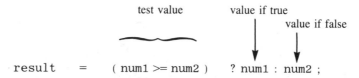

Here *result* is assigned one of two possible values. If *num1* is greater than or equal to *num2* (that is, the test is true) then *result = num1,* otherwise *result = num2.*

The rules for using **?** are simple. The test part can be any legal expression that yields a *zero/nonzero* value:

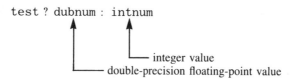

The parentheses surrounding the test expression, though optional, are recommended for clarity.

The two *alternative* values, each separated by a **:**, can be any expression. If the types yielded by the two differ, the compiler will promote both to a type able to handle both. For example:

```
test ? dubnum : intnum
```
            integer value
   double-precision floating-point value

will yield a value of type **double,** regardless of which of the two is selected.

Finally, note that only one of the two alternate expressions will ever be evaluated. In an expression like:

```
test ? a++ : b++
```

either *a* or *b* will be incremented, never both.

The program "maxdemo.c", in Fig. 18–1, illustrates a few of the many ways to use this handy set of operators. First, the **?** expression yields a value that is assigned to *result,* and that variable is printed. Then the **?** expression is passed as an argument directly to *printf().* Finally, it is used to drive *printf()* as part of its own evaluation.

FIGURE 18-1 maxdemo.c

```
/* maxdemo.c:   demonstrates the ?: operators */

main()
{
    int result, num1, num2;

    while( 1 )
    {
        printf( "Enter two numbers (0's to quit): " );
        scanf( "%d%d", &num1, &num2 );

        if ( num1 == 0 )
            break;

        result = (num1 >= num2) ? num1 : num2;
        printf( "1) %d is greater\n", result);

        printf( "2) %d\n", (num1 >= num2) ? num1 : num2 );

        printf( "3) " );
        (num1 >= num2) ? printf("%d", num1) : printf("%d",num2 );
        printf( "\n" );
    }
}
```

18.2 THE OP= SHORTHAND

A Way to Save Typing, with a Possible Pitfall Whenever a variable can be changed by performing an operation on itself, the shorthand ''op='' may be used, where *op* is any arithmetic operator (+, -, *, /, %). For example:

num = num + 1;

can be written:

num += 1;

with the same meaning and result. For any operator where you would ordinarily write:

num = num *op* val;

you may equally well write:

num *op*= val;

Or more specifically:

Where You Would write	*You Can Also Write*
num = num + val;	num + = val;
num = num − val;	num − = val;
num = num * val;	num * = val;
num = num / val;	num / = val;
num = num % val;	num % = val;

where **val** can be any legal expression that yields a value.

But beware! A pitfall lurks when **num** and **val** are of different types. Although not a problem with all compilers, some will give erroneous results if the type difference involves floating point and integer. The following, for example, if written in our old form:

```
intnum = intnum * 0.5;
```

will correctly yield an integer result for **intnum** that is half its original value. This is because the compiler automatically promotes the **int** to a **float** before the multiplication. However:

```
intnum *= 0.5;
```

will assign **intnum** a value of 0 on some compilers, because the 0.5 is *demoted* to an **int** before the multiplication, making it 0.[1]

The program "opprob.c", in Fig. 18–2, can be used to see if this pitfall is present in your compiler.

FIGURE 18-2 opprob.c

```
/* opprob.c: detect a problem with int op= float */

int i = 8, j = 8;

main()
{
    i *= 0.5;
    j = j * 0.5;

    printf( "These two numbers should be the same:\n" );
    printf( "%d, %d\n", i, j );
    printf( "If they are not, you have a compiler bug.\n" );
}
```

18.3 PREPROCESSOR MACROS

Functions in Disguise Produce In-Line Code Let's take a look at what happens when you call a function. The precise steps will vary from machine to machine, but the idea remains the same. When a function is called, the arguments you want to

---

[1] Some might call this a compiler bug. They would be right.

pass to it are *set aside* somewhere in memory where that called function will be able to find them. Then the automatic variables of the calling function are *hidden* so they will not be affected by the called function. The function is then called and a value returned. Finally, the *hidden* automatic variables are restored for use by the calling function.

All of this requires time (not a lot of time in human terms, but time nonetheless). Each operation a computer performs requires only a small part of a second. But a computer performs many, many such operations. Look at the time required for a call to the function *max():*

```
top = max ( temp1, temp2 ); /* larger of two values */
```

The time required for each step might be:

step 1:	set aside a and b	2 operations
step 2:	hide auto variables	4 operations
step 3:	call max	1 operation
step 4:	do max itself	3 operations
step 5:	restore autos	4 operations
	total	14 operations

The *additional time* created by a function call (that is, the time taken in addition to that used by the *max()* function itself) is (14 minus 3) or 11 operations. If *max()* was inside a loop, and that loop was executed a million times, and if your computer performed one operation every millionth of a second, then the overhead of the *call* would be 11 seconds! Compared to the 3 seconds taken by *max()* itself, that represents 11 seconds where nothing useful is happening.

The alternative to writing *max()* as a function is to write it as *in-line code.* That is, use the **?** operators to do the job where needed, rather than as a time-consuming function call:

```
top = ( ( temp1 >= temp2 ) ? temp1 : temp2 );
```

A function call to *max()* consumes 11 operations, but this in-line code consumes only 3. In time-critical application (loops with a million iterations, for example) execution time can be significantly improved by using in-line code. This does not mean that you should throw functions to the wind, only that there are times when a function call is best rewritten in-line.

Introducing #define Macros

The C preprocessor provides a means of making in-line code *look* like a function call. It is a variation on **#define,** called ''**#define** with macro expansion,'' or ''macro'' for short. The form for a macro is:

```
#define token(sub1, sub2, . . . . ) replacement text
```

or more specifically:

```
#define max(a,b)   (a >= b) ? a : b
top = max( temp1, temp2 );
```

When the preprocessor encounters the line:

```
top = max( temp1, temp2 );
```

in the source text, it will first expand the original macro:

```
max(a,b)
```

substituting, in the replacement text:

```
(a >= b) ? a : b
```

temp1 for each occurrence of *a* and *temp2* for each occurrence of *b.* After all the parameters have been substituted, the source text:

```
max( temp1, temp2 )
```

is replaced with the expanded definition:

```
( temp1 >= temp2 ) ? temp1 : temp2
```

yielding the final code:

```
top = ( temp1 >= temp2 ) ? temp1 : temp2;
```

The program ''macdemo.c'', in Fig. 18–3, is a rewrite of the earlier ''maxdemo.c''. It illustrates the use of macros as a labor-saving device. Notice that *max()* looks just like a function call.

Macro Rules and Pitfalls

When you **#define** a macro, there can be no space between the token name and its parenthesized parameter list, nor should there be any spaces within that list. ''Air'' within the comma-separated parameter list is optional, but not recommended:

no air in token and parameter list

```
#define max(a,b)  (a >= b) ? a : b
```

air here optional

Generally, macro definitions should not end with a semicolon:

bad news

```
#define max(a,b)  (a >= b) ? a : b;
```

Note that the expression to be replaced begins with the token name and ends with the rightmost parenthesis:

FIGURE 18-3   macdemo.c

```
/* macdemo.c: demonstrate #define macros */

#include <stdio.h>

#define max(a,b) (a >= b) ? a : b
#define P1(x)    fprintf( stderr, x )
#define P2(x,y) fprintf( stderr, x, y )
main()
{
    int result, num1, num2;

    while( 1 )
    {
        P1( "Enter two numbers (0's to quit): " );
        scanf( "%d%d", &num1, &num2 );

        if ( num1 == 0 )
            break;

        result = max(num1, num2);
        P2( "1) %d is greater\n", result);

        P2( "2) %d\n", max(num1, num2) );

        P1( "3) " );
        (num1 >= num2) ? P2("%d", num1) : P2("%d",num2 );
        P1( "\n" );
    }
}
```

$$\text{top} = \underbrace{\text{max(temp1, temp2)}}_{\text{replaced}};$$

Nothing is hurt by an extra semicolon in this instance, but examine:

```
                                        ┌─ extra semicolon
                                        ↓
#define max(a,b)  (a >= b) ? a : b;
for ( i = max(x, y) ; i < end; i++ )
```

which, when the erroneous macro definition above is expanded, would yield a **for** statement with one too many semicolons:

```
for ( i = x >= y ? x : y;; i < end; i++ )
                         ↑
                         └── extra semicolon
```

In the first stage of macro expansion (the substitution of parameters into the definition), quotation marks are ignored. For example:

```
#define BIG 1000
#define bigis(x)   "big is x"
printf( bigis(BIG) );
```

will substitute and expand to:

```
printf( "big is 1000" );
```

This works because the parameters are substituted first, *ignoring quotation marks,* and then that definition replaces the macro.

A pitfall to beware of when using macros is that they don't pass copies of variables like functions do. Try to avoid situations where you will affect variables directly within macros. To illustrate, compile and run the program in Fig. 18–4, called ''effectdemo.c''. In it, the macro *doub1()* changes the value of *num,* while the function *doub2()* does not.

FIGURE 18-4 effectdemo.c

```
/* effectdemo.c: demonstrate macro side-effects */

#define doub1(x) (x *= 2)
#define NL  printf( "\n" )

main()
{
    int num;

    printf( "num = %d\n", num = 2 );
    printf( "doub1() yields %d\n", doub1( num ) );
    printf( "and makes num now = %d\n", num );
    NL;
    printf( "num = %d\n", num = 2 );
    printf( "doub2() yields %d\n", doub2( num ) );
    printf( "and makes num now = %d\n", num );
}

doub2( val )
{
    return( val *= 2 );
}
```

Whenever a macro or function directly causes a change in the value of one of its arguments, it is said to have *side effects.* You should try to avoid creating macros with side effects.

Macros represent both a strength and a weakness in the C language. Their strength lies in providing a means to write in-line code in a concise and readable manner. Their weakness is that they are easily abused, can create difficult to locate errors, and are often confused with actual function calls.[2]

18.4 THE FAST VARIABLE: register

Speed Up Variables in Time-Critical Positions   In Chapter 6, you learned that variables could be allocated a permanent, fixed place in memory (**static**), or could be allocated dynamically (**auto**). One of the nicer features of C is also the ability to specify the placement of a variable into one of the computer's *registers*. Registers are special, fast locations that exist because the computer needs to do certain things faster than others. There is no need to know where these registers are on your machine. Just think of them as places where operations on variables stored there will be at their fastest and that some of them are available for you to use in your programs.

The rule for allocating a fast **register** variable is:

```
register type name;
```

as, for example:

```
register int count;
```

This places the **int** variable *count* into a special fast location in the computer, thereby creating a **register** variable.

Compile and run "regdemo.c", in Fig. 18–5, to witness the difference in speed between **register** and non-**register** variables. In it, the variables *r1, r2,* and *r3* are placed into special fast locations by the declaration **register.** The variables *i1, i2,* and *i3* are ordinary **auto** integers. In two loops, first the **register** variables are multiplied one million times, then the ordinary variables are. You should see a visible difference between the speeds of the two loops. You may have to adjust the size of LOOP.

It is generally safe to assume your machine will have at least three fast locations available for use as **register** variables. Some have more, some fewer. However many yours has, **register** variables are placed into them on a first-come, first-served basis. Suppose, for example, you declared seven variables to be **register,** as:

```
register int a, b, c, d, e, f, g;
```

On a machine with three fast locations, only *a, b,* and *c* would become **register,** while the rest would become the default class **auto.**

There are a few restrictions on the use of **register:**

1. A variable can be declared **register** only if it would otherwise be of class **auto.** A declaration like:

```
static register int xxx;
```

---

[2]As with many such speedups, use them when they are important for *major* efficiency improvements, and eschew them otherwise.

FIGURE 18-5   regdemo.c

```
/* regdemo.c: demonstrate the speed advantage of register */

#include <stdio.h>

#define MARK(x)  fprintf( stderr, "mark %s:\n", x )
#define END(x)   fprintf( stderr, "end %s:\n", x )
#define BELL     putchar( 7 )
#define LOOP     100000L
#define R1       r1=r2*r3
#define R5       R1;R1;R1;R1;R1
#define RSTUFF   R5;R5
#define I1       i1=i2*i3
#define I5       I1;I1;I1;I1;I1
#define ISTUFF   I5;I5

main()
{
    register int r1, r2, r3;
    int i1, i2, i3;
    long cnt;

    MARK( "register: any key to start" );
    getchar();
    BELL;
            for ( cnt = 0; cnt < LOOP; cnt++ )
            {
                r2 = 10;
                r3 = 20;
                RSTUFF;
            }
    BELL;
    END( "register" );

    MARK( "auto: any key to start" );
    getchar();
    BELL;
            for ( cnt = 0; cnt < LOOP; cnt++ )
            {
                i2 = 10;
                i3 = 20;
                ISTUFF;
            }
    BELL;
    END( "auto" );
}
```

is illegal, because it is an attempt to tie up a **register** for the duration of the program. Since there are a mere handful of fast locations in any machine, it makes sense that you should not be able to do this.

2. You cannot access the address of a **register** variable. That is, if *num* is declared as:

```
register int num;
```

then you cannot fetch its address with:

&num

The fast **register** locations are usually not in ordinary memory. They are in a special place, where the concept of address does not usually apply.

3. Neither **longs,** nor **structures,** nor **unions,** nor arrays can be put in **registers.** However, **pointers to** them can. Unless your machine has special floating-point hardware, it is possible that neither **floats** nor **doubles** can be placed into **registers** either. You should check your documentation on this point.

As a rule of thumb, you can improve a program's execution speed by declaring as **register** any variable that will be used often. Frequently, pointers and array indices are the best choices, as regular variables get a much smaller improvement. But remember, this is a first-come, first-served situation, and those variables most needed for speed should be declared first. Also note that the declaration **register** does not *cause* variables to be handled specially, it merely notifies the compiler that you *desire* them to be. The number of special fast locations your compiler offers (if it offers any at all) is something you will have to discover for yourself. So, once again, refer to your documentation.[3]

18.5 ANOTHER ALIAS: typedef

Create a New Type from Existing Types and Give It a Name   Superficially, **typedef** resembles the simple **#define** directive of the preprocessor in that it assigns an alternative name to an existing type. Generally, it is used to clarify the role a variable will play in a program. For example:

```
typedef short BOOL;
```

defines a new type named *BOOL* to be the equivalent of the type **short.** Here the name *BOOL* is meant to stand for *Boolean*—a variable used to store values that are either zero, for "false," or 1 for "true." There is no difference between *BOOL* and **short,** except that the name *BOOL* conveys a clearer picture of its intended use. The compiler will treat them identically, and the program will run no differently. In fact, the same thing could have been done with a **#define,** as:

```
#define BOOL short
```

The **typedef** statement, however, is not limited to simple one-for-one substitutions. Unlike **#define,** it can be used to assign new names to more complex types such as arrays, **structures,** and **unions.** For example:

```
typedef int MATRIX[MAX][MAX];
```

defines the new type named *MATRIX* to be a doubly-dimensioned array containing MAX by MAX elements, each of type **int.** Thereafter, you can declare:

---

[3]Given the sad state of some documentation, you may need to work this out experimentally.

```
MATRIX board1, board2;
```

which will convey to the compiler the same thing as if you had declared:

```
int board1[MAX] [MAX], board2[MAX] [MAX];
```

The procedure for defining a new type name with **typedef** is similar to the way you ordinarily declare a variable's type. First, write that declaration as though the *name* were the name of a variable:

```
char name[80];
```

Then replace *name* with the typedef name (for example, STRING), and insert **typedef** at the front:

```
typedef char STRING[80];
```

Voilà! A new data type has been defined!

Use of the **typedef** keyword is best reserved for those situations where it truly clarifies a type's role. It might, for example, be necessary for a variable to always be a particular number of bytes long for a program to properly work. For such a case, consider:

```
#ifdef vax
typedef int LONGINT;
#else
typedef long LONGINT;
#endif
```

which makes *LONGINT* an **int** if compiled on a Vax, and a **long** if compiled on any other machine.

For clarity, new names defined with **typedef** should be uppercase. Just as with the simple **#define** tokens, uppercase signals to the reader that substitution of some sort is occurring.

As an example of one common application for **typedef,** examine the program in Fig. 18–6, ''complex.c''. Here, complex numbers are represented by a structure containing two **double** variables, one for the real part and one for the imaginary part. Note how **typedef** clarifies the declaration of this ''type.''

Remember that **typedef** merely gives a new name to an existing type. It is a form of shorthand, and cannot be used to create anything really new. If used capriciously, it can confuse rather than enlighten the reader.

18.6 LOW LEVEL I/O

File I/O One Step Closer to the Machine's Guts   Most versions of the standard library contain functions for performing input and output (I/O) on the same efficient level as your operating system. Such *low-level I/O* is generally faster than the so called high-level I/O you learned about in Chapter 11. In fact, the higher level I/O functions of that chapter were, in all likelihood, created using calls to these low-level routines.

FIGURE 18-6 complex.c

```
/* complex.c: illustrate typedef struct COMPLEX */

typedef struct {
    double real;
    double imag;
} COMPLEX;

main()
{
    COMPLEX num;                   /* declare with new type */

    printf( "Enter a complex number," );

    printf( "real part first: " );
    scanf( "%lf", &(num.real) );

    printf( "imaginary part : " );
    scanf( "%lf", &(num.imag) );

    printf( "\nnumber = %lf + j%lf\n", num.real, num.imag );
}
```

For low-level I/O, you will be using a *file descriptor* of type **int,** instead of a *file pointer* of type **(FILE *).** The standard input, output and error output are predefined as **int** file descriptors:

File Descriptor (int)	Describes
0	standard input
1	standard output
2	standard error output

Unlike the file pointers **stdin, stdout,** and **stderr,** these file descriptors are not **#define'd** in the system header "stdio.h". To use them in a program you should **#define** them yourself, as for example:

```
#define STDIN  0
#define STDOUT 1
#define STDERR 2
```

Making them uppercase prevents their being confused with the **file pointers** of the same names.

The read() and write() Functions

The functions **read()** and **write()** are used for low-level reading and writing of files. Each requires three arguments: a file descriptor (an **int**); the address of a buffer where the data will be placed into or taken from; and the number of bytes to read or write. Those arguments are passed as:

```
read( fd, buff, nbytes );
write( fd, buff, nbytes );
```

Each returns the number of bytes (an **int**) actually read or written or a negative value if there was some error. Like *fread()*, *read()* does not return 0 when end-of-file is first reached. If any usable data was read, that number is returned. The next time *read()* is called, it will return 0 for end-of-file.

The short program "lowcopy.c", in Fig. 18–7, demonstrates use of these low-level functions. Since no appropriate definitions are contained in "stdio.h", it is not **#include'd**. Instead, *STDIN, STDOUT,* and *BUFSIZE* are **#define'd** as part of the program.

FIGURE 18-7 lowcopy.c

```
/* lowcopy.c: copies stdin to stdout with read() & write() */

#define STDIN  0
#define STDOUT 1
#define BUFSIZE 512

main()
{
    char buf[BUFSIZE];
    int  numbytes;

    while ( (numbytes = read( STDIN, buf, BUFSIZE )) > 0 )
        write( STDOUT, buf, numbytes );
}
```

As an exercise, rewrite "lowcopy.c" using different values for *BUFSIZE*. How is the speed of the copy affected? Look at how *BUFSIZE* is **#define'd** in "stdio.h". Why do you think *BUFSIZE* was given that value?

The open() and creat() Functions

To open a file or device for reading or writing, you must first declare a variable to receive the **file descriptor:**

```
int fd;
```

The function *open()* is then used to perform the actual open. The call to *open()* is very similar to that for *fopen():*

```
open( name, mode );
```

where *name* is again the address of a zero-terminated string, a pointer, or a quoted string constant that is the file or device name. However, *mode* is an integer. A *mode* value of 0 opens the file for reading, 1 opens it for writing, and 2 opens it for both. Note that you cannot use *open()* to open a file in append mode. Instead, you must open it with a *mode* of 2 (reading and writing), then position yourself at the end of the file by using *lseek(),* the low-level version of *fseek().*

The value returned by *open()* is of type **int,** and is the **file descriptor** you will be using for reading and writing. Any error returns a negative value. Thus, a typical call to *open()* looks like:

```
if ( (fd = open ( name, mode ) ) < 0 )
     . . . . error stuff here
```

When opening a file for writing, *open(),* unlike *fopen(),* does not create a file if it cannot be found. To create a new file, you must use the function *creat().* Like *open(),* it requires a file name and a mode number. The *mode,* however, has differing meanings depending on your system. Under Unix, for example, a *mode* of \777 creates a file with read, write, and execute *permission.* Under Aztec C65 on an Apple II, a *mode* of 0 creates a *text* file.

If successful, *creat()* returns a file descriptor and opens the file for writing. Any error returns negative file descriptor value. Thus, to open a file for writing (creating it if it doesn't exist), you could state:

```
if ( (fd = open ( filename, WRITE ) ) < 0 )
{
     if ( (fd = creat ( filename, CMODE ) ) < 0 )
          . . . can't open for writing or create
}
```

Compile the following program, ''lowfilecopy.c''. (See Fig. 18–8.) It demonstrates one approach to using low-level I/O. Notice how the function *quit()* uses *write()* to print diagnostics to the standard error. The *strlen()* function (Chapter 9) is used to determine how many characters to print.

For a complete picture of the rest of the low-level I/O functions, take a tour through your documentation. We recommend *close(),* to close a file using a **file descriptor,** and *lseek(),* to position your I/O within a file. Many libraries also offer nonstandard low-level I/O routines to handle problems specific to a particular machine or system. CP/M libraries, for example, usually contains functions that allow direct *BDOS* calls. Other nonstandard functions to look for are those that provide information about files, produce directory listings, and read the keyboard without echoing characters. Note that most low-level I/Os tend to be machine specific. If you want to write portable code, stick to the high-level routines described in Chapter 11.[4]

---

[4] It is also sometimes true that the high-level routines (*fread, fwrite,* and so forth) are just as fast or faster than low-level ones (*read, write,* and so forth). This just depends on your machine and operating system.

FIGURE 18-8 lowfilecopy.c

```
/* lowfilecopy.c: low level I/O file copying program */

#define STDIN   0
#define STDOUT  1
#define STDERR  2
#define READ    0
#define WRITE   1
#define BUFSIZ 512

main( argc, argv )
int  argc;
char *argv[];
{
    int infd, outfd, nbytes;
    static char buffer[ BUFSIZ ];

    if( argc < 3 )
    {
        outfd = STDOUT;
    }
    else if( (outfd = open( argv[2], WRITE )) < 0 )
        quit( "doesn't exist to overwrite", argv[2] );

    if( argc < 2 )
    {
        infd = STDIN;
    }
    else if( (infd = open( argv[1], READ )) < 0 )
        quit( "can't open to read", argv[1] );

    while( (nbytes = read( infd, buffer, BUFSIZ)) > 0 )
        write( outfd, buffer, nbytes );

    exit( 0 );
}

quit( msg, name )
char *msg, *name;
{
    write( STDERR, name, strlen( name ) );
    write( STDERR, ": ", 2 );
    write( STDERR, msg, strlen( msg ) );
    write( STDERR, "\n", strlen( "\n" ) );
    exit( -1 );
}
```

19. BITS AND THE BITWISE OPERATORS

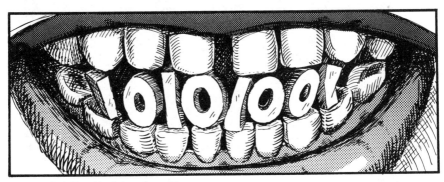

Time to Sink Your Teeth into Some Bits.

19.1 A BRIEF OVERVIEW OF BINARY NUMBERS

How to Count Using Only 1s and 0s   Recall from Chapter 2 that the basic storage unit in a computer's memory is called a byte. Each byte is composed of eight bits, and each of those bits is something like a light switch in that it can either be "on" or "off." For the examples in this chapter, we will identify each bit's position in a byte by numbering those positions from right to left:

a byte

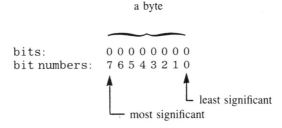

```
bits:          0 0 0 0 0 0 0 0
bit numbers:   7 6 5 4 3 2 1 0
```

least significant

most significant

This is the usual way a byte's bits are depicted. Notice that bits, like arrays, are numbered beginning with zero. When a bit is *set,* it has a value of 1. When it is *clear,* it has a value of 0. Since all the bits in this byte are clear, it represents the value zero. But by setting combinations of those bits, it can be made to represent other values.

A number system that uses only ones and zeros is called the binary number system. Examine the way a byte's value is progressively increased by 1, when counting in binary:

Binary	Decimal
00000000	0
00000001	1
00000010	2
00000011	3
00000100	4
00000101	5
00000110	6
00000111	7
00001000	8
00001001	9
00001010	10
etc.	etc.

Notice that for the decimal values 1, 2, 4, and 8, only a single bit is set. These values represent the powers of 2. For example, 2 to the power of 3 equals 8 (2 multiplied by itself 3 times, or 2 * 2 * 2). In the following list, observe how each bit position represents a unique power of two:[1]

Binary	Decimal	Power of Two
00000001	1	anything to the power of 0 = 1
00000010	2	2
00000100	4	2 * 2
00001000	8	2 * 2 * 2
00010000	16	2 * 2 * 2 * 2
00100000	32	2 * 2 * 2 * 2 * 2
01000000	64	2 * 2 * 2 * 2 * 2 * 2
10000000	128	2 * 2 * 2 * 2 * 2 * 2 * 2

Using this observation, it is easy to calculate the value of a byte from its set bits. Merely add together each set-bit's value as a power of 2. For example:

00000011 = 3   = 2 + 1

01000100 = 68 = 64 + 4

00000000 = 0   = 0

11111111 = 255 = 128 + 64 + 32 + 16 + 8 + 4 + 2 + 1

This demonstrates how a byte can have positive values ranging from 0 to 255. Earlier, however, you learned that a byte could have values ranging from −128 to +127. A byte can be made to *represent* negative as well as positive values by assigning negative values to those bytes that have the *most significant bit* set.

---

[1] This is entirely analogous to the way each place represents a power of 10 in the decimal system.

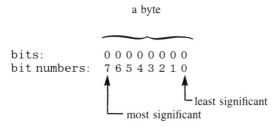

```
bits:            0 0 0 0 0 0 0 0
bit numbers:     7 6 5 4 3 2 1 0
```

least significant

most significant

Bit number 7 is called the most significant bit because it contributes most to the value of a byte. Bit number 0 is called the *least significant bit* because it contributes least to the value of a byte. If the most significant bit is set, the value of the byte is negative. If it is clear (that is, 0), the value of the byte is positive. The negative value, or "negation," of a byte, using this convention, is most commonly represented in *two's complement notation*. Two's complement "negation" is accomplished by inverting all the bits in a byte, then adding 1. For example, to convert a +1 to a −1:

```
                00000001  =  +1
invert bits     11111110
     add one    11111111  =  -1
```

Here the bits representing the value 1 are first inverted (all 1s become 0s and all 0s become 1s). Then 1 is added to yield a −1, which is two's complement of 1. To find the value of a negative byte, take the two's complement of that byte, which yields the equivalent positive number:

```
                11111111  =  -1
invert bits     00000000
     add one    00000001  =  +1
```

Larger ranges of values can be represented by grouping bytes into larger units. The same method of organizing values is used, but with more bits. Take the example of a two-byte (16-bit) integer:

```
high byte      low byte

01111111       11111111    = 32767
00000000       00000001    = 1
00000000       00000000    = 0
10000000       00000000    = -32768
11111111       11111111    = -1
```

When you declare a variable to be of type **char, short, int,** or **long,** you are reserving a machine-dependent number of bits, where the most significant bit serves as a sign bit. When you declare a variable to be of type **unsigned,** the most significant bit contributes to the value (as a power of two), so larger positive values can be represented.

The C language contains a number of operators that deal directly with bits.

They allow you to turn bits on and off (called *masking*) and move them left or right (called *shifting*). Some compilers also allow you to give names to individual bits. This feature is called *bit fields*.

19.2 THE BITWISE OPERATORS

Changing Bits in a Byte with a Single Stroke   In C there are four bitwise operators. They are called bitwise because they operate on variables in a manner that directly and predictably affects bits. They are: the bitwise-and (&); the bitwise-or (::); the bitwise exclusive-or ($\wedge$); and the ones-complement operator ($\sim$).

The bitwise-and Operator: &

The bitwise-and operator is the **&** symbol. Remember that we have two other operators using **&**—the logical-and is **&&,** and the address operator is also **&**. Fortunately, the different usages are obvious from their context in your source code:

```
if ( ab = = 0 && bc = = 0)   (the logical-and)
ptr = &array[0];             (fetch address operator)
res = ab & bc;               (the bitwise-and)
```

The bitwise-and operator compares two values, bit by bit, and yields an appropriate value as a result. If corresponding bits, in the two values compared, are set (1) then the corresponding bit in the result is set. If only one bit of the two, or neither, is set then the corresponding bit of the result is cleared (made 0). For example, take three variables of one byte each:

```
result = num1 & num2;
```

where:

	Binary	*Decimal*	
num1	= 01001111	= 79	
num2	= 00110001	= 49	
result	= 00000001	= 1	= num1 & num2

or

	Binary	*Decimal*	
num1	= 01111111	= 127	
num2	= 00000010	= 2	
result	= 00000010	= 2	= num1 & num2

Notice in the last example that the presence of a single set bit (in ***num2***) can be used to discover the presence of a corresponding set bit in ***num1***. This process of turning all but selected bits off with a bitwise-and is one form of masking. Masking can be used to determine whether a bit is set in some variable. To see, for example, if the third from the lowest bit is set in the variable ***foo,*** you can use the fragment:

```
#define MASKTHIRD 4
if ( (foo & MASKTHIRD) != 0 )
{
       . . . . bit was set stuff here
}
```

The C language has no standard library function that will print the individual bits of a variable. In a way, this is fortunate because writing one will help you to understand the properties of a bitwise-and. In the following function, *showbits()* (Fig. 19–1), an array is made up of the eight possible masks, one for each bit of a byte. In a loop, each mask is bitwise-and'ed with the single byte of the variable *var*. The result will be 0 if that bit was clear and not 0 if it was set. The appropriate '1' or '0' is then printed.

FIGURE 19-1   showbits()

```
/*
** showbits(): print a char in binary to file/device indicated.
*/

#include <stdio.h>

static unsigned char mask[8] = { 1, 2, 4, 8, 16, 32, 64, 128 };

showbits( to, var )
FILE *to;
char var;
{
    int bit;
    unsigned onezero;

    for( bit = 7; bit >= 0; bit-- )
    {
        onezero = mask[bit] & var;
        fprintf( to, "%c", onezero ? '1' : '0' );
    }
}
```

Now compile the program "bitdemo.c" (in Fig. 19–2) and link it (Chapter 17) with "showbits". This program illustrates all four bitwise operators in action and will help you follow our discussion of the three remaining bitwise operators.

The bitwise-or Operator: |

While the bitwise-and is generally used to turn bits off, the bitwise-or is used to turn them on. The bitwise-or operator is the | symbol. Don't confuse it with the logical-or operator "||". Again, the difference will be clear from the context in which each appears:

FIGURE 19-2 bitdemo.c

```c
/* bitdemo.c: demonstrates the bitwise operators */

#include <stdio.h>
#define BITS(x) showbits( stdout, x )
#define P(x) printf( " %c ", x )

main()
{
    int num1, num2, result;

    while( 1 )
    {
        printf( "\nEnter two integers (0 quits):\n1) " );
        scanf( "%d", &num1 );
        if( num1 == 0 )
            exit();
        printf( "2) " );
        scanf( "%d", &num2 );

        printf( "\nnum1 = " );      BITS(num1);
        printf( "    num2 = " );    BITS(num2);

        printf( "\n\nBitwise AND:\n" );
        result = num1 & num2;
        BITS(result); P('='); BITS(num1); P('&'); BITS(num2);

        printf( "\n\nBitwise OR:\n" );
        result = num1 | num2;
        BITS(result); P('='); BITS(num1); P('|'); BITS(num2);

        printf( "\n\nBitwise exclusive-OR:\n" );
        result = num1 ^ num2;
        BITS(result); P('='); BITS(num1); P('^'); BITS(num2);

        printf( "\n\nBitwise ones-complement:\n" );
        result = ~num1;
        BITS(result); P('='); P('~'); BITS(num1);

        printf( "\n" );
    }
}
```

```c
if ( ab == 0 || bc == 0)          (logical-or operator)
res = ab | bc;                    (bitwise-or operator)
```

In the bitwise-or, if *either* one or both compared bits are set, the corresponding bit in the result byte is set. If both compared bits are clear, the corresponding result bit is cleared. Again examine the example of 3 one-byte variables:

```
          Binary       Decimal
num1   = 00011000    = 24
num2   = 00001011    = 11
result = 00011011    = 27    = num1 | num2
```

or

```
          Binary       Decimal
num1   = 00000000    = 0
num2   = 00001000    = 8
result = 00001000    = 8     = num1 | num2
```

In the second example, notice how the bitwise-or can be used to turn on (set) a selected bit. This provides a means, for example, to convert the values 0 through 9 into the characters '0' through '9'. Simply bitwise-or each value with the character constant '0', and presto, that value is now a character:

```
          Binary       Decimal
num1   = 00000101    = 5
 '0'   = 00110000    = 48
char   = 00110101    = 53    = '5' = num1 | '0'
```

The exclusive-or Operator: ^

The bitwise exclusive-or operator is the carate ^ symbol. When two bits are compared under exclusive-or, the result bit is set if one or the other, but not both, of the compared bits is set. The corresponding result bit is cleared if both compared bits are set or if both compared bits are clear. For example:

```
          Binary       Decimal
num1   = 00011000    = 24
num2   = 00001011    = 11
result = 00010011    = 19    = num1 ^ num2
```

or

```
          Binary       Decimal
num1   = 00000001    = 1
num2   = 00000001    = 1
result = 00000000    = 0     = num1 ^ num2
```

One application for the bitwise exclusive-or is in toggling a flag. In a loop, for example, you might wish to perform some action every other time:

```
flag = 1;
for ( time =0; time < END; time ++ )
{
    flag = flag ^ 1;
    if ( flag == 0 )
```

```
        . . . . do this every other time
    . . . .
}
```

The ones-complement Operator: ˜

The ones-complement operator is the tilde (˜) symbol. This is called a unary operator because it affects only a single variable. Ones-complement yields a value in
which all the bits are inverted. All the set bits are made clear, and all the clear bits
are made set. For example:

	Binary	*Decimal*
num1	= 00011000	= 24
result	= 11100111	= 231 unsigned or −25 two's complement = ~num1

or:

	Binary	*Decimal*
num1	= 00000001	= 1
result	= 11111110	= 254 unsigned or −2 two's complement = ~num1

The latter example illustrates that the ones-complement of 1 results in every bit but
the zeroth bit being made set. To illustrate one application, consider the problem of
turning off (making 0) the zeroth bit in a variable. Since ˜ 1 yields a value in which
every bit but the zeroth is set, bitwise-and'ing with ˜ 1 will always clear the zeroth
bit, *regardless* of the number of bytes occupied by a variable:

```
result = num & ( ˜1 );
```

Bitwise op= Shorthand

Most bitwise operators can utilize the ''op='' shorthand (Chapter 18). Only the
ones-complement cannot, and that is because it is a unary operator. To illustrate this
''op='' shorthand, first review the table from the last chapter:

Where You Would Write	*You Can Also Write*
num = num + val;	num + = val;
num = num − val;	num − = val;
num = num * val;	num * = val;
num = num / val;	num / = val;
num = num % val;	num % = val;

now add the bitwise operators to that table:

num = num & val;	num & = val;
num = num | val;	num | = val;
num = num ˆ val;	num ˆ = val;

19.3 SHIFTS

Move Bits Left and Right   C offers two operators to shift bits left and right. The left-shift operator is the $<<$ symbol and the right-shift operator is $>>$ symbol. Both require a positive value specifying how many bits to shift. For example, $<<2$ means to shift left by two bits, and $>>1$ means to shift right by one bit.

The Left-Shift Operator: $<<$

The left-shift operator $<<$ shifts a value left by the number of bits specified. For example:

```
result = num <<2;
```

assigns to **result** the value of **num** shifted left by two bits.
That is:

	Binary	*Decimal*	
num	= 00000001	= 1	
result	= 00000100	= 4	= num $<<2$

or

	Binary	*Decimal*	
num	= 10000000	= 128 unsigned or -12 two's complement	
result	= 00000000	= 0	= num $<<2$

When a number is left shifted, zeros always fill the right side, and the left bits that are shifted off are simply discarded. As you can see, in the second example, left shifting negative values can be tricky because the sign bit is always thrown away. If you need to left shift a negative value, you should first save the sign bit, shift, then restore the sign bit. The following fragment shows one approach to left shifting a signed variable while preserving the sign bit:

```
sign = (num < 0) ? -1 : 1;
num = num <<2;
num *= (num < 0) ? -sign : sign;
```

Care should also be taken to avoid shifting a bit *into* the sign position when using signed variables. Just to be on the safe side, declare any variable you expect to shift as **unsigned.**
Observe that left shifting is the equivalent of multiplying by powers of two:

Binary	*Decimal*	*Power of Two*
00000001	1	anything to the power of 0 = 1
00000010	2	2
00000100	4	2 * 2
00001000	8	2 * 2 * 2

Binary	Decimal	Power of Two
00010000	16	2 * 2 * 2 * 2
00100000	32	2 * 2 * 2 * 2 * 2
01000000	64	2 * 2 * 2 * 2 * 2 * 2
10000000	128	2 * 2 * 2 * 2 * 2 * 2 * 2

The left-shift operator can also be written using the ''op='' shorthand. Thus:

Where You Would Write	*You Can Also Write*
num = num << val;	num <<= val;

The Right-Shift Operator: >>

Right shifting >> moves bits to the right. The bits shifted off the end are discarded. What gets filled in on the left, however, depends on your compiler. All compilers left fill with clear bits when the sign bit is clear. If the sign bit is set, however, some machines will fill with clear bits while others will fill with set bits. When right shifting, care should be taken to shift only **unsigned** or positive values. The right shift is handy because it *divides* a value by two for each shift.

To illustrate the right shift, take a moment to rewrite the function *showbits()* (see Fig. 19–3). Note how the use of a shift eliminates the need for a table of masks.

FIGURE 19-3   showbits() (revision 1)

```
/*
** showbits() (revision 1): illustrates the right shift
*/

#include <stdio.h>

showbits( to, var )
FILE *to;
char var;
{
    int bit;
    unsigned onezero;

    for( bit = 7; bit >= 0; bit-- )
    {
        onezero = (var >>bit) & 1;
        fprintf( to, "%c", onezero ? '1' : '0' );
    }
}
```

The right shift operator can also be written using the ''op='' shorthand. Thus:

Where You Would Write	*You Can Also Write*
num = num >> val;	num >>= val;

Shifting and Packed Data

A common application for shifts is accessing packed data—data that is represented by individual bits in a variable. Suppose, for example, you wanted eight individual flags packed into a byte to use with a text-formatting program:

Bit	Means	
0	right adjust	if set
1	left adjust	if set
3	print page numbers	if set
4	fill paragraphs	if set
5	fill other text	if set
6	double space	if set
7	add linefeed	if set

You might create a variable called *flags* of type **char** to hold all this information. Then, to see if the bit representing page numbering is set, you could write:

```
if ( (flag >>2) & 1)
    . . . . yes, number pages
```

or more graphically:

```
               ┌──────────"print page numbers" bit
             ▼
1101101 flag
0011011 >>2
0000001 &1
```

The function in Figure 19–4, *setbit()*, illustrates a more general method of testing and setting individual bits. You pass it the address of a **char** being used to hold packed data and a number indicating which bit (0 through 7) you wish to set. If that number is within legal range, the bit is set. The *setbit()* function returns 1 if that bit was already set, 0 if it was clear, and −1 if the bit specification was out of range.

19.4 BIT FIELDS

Some Compilers Let You Give Names to Bits Most C compilers provide an alternative method of dealing with packed data. Called bit fields, it provides a means of accessing bits by name.

Bit fields can be used to pack data into bits and give each of those bits a name as a member of a structure. The process is perhaps best illustrated specifically before it is described generally:

```
struct packed {
    unsigned int radj:1; /* right adjust if set       */
    unsigned int ladj:1; /* left adjust if set        */
    unsigned int pnum:1; /* print page numbers if set */
    unsigned int fill:1; /* fill paragraphs if set    */
```

FIGURE 19-4 setbit()

```
/*
** setbit(): set and report previous setting of a bit
*/

setbit( flags, bit )
char *flags;
int bit;
{
    unsigned orig;

    if ( bit < 0 || bit > 7 )
        return( -1 );

    orig = *flags;
    *flags |= 1<<bit;
    orig >>= bit;
    orig &= 1;
    return ( orig );
}
```

```
                unsigned int filo: 1; /* fill other text if set    */
                unsigned int dspc: 1; /* double space if set        */
                unsigned int adlf: 1; /* add linefeed if set        */
        };
```

This defines *packed* to be a structure containing a single integer whose bits have been individually named (*radj, ladj, pnum,* and so on). In general, the expression:

```
name: 1
```

defines *name* to be a member of that structure and specifies that it is composed of one bit.

If the variable *flags* is declared to be of type *struct packed,* as:

```
struct packed flags;
```

then any of its members (each representing a bit) can be accessed using the normal structure notation:

```
flags.member
```

To see, for example, if *flags* has the bit set for page numbering, you could state:

```
if ( flag.pnum )
    .... yes, print page numbers
```

A nice aspect of bit fields is that they are not limited to a single bit. They are, however, sometimes limited to no more than the bits in an **unsigned int.** For example, you could define:

```
struct packed_alpha {
    unsigned int chr1: 5;
    unsigned int chr2: 5;
```

```
        unsigned int chr3:5;
    } palpha;
```

as a means of packing three characters into a single two-byte integer. The notation:

```
    char1:5
```

causes the compiler to set aside five bits for the member ***char1***. In general, the number of bits reserved for any member is specified by the form:

```
    member:bits;
```

where *bits* is an integer constant expression.

There are two rules that limit your use of bit fields: You cannot fetch their addresses (using &), and you cannot create pointers to them. Other than these two restrictions, they are handled in the same way as ordinary variables. That is, the compiler produces the code to properly insert and extract them. All you have to do is state:

```
    structure.member
```

and the compiler produces all the necessary shifts and masks needed to access the value stored in ***member's*** bits.[2]

19.5 HEXIDECIMAL AND OCTAL

Other Ways of Counting Can Make Life Easier   When dealing with bits, it is difficult to visualize their arrangement when they are described by the decimal numbers they represent. For example, from what you've learned so far, how are the bits arranged for the following decimal values?

```
    123456
    876543
    111111
```

Not very easy, eh?

Fortunately, C supports two other methods of counting that lend themselves to the conceptualization of bit arrangements. Decimal is a method of counting in base 10, octal is a method of counting in base 8, and hexadecimal is a method of counting in base 16.

In octal, each digit represents three bits and the digits count from 0 to 7. In C, an octal number is indicated by merely making the first digit 0, as:

```
    num = 0777;
```

Examine the following short table comparing binary to octal:

---

[2]Since bit fields are not supported by some compilers, their use should be minimized for portability. Their compactness comes with a very real cost—the hidden time required for the computer to access the bits. Best to use bytes (char) as flags unless you are very short on space.

Binary	Octal
0 000	0
0 001	01
0 010	02
0 011	03
0 100	04
0 101	05
0 110	06
0 111	07
1 000	010

Notice that each bit position is represented by the octal numbers 01, 02, and 04. This correspondence makes it easy to convert binary to octal and octal to binary. For example, the octal number 0777 converts to:

```
111 111 111
```

and the binary number 10011011 (imagine a lead 0 to group in threes) converts to:

```
0133
```

The disadvantage of octal numbers is that dividing a byte into three-bit groups leaves one group with only two bits. The hexadecimal numbering system, on the other hand, uses base 16, or four bits, thus perfectly dividing a byte in half.

Hexadecimal (or hex) digits count from 0 to f. That is:

```
0 1 2 3 4 5 6 7 8 9 a b c d e f
```

In C, a hex number is indicated by beginning it with a ''0x'', as:

```
num = 0x7f;
```

Examine the following table of binary versus hex numbers. Octal and decimal have been thrown in to emphasize the differences:

Binary	Hex	Octal	Decimal
0 0000	0x0	0	0
0 0001	0x1	01	1
0 0010	0x2	02	2
0 0011	0x3	03	3
0 0100	0x4	04	4
0 0101	0x5	05	5
0 0110	0x6	06	6
0 0111	0x7	07	7
0 1000	0x8	010	8
0 1001	0x9	011	9
0 1010	0xa	012	10
0 1011	0xb	013	11
0 1100	0xc	014	12
0 1101	0xd	015	13

Binary	Hex	Octal	Decimal
0 1110	0xe	016	14
0 1111	0xf	017	15
1 0000	0x10	020	16

Again, note that the bit positions in a group of four correspond to the hex digits 0x1, 0x2, 0x4 and 0x8. The choice of octal or hexadecimal will depend on your particular outlook and needs. Often programs will be written that mix the two.

In Appendix 3 you will find a table of corresponding ASCII, binary, octal, hexadecimal, and decimal values. The program in Figure 19–5, "asciitable.c", was used as a step in generating that table.

FIGURE 19-5 asciitable.c

```
/* asciitable.c: prints ascii binary decimal octal hex */

#include <stdio.h>

main()
{
    int count;

    for ( count = 0; count < 128 ; count++ )
    {
        count &= 0x7f;  /* mask off hi bits just in case */

        /*
        ** special handling for control characters
        */
        if ( count < ' ' )
            printf( " cntl-%c  ", count + '@' );
        else if ( count == 0x7f )
            printf( " cntl-?  " );
        else
            printf( "     %c  ", count );

        /*
        ** binary
        */
        showbits( stdout, count );

        /*
        ** octal, hex, and decimal
        */
        printf( "  %04o  0x%02x  %3d\n", count,count,count );
    }

    exit( 0 );
}


/** place showbits() here or link it **/
```

Remember that *printf()* and *scanf()* have the built-in means of handling both octal and hexadecimal numbers. The **%o** directive is used for octal and the **%x** directive for hexadecimal. You might wish to review the discussions of *printf()* in Chapter 3 and *scanf()* in Chapter 9.

20· EPILOG

Looking Ahead: Where to Go from Here.

20.1 ADVANCED TOPICS

Introducing Further Avenues for Exploration   This chapter marks the end of your introduction to the C programming language. You now have the tools you need to write useful, meaningful, even complex programs. More important, you have a real grasp of the language, and that will enable you to move on to C's subtler and more advanced aspects. In this chapter, we will touch on a number of those aspects.

20.2 RECURSION

How a Function Can Usefully Call Itself   Recursion is the ability of a function to call itself. Other languages, like Lisp and Logo, make extensive use of recursion. C, too, can use this technique.

Examine this simple function, which demonstrates recursion:

```
timeout( from )
int from;
{
        if ( from <= 0 )
            return;
        printf( "%d\n", from );
        timeout( from - 1 );     /* calls itself */
}
```

Given, for example, an initial passed argument value of 3, *timout()* will print that value, and then call itself. The value it passes, when it calls itself, is 1 less than the value it received. That new argument creates a brand new **auto** variable *from,* one completely different from the first. This continues until an argument value of 0 is received. A **return** is then executed, which returns the flow to the previous incarnation of *timeout()* that called it. That incarnation returns to its predecessor, and so on, until the original *timeout()* is returned to and exited for good.

The key to using recursion in C lies in understanding **auto** variables. Recall that **auto** variables are created anew each time a function is called and that arguments are passed by value. When a function receives an argument and places it into an **auto** variable, that variable is freshly created and placed into a free space in memory. If that function then calls itself, another brand new **auto** variable is created and placed in yet another free space in memory. Neither knows of the existence of the other, and neither incarnation of the function can affect the other's **auto** variable.

Recursive functions tend to be inefficient because they consume significant time in function calls. They also make heavy demands on the runtime stack—the place where **auto** variables are created and destroyed. You will find that recursion is seldom used in C programs. This is not to say that you should avoid it. Despite its costs, it may prove to be the cleanest and most concise approach to solving some problems.

As a practical illustration of one application for recursion, examine the function *member(),* which is in Fig. 20–1. Passed two strings, it checks to see if the first is contained in the second. If so, a **pointer to** where the match begins is returned. Otherwise, NULL is returned.

Take the time now to write a *main()* to test *member().* As a suggestion, consider the fragment:

```
gets ( string, MAX ) ;
scanf ( "%s", word ) ;
if ( member ( word, string ) = = NULL
}
    printf ( "nope, not a member\n") ;
}
printf ( "yep, it is a member\n" ) ;
```

Once you've gotten *member()* and *main()* working together, try rewriting *member()* without recursion. The exercise of creating a nonrecursive *member()* function will underscore how recursion may prove to be the best approach to solving some problems.

20.3 SCREEN CONTROL

Cursor Positioning and Related Topics[1]   ''Screen control'' generally means being able to print things to your terminal's video screen anywhere you please. It means being able to clear the entire screen, a part of the screen, or just to the end of a line. But be careful. All compilers handle screen control differently.

Programs that use the screen-control routines provided by Unix libraries and

---

[1]This is *not* a section on where to put people with foul mouths.

FIGURE 20-1 member()

```
#include <stdio.h>

/*
** member(): returns pointer to substr found in string, else
**           returns NULL.
*/
char *member( substr, string)
register  char *string;
char *substr;
{
    register char *str, *sub;
    char *temp;

    if ( !*substr) return(NULL);            /* nothing to look for */

    str = string;
    while ( *str && *str != *substr )   /* scan for 1st letter */
        ++str;
    if ( *str == 0 ) return(NULL);      /*            not found */

    temp = str;

    while ( *temp  &&  *sub  &&  *sub == *temp )
    {
        ++temp; ++sub;                      /* compare all letters */
    }

    if( *sub == 0 )
        return( str );                      /*          match found */
    else
        return( member( substr, str+1 ));  /* else recursion */
}
```

headers will generally compile and work properly on all Unix machines. The same thing can be said for the Aztec C compiler within the family of Apple II products. However, if you want to transport a screen-control package from, say Unix to any non-Unix environment, it will probably not work without extensive revision.

If you need to transport a program with screen control to another system, be sure to place your screen-control routines in a separate file. Call it something like "screenstuff.c", and use many comments, so only that file will have to be rewritten after the move.

You'll have to discover for yourself the ins and outs of your particular screen control, but there are several common places to begin looking. In addition to your documentation, you may find, in your standard library or elsewhere, one or more of the following:

```
ioctl() and ioctl.h
screen    or  screen.lib
curses() and termcap()
```

As a last resort, look through the advertisements that came with your compiler. A separate package of screen-control routines may be available for purchase.

20.4 ENUMERATED VARIABLES: enum

A Way to Limit What Values a Variable Can Have   The enumerated variable type **enum** is a relatively new addition to the language. It is not available on all compilers and doesn't work properly on some that allow it. This section is for those of you whose compilers support **enum.**

As programs become more complex, the tendency to assign the incorrect value to a variable increases. Suppose, for example, you declared an integer variable called *flag,* and suppose that this variable should be assigned only one of two possible values: 1 for true or 0 for false. Knowing this, you design all the functions dealing with that variable to test for equality to 1 or to 0. Months pass and you design a new function that assigns it a value of −1. This is an easy mistake to make, as −1 is often used to represent an error condition. Unfortunately, this creates a bug that's very difficult to track down.

Herein lies the utility of the keyword **enum.** It prevents this kind of bug from happening in the first place. Had *flag* been declared, for example, as:

```
              ┌──── name of pattern
          ▼
enum tfonly {
      true,  ⎫
      false  ⎬──────► list of legal variables
} flag;      ⎭
   ▲
   └──── name of enumerated variable
```

a later assignment of:

```
flag = err;
```

or

```
flag = -1;
```

would result in a compiler error, since the variable *flag,* when declared as type **enum,** can be assigned only the values of the variables named *true* and *false.*

Notice that the **enum** definition looks like a structure definition. The line:

```
              ┌──── name of pattern
          ▼
enum tfonly {
      true,   ⎫
      false   ⎬        list of legal variables
};            ⎭
```

defines *tfonly* as the name of an enumerated *pattern* that can be assigned only the values of the variables listed. The statement:

```
enum tfonly flag;
```

then, declares *flag* to be a variable of type **enum tfonly.** The actual type of *flag* is defined by the type of the variables named in the list. That is, if *true* and *false* are both declared elsewhere as type **int,** then *flag* is also of type **int.** All the names in the list must, of course, be the same type.

If your compiler lacks **enum,** and you wish to transport a program that uses it to your machine, you can substitute a simple variable declaration, as:

```
int true, false, flag;
```

All you will sacrifice is a form of "rule checking" done by the compiler.[2]

20.5 COMPUTED goto

Vectoring with Arrays of Pointers to Functions   Two facets of C can be combined to create an alternative means of selecting functions.

First, notice that a pointer can be declared that points to a function:

```
(char * fptr) ();
```

Note, too, that a pointer can be assigned the address of a function:

```
fptr = dozero;
```

where *dozero* is the name of the function *dozero().* That function can then be called using the pointer, as:

```
(*fptr) ();
```

Second, note that an array can be an array of pointers:

```
(char *funs) [2];
```

and that the pointers in that array can each be assigned a value that is the address of a function:

```
funs[0] = dozero;
```

The functions these array elements point to can then be called using an offset into that array, as:

```
(*funs[0]) ();
```

Putting this all together yields a *computed goto,* wherein the function called is directly determined by the value of the offset. To illustrate this process, examine the two following segments of code. In the first, the selection of which function is called is made with a **switch-case** statement:

```
num = getchoice() /* 0 or 1 */
switch ( num )
{
  case 0:
          dozero();
          break;
```

---

[2]If you have used it heavily, though, you will have a lot of rewriting to do. Best to limit its use.

```
        case 1:
                doone();
                break;
    }
```

In the second, the offset into an array of pointers to functions is used to call the appropriate function indirectly:[3]

```
(static char *funs) () [2] = {
        dozero,
        doone
};
```

```
num = getchoice();        /* 0 or 1 */
(*functs[num]) ();        /* call the num function */
```

The *computed goto* is most useful in situations in which compactness of code is critical. You will find it used, for example, in word processors, compilers, and complex games.

20.6 THE MATH LIBRARY AND math.h

Accessing and Using Things Like sin() and sqrt() Many compilers offer a library of double-precision floating-point math routines. In that library, you will find such useful functions as:

double acos(x)	inverse cosine of x
double asin(x)	inverse sine of x
double atan(x)	inverse tangent of x
double atan2(x,y)	arctangent of x divided by y
double ceil(x)	smallest integer not less than x
double cos(x)	cosine of x
double cosh(x)	hyperbolic cosine of x
double cotan(x)	cotangent of x
double exp(x)	exponential of x
double fabs(x)	absolute value of x
double floor(x)	largest integer not greater than x
double log(x)	natural log of x
double log10(x)	logarithm base 10 of x
double pow(x,y)	raise x to the y'th power
double sin(x)	sine of x
double sinh(x)	hyperbolic sine of x
double sqrt (x)	square root of x
double tan(x)	tangent of x
double tanh(x)	hyperbolic tangent of x

Since these functions are all type **double,** they must be declared **extern** in your program before they can be called (Chapter 12). For your convenience, those **ex-**

---

[3]Of course, this approach is less clear (especially for our simple example) than the first one. But it should tantalize you with the potentials of C.

tern declarations will usually be found in a system header file called "math.h". That file can be **#include'd** as a part of your program as:

```
#include <stdio.h>
#include <math.h>
```

where "stdio.h" should precede all other header files.

On some systems, these math functions are offered as an additional package you must purchase. If your system already has a math library, it may require special linking (Chapter 2) or special compile-time flags. Check your documentation.

20.7 WHERE TO GO NEXT

Hungry for More? Some Suggestions   There are many rich sources of information on the C language. Here we suggest a few possible resources you may find rewarding.

Looking at how others have gone about solving common programming problems can reveal much about the inner workings of the language. Many compilers, for example, supply source listings for their library functions.

Source listings are also available in a few magazines. *Dr. Dobbs Journal* carries many articles that feature C programs for microcomputers. *Unix World Magazine* carries a C tutorial section and features articles dealing with Unix-specific C programs and problems.

Another place to look for C source listings is on the UUCP network in net.lang.c and net.sources. This is an electronic bulletin board available at many Unix sites such as universities.

Depending on your city, there may also be a C users' group nearby. These groups often offer public domain C programs and source listings. As a bonus, if you're really interested in learning the ins and outs of the C language, nothing beats being around others who feel the same way.

Finally, we recommend certain other books that no would-be C programmer should be without.[4] First and foremost is *The C Programming Language*, by Kernighan and Ritchie. This is the "official" word by the author of the language, Dennis M. Ritchie. Two other books about programming in general, which teach good habits of content, style, and utility, are *Software Tools* and *The Elements of Programming Style*, both by Kernighan and Plauger. For fun and inspiration, don't pass up *The C Puzzle Book* by Allen Feuer. And, finally, for a well-organized overview of C, investigate the brief but informative *C Notes* by C. T. Zahn.

---

[4]Alternatively, buy several copies of this book and read them from different angles.

APPENDIX 1
A SMALL STYLE SHEET

Prior to writing this book, we decided that all the examples in it should have a single, consistent style or "look." Trying to be clear was, and is, the goal. The "look" we prefer results from adherence to a number of fine points, but each of them should be considered a rule of thumb—our recommendation or preference.

Rule of Thumb 1

Generally, use lots of "air" (white space) to separate one idea from another. Air is like the spaces in a sentence, in that it helps to separate and clarify. Observe that:

```
if ( (c = getchar ()) != NEWLINE )
```

is preferred over:

```
if ((c=getchar()) !=NEWLINE)
```

Air helps to clarify how the parentheses are grouped and makes the flow of logic easier to follow. Give your programs room to breathe.

Rule of Thumb 2

Place separate ideas on separate lines and indent to show flow of control. Just as air clarifies meaning in a line, newlines give clarity to separate ideas. Imagine how confusing a poem would be if it were written as one long line! Indenting helps to

256

show what idea "belongs" to other ideas and which ideas are independent. Notice that:

```
while ( *s1 = *s2 )
{
    ++s1;
    ++s2;
}
```

is preferred to:

```
while ( *s1 = *s2 ) { ++s1; ++2; }
```

The former shows more clearly that "++s1;" and "++s2;" are subsets of the **while** statement.

Rule of Thumb 3

Use comments as often as necessary to clarify your intent. When selecting names, choose names that best reflect their usage:

```
int guess;              /* player's guess (1-99) */
guess = getguess();  /* getguess() returns 1-99 */
```

is preferred over:

```
int zz;         /* choice */
zz = inz();     /* get it */
```

Certainly, "guess" as a name is much more meaningful than "zz".

Rule of Thumb 4

Use the **#define** directive to clarify obscure constructs.

```
#define DELKEY 0x7f       /* terminals delete key */
if ( keypressed == DELKEY ) /* test for delete */
```

is preferred to

```
if ( keypressed == 0x7f )
```

Rule of Thumb 5

Line things up on the screen. Try to make the program look good. No matter how much extra air you place in your programs, they will compile to the same size and run just as fast. The reward for neatness is worth the extra effort. Thus:

```
int  maxtemp,     /* highest temperature */
     mintemp;     /* lowest temperature  */

char fctoken;     /* fahr/celcius token   */
```

is preferred to:

```
int maxtemp, mintemp; /* highest, lowest temperature */
char fctoken; /* fahr/celcius token */
```

Rule of Thumb 6

Whatever look you wish to give your programs, be consistent. The eye grows accustomed to seeing patterns of style. Changing styles in midstream can be not only distracting, but can cause misinterpretation of what was intended.

For example, consider the following alternative placements of curly braces:

Method 1:

```
while( foo )
{
    bar();
}
```

Method 2:

```
while( foo )
    {
    bar();
    }
```

Method 3:

```
while( foo ) {
    bar();
}
```

We, of course, chose the first method and stuck to it throughout this book. However, method 2 is preferred by some because it seems to more clearly indicate what is controlled by the **while** statement. The last method is often used by people programming under Unix, because their text editor contains a means to automatically match curly braces, and because this method allows more of the program to be visible on the video screen at one time.

No one look is better than another. Just don't mix them in a single program or project.

APPENDIX 2
A PSEUDO-RANDOM FUNCTION

The following function is a software implementation of a pseudo-random bit sequence generator. When you enter this listing DO NOT include the line numbers at the left. They are for your reference and will be used in the explanation that follows.

```
[01] #ifdef vax
[02] #define int short
[03] #endif
[04]
[05] /* rand( val ): return a pseudo-random value between 1
[06] **          and val. If val negative, it is used as a seed.
[07] **   Note: an int must be 16 bits for this function to work!
[08] */
[09] rand( val )
[10] int val;
[11] {
[12]     int bit0, bit1, bit14, num, i;
[13]     static int rndval = 2;
[14]
[15]     /* see if val is negative
[16]     */
[17]     if ( val < 0 )
[18]         rndval = -val;
[19]
[20]     /* repeat 10 times to prevent clumping
[21]     */
[22]     for ( i = 0; i < 10; i++ )
[23]     {
```

```
[24]          bit0 = rndval & 1;
[25]          bit1 = (rndval & 2) >>1;
[26]          bit14 = bit0 ^ bit1;
[27]          rndval >>=1;
[28]          rndval |= (bit14 <<14);
[29]      }
[30]
[31]      num = rndval % val;
[32]      return ( num ? num : val );
[33] }
```

This 15-bit sequence generator provides a mechanism for producing "pseudo" random values. The process begins with the signed **int** passed value *val* [9–10]. If that value is negative [17], it is made positive and used to seed the random number variable *rndval* [18]. Regardless of whether *rndval* was seeded, a loop is entered to generate a new "pseudo" random number. That loop is repeated 10 times to prevent clumping—that is, to even out the spread (reduce correlation) of selected values [22]. Each time through the loop produces a new value in three steps:

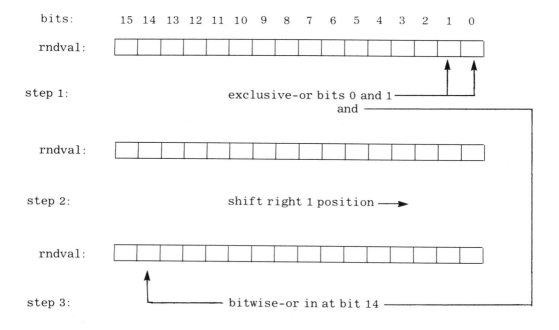

First, bits 0 and 1 of *rndval* are exclusive-or'd together and the result saved [24–26]. Second, *rndval* is shifted right one bit [27]. And third, the result saved in step 1 is bitwise-or'd into *rndval* at bit 14 [28]. This final value is taken modulo *val,* which yields a number 0 through *val - 1* [31]. If that number is 0, *val* is returned, thereby returning a number in the range 1 through *val* [32].

This algorithm provides a period of 32,767 values before it begins to repeat. For information about the theory involved, refer to *Integrated Circuits in Digital Electronics,* by Arpad Barna and Dan I. Porat, Chapter 9, John Wiley and Sons Publishers.

APPENDIX 3
HANDY TABLES

This appendix contains two tables. First is a table illustrating the order of precedence and grouping of the C operators as discussed in Chapter 4. Second is a table of equivalent values for the ASCII character set as discussed in Chapters 2 and 19.

OPERATOR PRECEDENCE AND GROUPING

Level	Operator	Grouping	Description
Highest	->	left to right	Structure member reference
			Structure member reference
	*	right to left	Pointer reference
	&		Address
	−		Unary minus
	!		Negation (not)
	~		Ones Complement
	++		Increment
	−−		Decrement
	(type)		Cast (conversion)
	sizeof		Size of
	*	left to right	Multiplication
	/		Division
	%		Modulo
	+	left to right	Addition
	−		Subtraction

>>	left to right	Right Shift	
<<		Left Shift	
<	left to right	Less Than	
>		Greater Than	
<=		Less Than or Equal	
>=		Greater Than or Equal	
==	left to right	Equal To	
!=		Not Equal To	
&	left to right	Bitwise-and	
^	left to right	Bitwise Exclusive-or	
|	left to right	Bitwise-or	
&&	left to right	Logical and	
||	left to right	Logical or	
?:	right to left	Conditional Operator	
=	right to left	Assignment Operators	
op=			
Lowest ,	left to right	Comma Operator	

THE ASCII CHARACTER SET AND CONVERSION TABLE

ASCII	Binary	Octal	Hex	Decimal	Comments
CTRL-@	00000000	0000	0x00	0	null, '\0'
CTRL-A	00000001	0001	0x01	1	SOH Start of Heading
CTRL-B	00000010	0002	0x02	2	STX Start of Text
CTRL-C	00000011	0003	0x03	3	ETX End of Text
CTRL-D	00000100	0004	0x04	4	EOT End of Transmission
CTRL-E	00000101	0005	0x05	5	ENQ Enquiry
CTRL-F	00000110	0006	0x06	6	ACK Acknowledge
CTRL-G	00000111	0007	0x07	7	BELL
CTRL-H	00001000	0010	0x08	8	Backspace, '\b'
CTRL-I	00001001	0011	0x09	9	Horizontal tab, '\t'
CTRL-J	00001010	0012	0x0a	10	Linefeed, Newline, '\n'
CTRL-K	00001011	0013	0x0b	11	VT Vertical Tab
CTRL-L	00001100	0014	0x0c	12	Formfeed, '\f'
CTRL-M	00001101	0015	0x0d	13	Carriage Return, '\r'
CTRL-N	00001110	0016	0x0e	14	SO Shift Out
CTRL-O	00001111	0017	0x0f	15	SI Shift In
CTRL-P	00010000	0020	0x10	16	DLE Data Link Escape
CTRL-Q	00010001	0021	0x11	17	DC1 Device Control 1
CTRL-R	00010010	0022	0x12	18	DC2 Device Control 2
CTRL-S	00010011	0023	0x13	19	DC3 Device Control 3

CTRL-T	00010100	0024	0x14	20	DC4 Device Control 4
CTRL-U	00010101	0025	0x15	21	NAK Negative Acknowledge
CTRL-V	00010110	0026	0x16	22	SYN Synchronous Idle
CTRL-W	00010111	0027	0x17	23	ETB End Transmission Block
CTRL-X	00011000	0030	0x18	24	CAN Cancel
CTRL-Y	00011001	0031	0x19	25	EM End of Medium
CTRL-Z	00011010	0032	0x1a	26	SUB Substitute
CTRL-[	00011011	0033	0x1b	27	Escape
CTRL-\	00011100	0034	0x1c	28	FS File Separator
CTRL-]	00011101	0035	0x1d	29	GS Group Separator
CTRL-ˆ	00011110	0036	0x1e	30	RS Record Separator
CTRL-_	00011111	0037	0x1f	31	US Unit Separator
	00100000	0040	0x20	32	Space
!	00100001	0041	0x21	33	Exclamation point
''	00100010	0042	0x22	34	Double quotation mark
#	00100011	0043	0x23	35	Number sign (pound)
$	00100100	0044	0x24	36	Dollar sign
%	00100101	0045	0x25	37	Percent sign
&	00100110	0046	0x26	38	Ampersand
'	00100111	0047	0x27	39	Apostrophe (half quote)
(	00101000	0050	0x28	40	Left Parenthesis
)	00101001	0051	0x29	41	Right Parenthesis
*	00101010	0052	0x2a	42	Asterisk
+	00101011	0053	0x2b	43	Plus sign
,	00101100	0054	0x2c	44	Comma
-	00101101	0055	0x2d	45	Hyphen or Minus Sign
.	00101110	0056	0x2e	46	Period or Decimal Point
/	00101111	0057	0x2f	47	Slant (Slash)
0	00110000	0060	0x30	48	
1	00110001	0061	0x31	49	
2	00110010	0062	0x32	50	
3	00110011	0063	0x33	51	
4	00110100	0064	0x34	52	
5	00110101	0065	0x35	53	
6	00110110	0066	0x36	54	
7	00110111	0067	0x37	55	
8	00111000	0070	0x38	56	
9	00111001	0071	0x39	57	
:	00111010	0072	0x3a	58	Colon
;	00111011	0073	0x3b	59	Semicolon
<	00111100	0074	0x3c	60	Less Than Symbol
=	00111101	0075	0x3d	61	Equal Sign
>	00111110	0076	0x3e	62	Greater Than Symbol
?	00111111	0077	0x3f	63	Question Mark
@	01000000	0100	0x40	64	At
A	01000001	0101	0x41	65	

B	01000010	0102	0x42	66
C	01000011	0103	0x43	67
D	01000100	0104	0x44	68
E	01000101	0105	0x45	69
F	01000110	0106	0x46	70
G	01000111	0107	0x47	71
H	01001000	0110	0x48	72
I	01001001	0111	0x49	73
J	01001010	0112	0x4a	74
K	01001011	0113	0x4b	75
L	01001100	0114	0x4c	76
M	01001101	0115	0x4d	77
N	01001110	0116	0x4e	78
O	01001111	0117	0x4f	79
P	01010000	0120	0x50	80
Q	01010001	0121	0x51	81
R	01010010	0122	0x52	82
S	01010011	0123	0x53	83
T	01010100	0124	0x54	84
U	01010101	0125	0x55	85
V	01010110	0126	0x56	86
W	01010111	0127	0x57	87
X	01011000	0130	0x58	88
Y	01011001	0131	0x59	89
Z	01011010	0132	0x5a	90
[	01011011	0133	0x5b	91	Left Square Bracket
\	01011100	0134	0x5c	92	Back Slash
]	01011101	0135	0x5d	93	Right Square Bracket
^	01011110	0136	0x5e	94	Caret or Circumflex
_	01011111	0137	0x5f	95	Underscore
`	01100000	0140	0x60	96	Grave Accent
a	01100001	0141	0x61	97
b	01100010	0142	0x62	98
c	01100011	0143	0x63	99
d	01100100	0144	0x64	100
e	01100101	0145	0x65	101
f	01100110	0146	0x66	102
g	01100111	0147	0x67	103
h	01101000	0150	0x68	104
i	01101001	0151	0x69	105
j	01101010	0152	0x6a	106
k	01101011	0153	0x6b	107
l	01101100	0154	0x6c	108
m	01101101	0155	0x6d	109
n	01101110	0156	0x6e	110
o	01101111	0157	0x6f	111

p	01110000	0160	0x70	112
q	01110001	0161	0x71	113
r	01110010	0162	0x72	114
s	01110011	0163	0x73	115
t	01110100	0164	0x74	116
u	01110101	0165	0x75	117
v	01110110	0166	0x76	118
w	01110111	0167	0x77	119
x	01111000	0170	0x78	120
y	01111010	0171	0x79	121
z	01111010	0172	0x7a	122
{	01111011	0173	0x7b	123	Left Curly Brace
|	01111100	0174	0x7c	124	Vertical Line
}	01111101	0175	0x7d	125	Right Curly Brace
~	01111110	0176	0x7e	126	Tilde
CTRL-?	01111111	0177	0x7f	127	Delete, Rubout

INDEX